The Domestic Airline Industry

The Domestic Airline Industry

D. Daryl Wyckoff
Harvard University

David H. Maister
University of British Columbia

Lexington Books
D.C. Heath and Company
Lexington, Massachusetts
Toronto

Library of Congress Cataloging in Publication Data

Wyckoff, D. Daryl.
    The domestic airline industry.

    Bibliography: p.
    1. Aeronautics, Commercial—United States. I. Maister, David H., joint author. II. Title.
HE9803.A4W92   387.7'4'0973   76-54612
ISBN 0-669-01307-2

To Our Parents

Contents

List of Figures

List of Tables

Preface

This book is one of a series published by Lexington Books, D.C. Heath and Company. Each book focuses on a selected industry through a general background description and specific cases directed at the operating programs and policies of companies within the industry. For the purposes of this series of books, an *industry* may be defined as a set of firms in competition, producing goods or services of a like function and nature.

The introductory note and glossary have been designed to provide a general background for individuals who are unfamiliar with the industry. Such readers might include students, members of the financial community, and members of government. Also, these sections have been included to help members of the industry who may be functional specialists, or those whose careers have been confined to one subsegment of the entire industry. The introduction and glossary also serve to define the use of terminology and provide reference material that will be useful in considering individual case studies.

The major portion of the book describes actual company situations and management decision-making processes in case studies. We stress the fact that these are actual cases, drawn from the experiences of real managers. They are not fabricated illustrations. We have disguised some names where it was appropriate, but all cases are used with the approval of the companies involved and with their agreement that the cases are a fair portrayal of the situations they faced, in all their complexities.

The cases have been selected to be representative of the vital decisions that influence the overall competitiveness of these firms. Most of these cases were developed as a response to a question posed to management: "What are the most important decisions that you have made in the recent history of your company?" By and large, the responses we received to this question, and consequently the selection of case studies included in this book, have focused on the issue of operating policy.

The approach of this book may be novel to some readers. Basically, we are presenting an inside look at an industry through "situational analysis" rather than the more conventional "theoretic construct" approach. We present the situation and the views of managers, but we leave the final analysis and conclusion to the reader, rather than present the actual outcome or "textbook" solution. By working through each of the case studies presented here it is possible to derive general principles of good management in this industry. Furthermore we believe that such an outcome is *only* possible by treating the book as a unit—considering all of the case studies together. The principle underlying this belief is that good decisions relating to one area within a company can only be made with reference to a comprehensive understanding of the goals and operations of the entire company, and that decisions by a single company cannot be taken independently of consideration of that company's role and position within the entire industry.

This approach is derived from the teaching methodology developed at the Harvard University Graduate School of Business Administration. These books were originally intended as texts to teach the elements of industry analysis, and, so far as is feasible, to place the students in the industrial climate so they could draw upon their own knowledge and simulate the decision-making process that might be expressed in the climate.

Our principal reason for making these books generally available is based on our observation, primarily through executive programs, that others have also benefitted from this approach.

In the industry approach, the reader should examine the technological and economic structures of the set of competitive firms producing goods or services in the industry. If an industry is not integrated to any extent from the final product back to the intermediate or raw materials, the executive does not need to know a great deal about the economic and technical aspects of stages preceding or following the particular phase in which he or she is engaged.

In the Harvard Business School approach to industry analysis, students are directed to study an industry to determine what characteristics are unique to it. What elements are within the control of the manager? How can the manager affect the outcome of a firm in the industry? We have found that the following questions or topics are often useful in approaching this task. Of course, not all topics are equally relevant or important to each industry. However, the following list has proven to be a reasonable point of departure.

Economics of the Industry (at Each Level of the Industry)

1. Labor, burden, material, depreciation costs
2. Flexibility to volume changes
3. Return on investment, prices, margins
4. Number and location of plants
5. Critical control variables
6. Critical functions (maintenance, production control, personnel, etc.)
7. Typical financial structures
8. Typical costs and cost relationships
9. Typical operating problems
10. Barriers to entry
11. Pricing practices
12. The concept of maturity of an industry
13. Importance of economies of scale
14. Importance of integrated capacities within corporations
15. Importance of balance of equipment

16. Ideal balances of equipment capacities
17. Nature and type of production controls
18. Government influences

Technology of the Industry (at Each Level of the Industry)

1. Rate and kind of technological changes
2. Scale of processes
3. Span of processes
4. Degree of mechanization
5. Technological sophistication
6. Time requirements for making changes

Competitive Situation in the Industry (at Each Level of the Industry)

1. Number and type of companies
2. Nature of competition
3. Marketing approaches
4. Job of the operating vice-president
5. Degree of linked or coupled operations
6. Possible strategies
7. Task of the operating function
8. Diversity of product lines
9. Interindustry sales and relations
10. Public policy towards the industry
11. Social expectations of the industry
12. Foreign competition
13. Competition from other industries
14. Historical and current problems
15. Company comparisons

Acknowledgments

We are grateful to John G. McLean who is credited with the conception and early development of the industry approach at the Harvard Business School in 1947. His original concept led to the course "Manufacturing Policy," which is still taught at the school as an elective in the two-year graduate program leading to the degree of Master of Business Administration. A number of other teachers have put their mark on this course in its development. Wickham Skinner, who taught the course and was co-author with David Rogers of a series of industry-oriented books that preceded this present series, has made a special contribution to the development of our thinking.

Professor Robert Hayes in 1972 made a substantial shift in the orientation of the course form exclusively focusing on the manufacturing industries. Although the course continued to be called "Manufacturing Policy," the operating policies of service industries were considered. The motor-carrier industry was the first "nonmanufacturing" industry included. We were the first instructors to develop and teach this new material. Although the course retains its manufacturing name today, the material, of which this book is an example, goes substantially beyond what the name might suggest.

We wish to thank several authors for contributing material to this book. Chapter 1, "Southwest Airlines," was contributed by Assistant Professor Christopher Lovelock of Harvard University. We wish to express our gratitude to Lewis Schneider of the consulting firm of Temple, Barker, and Sloane for Chapter 8, "Manning the 737." Coauthors and research assistants who made important contributions to various chapters include Joseph B. Fraser III, Daniel D'Aniello, Leslie Buck, Richard Horne and Nancy Van Broekhoven. We wish to specially thank Associate Professor W. Earl Sasser of Harvard University and Assistant Professor William Berry of Ohio State University for their contributions.

The cases and introduction material were possible because of the hours and days of time donated to us by executives of the domestic airlines of North America. We thank them for this contribution to a better understanding of this industry.

Both of us have received valuable assistance for our research from the UPS Foundation (previously known as the 1907 Foundation). This foundation has provided vital support to many transportation scholars throughout the United States of America and Canada.

One author particularly wishes to express his appreciation to Donald W. Douglas Sr. who was an alumnus of M.I.T. and helped the author as a young aeronautical engineering student fron Santa Monica, California at that school. Also, he wishes to express his gratitude to the William Barclay Harding Memorial Fellowship for aviation studies at Harvard University.

The other author gratefully acknowledges the assistance of Ian Gray, president, Gerry Manning, vice president of customer service, and Bill Murphy, director of customer service development (all of CP Air), not only in the development of the case study appearing in this volume but also for other contributions of time and effort to the Air Transport course taught at the University of British Columbia.

We wish to thank Dean Lawrence Fouraker of the Harvard Business School for providing the resources and opportunity to write this book. We are particularly grateful to the president and fellows of Harvard College, and to the Centre for Transportation Studies, University of British Columbia, by whom several of the cases included in this book are individually copyrighted. These cases are published here with their permission.

Introduction
The Domestic Airline
Industry

The Relative Importance of Air Transport in
Domestic Transportation

Expenditures on transportation in the United States, including private and public transportation, passenger and freight transport, and each of the five basic "modes" (rail, highway, air, water, and pipeline) account for approximately 20 percent of the Gross National Product, a total of $300 billion in 1974. As Table I-1 shows, movement of passengers constituted 54 percent of this total. Air transport accounted for 11 percent of passenger transport expenditures and 89 percent of for-hire passenger domestic intercity expenditures (Table I-2). Of total freight transport expenditures, the air mode accounted for only 1.2 percent (Table I-3).

Employment in transportation and related industries in 1974 accounted for approximately 12 percent of the civilian labor force, or 10.1 million people. Of these, approximately 360,000 were directly involved in airline operations and another 530,000 were employed in aircraft manufacturing and parts supply (Table I-4).

In terms of volume carried, there have been wide, and constantly changing, variations between the modes. In 1940, air transport accounted for 0.004 percent of intercity passenger-miles, but by 1975 the volume had grown to over 10 percent (Table I-5). In the same period, rail travel fell from 7.5 percent of passenger-miles to 0.007 percent. Similar rapid growth took place in the air mode's participation in freight transportation, which increased from 0.00003 percent of ton-miles in 1940 to 0.19 percent in 1975 (Table I-6).

Passenger Transport

The relative importance of each mode in passenger transport lies partially in its cost and service characteristics. Among the major determinants of passenger mode selection are cost, speed, length of journey, size of group traveling, required frequency of departure, and availability of service between the desired origin and destination.

As Table I-7 shows, air is the most expensive of the for-hire passenger modes; it cost an average of 7.52 cents per passenger-mile in 1974, compared with 4.41 cents for bus travel. Air is also the speediest of the modes over long distances, although due to the (fixed) time involved in obtaining access to airports, this speed advantage is somewhat reduced for shorter distances. Table I-8 shows the distribution of travel between automobile and for-hire carriers for

Table I-1

Transportation Outlays and Gross National Product, 1965-1974

($ billions)

	1965	1970	1974
Passenger transport	88.0	110.3	162.6
Freight transport	64.0	90.5	139.4
Total	145.0	200.8	302.0
Adjustments[a]	−1.5	−0.8	−1.4
Adjusted total	143.5	200.0	300.6
GNP	688.1	982.4	1406.9
Transport as a percentage of GNP[b]	20.02	19.78	20.90

Source: Adapted from *Transportation: Facts and Trends*, 12th Ed. (Washington, D.C.: Transportation Association of America, 1976), p. 3.

[a]Government expenditures not included in passenger or freight transport outlays, less duplications.

[b]Interest on debt for private automobiles excluded from calculation.

Table I-2

U.S. Passenger Transportation Expenditures, 1965-1974

($ millions)

	1965	1970	1974
Private transportation			
Auto	70,714	93,276	137,379
Air	1,370	2,629	4,262
Total private	72,084	95,905	141,641
For-hire transportation			
Local	3,142	4,509	5,542
Intercity			
Air	3,315	6,605	10,823
Bus	631	779	999
Rail	462	264	339
Water	12	12	16
Total intercity	4,420	7,660	12,177
International			
Air	997	1,925	3,003
Water	333	275	259
Total international	1,330	2,200	3,262
Total, private and for-hire	80,976	110,274	162,662

Source: Adapted from *Transportation: Facts and Trends*, 12th Ed. (Washington, D.C.: Transportation Association of America, 1976), p. 5.

Table I-3

U.S. Freight Transportation Expenditures, 1965-1974

($ millions)

	1965	1970	1974
Highway			
Truck—intercity			
ICC regulated	10,068	14,585	22,700
Other	13,560	18,968	26,112
Truck—local	23,041	35,531	59,847
Bus	70	122	145
	46,739	69,206	108,804
Rail	9,923	11,869	16,873
Water	3,758	5,109	7,838
Oil pipeline	1,051	1,396	1,861
Air	708	1,171	1,745
Forwarders	470	358	431
Other shipper costs	1,399	1,433	1,808
Total	64,048	90,542	139,360

Source: Adapted from *Transportation: Facts and Trends*, 12th Ed. (Washington, D.C.: Transportation Association of America, 1976), p. 4.

Table I-4

Employment in Transportation and Related Industries, 1965-1974

(thousands)

	1965	1970	1974
Transportation service			
Air	229	351	363
Trucking	882	998	1,087
Railroads	735	627	583
All other	485	460	430
Transportation equipment			
Manufacturing			
Aircraft and parts	624	669	532
All other	1,216	1,246	1,388
Total	1,840	1,915	1,920
Transportation-related industries[a]	4,306	4,693	4,978
Government transportation employees	715	789	781
Total transportation employment	9,192	9,833	10,142

Source: Adapted from *Transportation Facts and Trends*, 12th Ed. (Washington, D.C.: Transportation Association of America, 1976), p. 23.

[a]Includes automotive dealers, wholesalers and service stations, highway and street construction, shipping and receiving clerks, and so on.

Table I-5

Intercity Travel, by Modes, 1940-1975

(billions of passenger miles)

	Private Carrier			Public Carrier					Total
	Auto	Air	Total	Air	Bus	Rail	Water	Total	
1940	292.7	0.1	292.8	1.2	10.2	24.8	1.3	37.5	330.3
1950	438.3	0.8	439.1	9.3	22.7	32.5	1.2	65.7	504.8
1960	706.1	2.3	708.4	31.7	19.3	21.6	2.7	75.3	783.7
1970	1026.0	9.1	1035.1	109.5	25.3	10.9	4.0	149.7	1184.8
1975	1164.0	11.1	1175.1	136.9	25.6	10.0	4.0	176.5	1351.6

Source: Adapted from *Transportation: Facts and Trends*, 12th Ed. (Washington, D.C.: Transportation Association of America, 1976), p. 18.

different mileages, and Table I-9 shows the average length of haul for each for-hire mode.

The relative importance of speed in modal choice depends upon the purpose of the trip. Although more detailed classifications are possible, it is conventional to divide the market for intercity travel into two groups: business travel (which accounts for 20 percent of all trips involving journeys of more than 100 miles and at least one night spent away from home) and pleasure travel. The first group of travelers values speed relatively highly in the modal choice decision.

The number of persons traveling primarily effects the choice between private and for-hire transportation because the costs of the latter are dependent on the number of persons in the family group. If a four-member family travels by automobile, however, the total costs vary only slightly from the costs a single person incurs traveling by automobile.

Table I-6

Intercity Freight, by Modes, 1940-1975[a]

(billions of ton miles)

	Rail	Truck	Oil Pipeline	Water	Air	Total
1940	379	62	59	118	0.02	618
1950	597	173	129	164	0.3	1063
1960	579	285	229	220	0.9	1314
1970	771	412	431	319	3.3	1936
1975	761	441	510	354	4.0	2070

Source: Adapted from *Transportation: Facts and Trends*, 12th Ed. (Washington, D.C.: Transportation Association of America, 1976), p. 8.

[a]Includes both for-hire and private carriers. Prior to 1969, includes mail and express.

Table I-7

Average Revenue of For-hire Carriers, per Passenger-mile, by Mode, 1950-1974
(cents)

	1950	*1960*	*1970*	*1974*
Rail[a]	2.74	3.03	4.02	5.85
Bus[a]	1.89	2.71	3.60	4.41
Air[a]				
First class	5.79	7.06	8.31	8.89
Coach	4.11	5.01	5.46	6.94
Total	5.56	6.09	6.00	7.52
Consumer Price Index[b]	108	133	174	221

Source: Adapted from *Transportation: Facts and Trends*, 12th Ed. (Washington, D.C.: Transportation Association of America, 1976), p. 7.

[a]Class I railroads, Class I motor buses, and domestic scheduled airlines.
[b]1947 = 100.

In terms of availability of service, measured by the extent of geographical coverage, the air mode ranks behind automobile travel and the bus mode, but ahead of rail travel. It is noteworthy that, from the traveler's point of view, the relevant measure of availability of service may be the availability of direct service (i.e., the fewest number of interchanges). In particular markets, this factor might alter the ranking of the air and bus modes.

Frequency of departure is an important factor in the modal choice decision because the traveler looks for availability of service *when* it is required. Private

Table I-8

Choice of Travel Mode, by Distance of Trip, 1972

	Percent of Person Trips	*Percent by Automobile*	*Percent by Public Transport*
200-399 miles	42	97	3
400-599	20	93	7
600-799	10	88	12
800-999	5	77	23
1000 or more	19	63	37
Outside continental United States	4	49	51
	100		

Source: Adapted from *Transportation: Facts and Trends*, 12th Ed. (Washington, D.C.: Transportation Association of America, 1976), p. 20.

Table I-9
Average Length of Haul of Class I Intercity Carriers of Passengers, 1950-1974

	1950	1960	1970	1974
Air	461	583	679	684
Bus	52	79	106	120
Rail	128	139	79	76

Source: Adapted from *Transportation: Facts and Trends*, 12th Ed. (Washington, D.C.: Transportation Association of America, 1976), p. 15.

transportation (automobile) is the most favorable mode in this respect, and rail travel clearly ranks last. However, the ranking of air and bus depends upon the particular market considered and air usually provides the greater frequency of departure. The variability of demand for air travel by hour of the day, day of the week, and month of the year are shown in Tables I-10, I-11, and I-12, respectively.

Freight Transport

The participation of each mode in freight transportation is a function of its basic characteristics. Railroads are basically long-haul, slow movers of raw materials and low-value manufactured products (Table I-13). Except for a small percentage, all rail shipments are in "carload" (CL) lots. This term is not well defined, but it usually refers to shipments exceeding 10,000 pounds. Water transport is limited in scope due to the confines of the inland waterway system (which is usually defined to include coastal routes). Being a slow but low-cost mode of transport, water carriers have specialized in products of generally low value per pound (coal, ore, gravel, iron, steel, and cement).

The specialities of trucking include fast movement (relative to rail and barge), a willingness to handle small shipments ("less than truckload," or LTL), and complete door-to-door service. The motor-carrier industry's geographical coverage is extensive, and its frequency of service is extremely high. Because of these services, trucks have been able to penetrate the market for freight transportation in spite of relatively high costs (see Table I-14 and Figure I-1).

Air-freight shipments are generally categorized as *emergency, routine perishable,* or *routine surface divertible.* Emergency services are unplanned with the emphasis on speedy ("next day") delivery. An example is the delivery of a part needed to repair an out-of-order machine that is critical to a manufacturing plant. Routine perishable service is a planned shipment that usually consists of fresh fruit, vegetables, fresh flowers, and so on, and emphasizes customers' demand and service more than cost. Routine surface divertible is also a planned

Table I-10
Variability of Demand for Air Travel, by Hour of Departure, 1969[a]

Hour of Departure	Traffic as Percent of Peak Hour	Average Load Factor[b]
1 A.M.	15.2	45
2	5.7	31
3	4.1	36
4	2.8	43
5	2.3	44
6	2.5	n/a
7	29.0	42
8	71.2	48
9	92.5	55
10	77.2	57
11	65.7	51
12 (noon)	74.4	66
1 P.M.	70.6	58
2	63.8	55
3	74.4	63
4	78.3	66
5	100.0	64
6	99.1	64
7	95.8	61
8	57.6	53
9	55.8	44
10	37.1	44
11	21.7	38
12 (midnight)	14.9	46

Source: U.S. Department of Transportation, CAB Dockets 21866-9 and 21866-6, quoted in Douglas and Miller, *Economic Regulation of Domestic Air Transportation: Theory and Policy* (Washington, D.C.: Brookings Institution, 1974), p. 34

[a]Based on samples taken during all of 1969 (traffic data) and during February and November 1969 (load factor data).
[b]Percent of available seats filled.

shipment, but the total cost factors are more important than the speed of delivery or demand. In this type of service, the savings in inventory and warehousing costs often offset the incremental increase in the cost of air freight over a competing surface carrier.

There is a distinction between the terms air freight and air cargo, at least as used in the United States. Air cargo consists of a variety of services including air freight, U.S. mail, Air Express, and priority reserved freight. Air Express refers to a service offered prior to November 1975 by a partnership of the airlines and

Table I-11
Variability of Demand for Air Travel, by Day of Week, 1969[a]

Day of Week	Traffic as Percent of Peak Day	Average Load Factor[b]
Monday	90.0	63
Tuesday	88.4	51
Wednesday	92.8	53
Thursday	97.7	57
Friday	100.0	56
Saturday	84.2	58
Sunday	98.0	53

Source: U.S. Department of Transportation, CAB Dockets 21866-9 and 21866-6, quoted in Douglas and Miller, *Economic Regulation of Domestic Air Transportation: Theory and Policy* (Washington, D.C.: Brookings Institution, 1974), p. 35.

[a]Based on samples taken during all of 1969 (traffic data) and during February and November 1969 (load factor data).
[b]Percent of available seats filled.

Table I-12
Variability of Demand for Air Travel, by Month, 1969[a]

Month	Travel as Percent of Peak Day	Average Load Factor[b]
January	86.2	
February	66.0	58
March	85.6	
April	94.6	
May	92.9	59
June	98.6	
July	95.2	
August	100.0	71
September	83.3	
October	86.7	
November	79.2	55
December	93.7	

Source: U.S. Department of Transportation, CAB Dockets 21866-9 and 21866-6, quoted in Douglas and Miller, *Economic Regulation of Domestic Air Transportation: Theory and Policy* (Washington, D.C.: Brookings Institution, 1974), p. 35.

[a]Based on samples taken during all of 1969 (traffic data) and during February, May, August, and November 1969 (load factor data).
[b]Percent of available seats filled.

Table I-13
Average Length of Freight Haul, 1940-1974[a]

	1940	1950	1960	1970	1974
Air[b]	N/A	720	953	1014	1050
Railroad[c]	351	416	442	490	533
Truck[d]	236	218	239	276	302
Oil pipeline[e]					
Crude	254	292	316	300	302
Product	249	296	271	357	345
Water					
Rivers and canals	N/A	N/A	282	330	359
Great lakes	N/A	N/A	522	506	540
Domestic deep sea	N/A	N/A	1496	1509	1383

Note: N/A = not available.

Source: Adapted from *Transportation: Facts and Trends*, 12th Ed. (Washington, D.C.: Transportation Association of America, 1976), p. 14.

[a]Figures shown here do not include any allowance for the additional mileage due to the circuitry of the mode.
[b]All certificated airlines.
[c]All operating line-haul railroads.
[d]Class I intercity common carriers.
[e]All oil pipelines subject to ICC regulation.

Table I-14
Average Revenue per Ton-mile, by Mode, 1950-1974
(cents)

	1950	1960	1970	1974
Rail (Class I)	1.33	1.40	1.43	1.85
Truck (Class I)	5.01	6.31	7.46	9.00
Air (domestic scheduled)	18.10	22.80	21.91	25.92
Oil pipeline	0.32	0.32	0.29	0.32
Wholesale Price Index[a]	107	124	144	209

Source: Adapted from *Transportation: Facts and Trends*, 12th Ed. (Washington, D.C.: Transportation Association of America, 1976), p. 7.

[a]1947 = 100.

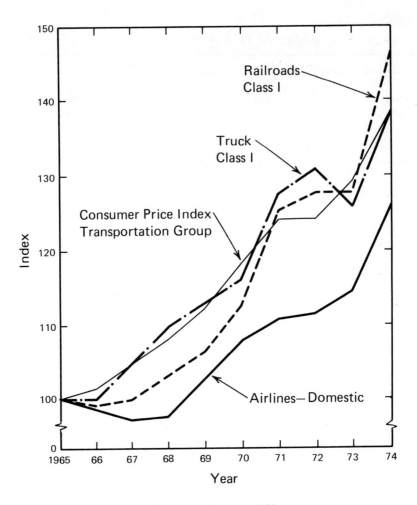

Sources: *Statistical Abstract—1975* and *Air Transport 1975.*

Figure I-1. Comparison of Freight Rates (1965 = 100)

REA Express for the priority movement of packages generally under 50 pounds. Priority reserved freight refers to similar services offered (mainly since 1975) by the individual airlines. In 1975, freight accounted for 80 percent of the air-cargo revenues of the scheduled airlines, and air mail for 19 percent.

The airport-to-airport (line-haul) movement of air freight is only a part of the air-freight system. The total operations also include pickup and delivery, containerization and packaging, and billing and collection.

The pickup and delivery service (i.e., movement of freight from the shipper's door to the originating airport, and the subsequent movement from the destination terminal to the consignee) is provided in a variety of ways. Some shippers deal with the airlines directly and deliver the shipment themselves to the cargo terminal, the consignee, or a local truck line performing pickup from the destination. Alternatively, the shipper may hire a motor carrier to deliver the shipment. The domestic trunk airlines jointly own and control a company called Air Cargo Inc. (ACI), which provides such services. The ACI service is provided by an independent trucking contractor who responds to a centrally located dispatcher at each major airport. However, because the individual airlines have no direct dispatch control and because there is no identification of the trucking contractor with a specific airline, some airlines operate their own fleets of trucks in major markets.

Shippers do have another alternative, one that has been growing rapidly in importance: the air-freight forwarder. Air-freight forwarders are licensed by the Civil Aeronautics Board as "indirect carriers" and provide a variety of services. The main source of their profitability is the *consolidating* function that they perform. Forwarders solicit freight—generally in small shipments—consolidate all the freight moving to the same destination, and purchase the line-haul movement from the direct carriers (i.e., the airlines). The forwarders' agents at the destination terminal pick up the consolidated shipment, break bulk, and perform local delivery. Because the air carriers' rates include a variety of weight and volume "breaks" (i.e., discounts), the forwarders are able to charge less for a small shipment than the airlines. In addition, by building sufficient volume to a single destination, forwarders are also able to take advantage of the low *containerized* freight rates offered by the airlines.

The forwarder provides a variety of additional services to the shipper. Because the forwarder can select the line-haul movement from any of the direct carriers, it can offer service between a greater variety of city-pairs than any individual airline, and because the shipment moves under the forwarder's own waybill, the forwarder takes on the responsibility of overseeing all transferrals of the shipment between the shipper's door and that of the final customer. The effect is to reduce the amount of documentation that the shipper must provide. In addition, by maintaining contact between terminals (via teletype, TWX, or computer), the forwarder can provide a tracing service for the shipper.

Forwarders are important to the airlines. By the early 1970s they accounted for approximately 30 percent of all domestic air-freight traffic. By reducing the number of individual shipments tendered at an airline's terminal and by increasing the use of containers, they reduce the complexity of the ground-handling task to the airlines.

Direct shipment (i.e., direct dealing with the airlines rather than with forwarders) is predominantly used for the larger-volume, routine-perishable-type shipments. Although the airlines have tried to improve their direct-service reputation, they have been only moderately successful. In a survey of traffic and distribution executives conducted by *Distribution Worldwide*,[1] 47 percent of the respondents answered negatively when asked whether the airlines were living up to their claims of providing dependable air-freight service. Some of their suggestions for the airlines were:

Improve delivery service. Often the short time gained does not warrant the considerable added expense over other means of transport.

Provide better forwarding and tracing information.

Ship (entire) large shipments on the same flight.

(Don't) give air freight a second-class status.

Deliver shipments when they say they will.

A comparison of air-freight services offered by airlines and freight forwarders is given in Table I-15.

The Structure of the Air-transport Industry

The air-transport industry may be structured according to a number of dimensions (Figure I-2). One dimension of interest distinguishes between

Table I-15
Comparison of Air-freight Services

| Comparison Factors | Direct Shipment | | | Forwarder | |
	Small Parcel Air Cargo	Air Express	Regular Air Service	Expedited Service	Regular Air Service
1. Freight pick-up from shipper	120 minutes after call	Same day	Varies	Same day	Same day
2. Shipment size and weight limitations	1 piece 50 pounds 90" (length plus girth)	No	No	1 piece 50 pounds 90" (length plus girth)	No
3. Delivery made	Arrival + 120 minutes	24 hours	48 hours	Possibly to-day or early tomorrow	48 hours
4. Comparison of cost (NYC to LA, 50 lbs. general commodity, Jan. '76)	$64.00	$50.45	$38.45	$127.15	$52.18

Source: Adapted from *Distribution Worldwide*, June 1976.

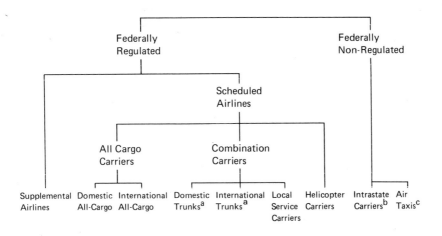

^aAll domestic trunks except United are also international trunks, and all international trunks have some domestic operations.

^bIntra-Alaska and Intra-Hawaii airlines are federally regulated.

^cAlso operating in this sector is Federal Express Corporation, an interstate all-cargo carrier operating small aircraft, and exempt from federal regulation under the "air taxi" (weight of aircraft) provision.

Figure I-2. Structure of the Air-transport Industry

(federally) regulated and unregulated carriers. Except for carriers that operate solely within the boundaries of a single state and certain "air taxis" operating aircraft below a set weight limit (net takeoff weight of 12,500 pounds), all air carriers must be "certificated" by the Civil Aeronautics Board (CAB), a regulatory agency of the federal government. Exceptions to this rule are intra-Hawaii and intra-Alaska operators, which are also federally regulated.

Among regulated carriers, a further distinction is made between scheduled and nonscheduled airlines (the latter being also known as "supplemental" or "irregular" air carriers). Scheduled air carriers provide regular service between designated city-pairs, whereas nonscheduled airlines offer irregular, charter services. It should be noted that most scheduled air carriers have the authority (from the CAB) to offer nonscheduled services, but nonscheduled carriers are normally prohibited from offering scheduled services. Nonscheduled airlines (or "nonskeds" as they are often called) operate primarily in international markets; domestic operations mainly concentrate on freight rather than passenger operations. Nonskeds account for approximately 4 percent of domestic air travel and approximately 9 percent of domestic air cargo.

Scheduled air carriers are divided into "combination" carriers, which transport both passengers and cargo, and "all-cargo" carriers, which are prevented (by the CAB) from transporting passengers.

Combination Carriers

The scheduled combination carriers are divided into two groups: the eleven trunk carriers (CAB Class I) that operate over wide geographical areas (an average length of haul of 810 miles in 1975 domestic operation) and the nine local service carriers that operate in more narrowly defined areas (an average length of haul of 312 miles in 1975). It is necessary to make a distinction between *international* trunk carriers and *domestic* trunks. As of 1976, all domestic trunks except United were also international trunks. Prior to 1970, Pan American was solely an international trunk. In 1970 the CAB revised its definition of domestic traffic to include operations between the United States mainland and Hawaii and Alaska. In consequence, Pan American became classified as a domestic trunk as well as an international trunk. A list of all carriers in each sector of the air-transport industry is given in Table I-16.

Cargo Carriers

In 1976 there were only two conventional[a] domestic all-cargo carriers (The Flying Tiger line and Airlift International) and one international all-cargo carrier (Seaboard World). Combination carriers participated in the cargo market either by carrying cargo in the "bellies" (lower holds) of passenger aircraft or by operating freighter (all-cargo aircraft). Table I-17 shows the structure of the cargo market in 1974.

In addition to the direct carriers (i.e., the airlines), there were approximately three hundred air-freight forwarders in 1976 as a result of an industry growth rate of 20 percent between 1962 and 1971. The industry is somewhat concentrated however, and Emery Air Freight clearly dominates the market. Total revenues in the air-freight-forwarder industry in 1973 exceeded $800 million, with operating profits (before taxes) of $16.3 million.

Local Service Carriers

The local service (CAB Class II) carriers originated in the post-World War II era when the CAB authorized an experimental feeder system to expand domestic

[a]Federal Express and several parcel carriers might also be considered all-cargo carriers, but they are not generally included in this category.

Table I-16
Classification of Airlines[a]

Trunk	Local Service	All Cargo
American (AA)	Air New England (NE)	Airlift International (RD)
Braniff International (BN)	Allegheny (AL)	Flying Tiger Line (FT)
Continental (CO)	Frontier (FL)	Seaboard World (SB)
Delta (DL)	Hughes Airwest (RW)	
Eastern (EA)	North Central (NC)	
National (NA)	Ozark (OZ)	
Northwest (NW)	Piedmont (PI)	
Pan American (PA)	Southern (SO)	
Trans World (TW)	Texas International (TI)	
United (UA)		
Western (WA)		

Source: Adapted from *Air Transport 1976* (Washington, D.C.: Air Transport Association of America, 1976), p. 31.

[a]Abbreviations for airline names are the official abbreviations.

mail and passenger service to small and intermediate-size cities. Seventeen carriers had gained temporary operating authority by 1950. In less than ten years the experiment proved successful, and in 1955 Congress granted the local service carriers permanent certification.

Many of the feeder airlines certificated between 1944 and 1950, including Piedmont, Ozark, and Allegheny Airlines, have prospered. Others, including Northeast and Mohawk airlines, have disappeared, although their routes have remained largely intact through mergers with trunk lines (e.g., Northeast with Delta) or other local service airlines (e.g., Mohawk with Allegheny). In 1972 there were ten regional carriers, as they were sometimes known. By 1976 there were only nine. The decline in the number of carriers was, in part, due to the deterioration of short-haul markets in the 1960s and 1970s. Population shifts away from smaller communities (served by local service airlines) to large cities (served by trunk lines) and intermodal competition from the interstate highway network had made many points less attractive to the airlines than when these points were first certificated. These phenomena, along with the rising cost of doing business, contributed to the difficulties of many local service carriers. Comparative statistics on the nine local service airlines operating in 1975 are given in Table I-18.

Air-Taxi and Commuter Airlines

The air-taxi and commuter airlines also developed in the post-World War II period, when many government aircraft were declared surplus and great numbers

Table I-17
Comparative Scheduled Domestic Air-freight Statistics, 1974

	Total Freight RTMs (000)	Total Freight Revenue (000)	Freight Yield (cents/RTM)	All-Cargo Freight RTMs (000)	All-Cargo Percentage of Total Freight	All-Cargo Load Factor (%)	Domestic Freighter Fleet
Domestic trunk lines							
American	447,553	$107,506	24.02	262,794	58.7	47.7	30
Braniff	58,897	18,343	31.14	23,414	39.8	71.5	13
Continental	164,881	32,573	19.76	None	0	–	None
Delta	172,296	64,033	37.16	None	0	–	None
Eastern	134,824	43,871	32.54	41,124	30.5	62.3	18
National	43,723	12,806	29.29	None	0	–	None
Northwest	205,825	47,293	22.98	41,899	20.4	49.7	5
Trans World	269,302	68,067	25.28	154,277	57.3	58.0	8
United	623,791	148,602	23.82	338,880	54.3	55.6	30
Western	66,467	18,937	28.49	None	0	–	None
Domestic all-cargo airlines							
Airlift	80,150	16,367	20.42	30,150	100.0	56.7	3
Flying Tiger	384,434	68,986	17.94	384,434	100.0	60.3	10

Source: *CAB—Quarterly Cargo Review*, December 1974, and *CAB—Trends in All-Cargo Service*, December 1975.

of skilled aviators were released from military service. Large numbers of small, one- and two-airplane carriers sought authority to provide charter and air-taxi services to certificated and noncertificated points. In a landmark decision, the CAB granted broad relief from strict regulatory controls to air-taxi and commuter air services. These airlines thus developed in a relatively competitive environment, subject only to CAB and Federal Aviation Administration (FAA) safety regulations and the restriction on aircraft size designed to protect the local service carriers. In 1975, the maximum takeoff weight for these aircraft was 12,500 pounds. Typically, this restriction meant that the aircraft had to carry less than twenty passengers in an environment lacking air-conditioning, pressurization, and lavatory facilities. In 1972 the CAB changed this restriction to 7,500 pound *payload* or 30 seats. Aircraft designers responded to this restriction by producing aircraft particularly suited to operations of air-taxi and commuter (CAB Class III) carriers. These aircraft, notably the DeHavilland, the DHC-6 (Twin Otter), and the Beechcraft B-99, were well suited to short-haul operations, short airstrips and minimal ground-service support at intermediate stops. As a special exemption, the CAB allowed commuter airlines to operate the larger Douglas DC-3 over routes not served by certificated carriers.

The relative sizes and growth of the sectors of the scheduled air-transport industry may be judged from Tables I-19, I-20, I-21, and I-22. Table I-19 shows revenue passenger-miles, a standard industry measure of passenger traffic, and Table I-20 gives the equivalent measure of cargo traffic (cargo ton-miles). The relative contributions of passenger and cargo traffic to airline revenues appear in Table I-21. The relative sizes of individual trunk airlines are listed in Table I-22.

The Regulatory Environment

Economic regulation of the air-transport industry, in its current form, dates from the Civil Aeronautics Act of 1938, which established the Civil Aeronautics Agency. Prior to this time, the federal government exerted a substantial degree of control over the infant industry through a variety of government departments, but primarily through the postal service, which granted air mail subsidies to promote the development of the industry. The historical context explains the fact that, in contrast to the Interstate Commerce Commission, which regulates the rail, highway, water, and pipeline modes, the Civil Aeronautics Agency and its successor, the Civil Aeronautics Board (formed in 1940), had (and have) the explicit responsibility not only for the regulation of the air-transport industry, but also for its promotion and development. Carriers under the CAB's jurisdiction must comply with certain regulations on matters of entry to and exit from individual markets, rates charged, finance, mergers and acquisitions, intercarrier agreements, and quality of service.

The CAB has five members, each of whom serves a six-year term. Members

Table I-18
Local Service Airlines Statistics, 1975

	Net Profit (Loss) ($000)	Total Operating Expense ($ per Revenue Ton-mile)	Total Operating Expense ($ per Revenue Ton-mile)	Operating Profit or (Loss) ($ per Revenue Ton-mile)	Average System Block-/ to-block Speed (mph)	Number of Aircraft Operated End of Year	Average Length of Flight (miles)	Passengers Emplaned per Departure
Air New England	(1527)	2.5048	2.6579	(0.1531)	158	22	81	6.5
Allegheny	(9886)	1.0382	1.0294	0.0088	330	81	230	33.9
Frontier	6800	1.0455	0.9735	0.0720	303	48	194	20.6
Hughes Air West	1703	1.1183	1.1009	0.0174	348	37	237	28.9
North Central	5224	1.3762	1.3154	0.0608	280	50	135	20.4
Ozark	546	1.2418	1.2094	0.0324	286	43	165	21.6
Piedmont	(1358)	1.1667	1.1452	0.0215	266	43	163	21.0
Southern	2743	1.1179	1.0865	0.0314	321	35	186	22.0
Texas International[a]	(4371)	1.2723	1.3197	(0.0474)	328	40	220	22.3

[a]Strikes affected Texas International during 1975.

are appointed by the president of the United States, subject to Senate approval. Like the Interstate Commerce Commission, the CAB is not itself a court but has recourse to the courts to enforce its orders. The CAB is not responsible for the safety regulation of aircraft and airline operations. These are the province of the Federal Aviation Administration (FAA), formed in 1958. The FAA is also responsible for airport-airway support functions. Since the formation of the Department of Transportation (DOT) in 1966, the FAA has been housed within the DOT, whereas the CAB has remained an independent regulatory agency.

Entry

No carrier may institute service in any market (i.e., between any two points) without first obtaining a certificate of authority from the CAB, which rules on the "public convenience and necessity" of certificating the carrier on that route. Carriers already serving the route or others desiring to initiate service may protest the application, and public hearings may be held by the CAB on the application. Such proceedings may be costly to all parties and, in some cases, might last for years.

The CAB has considerable discretion in interpreting "public convenience and necessity," and it can use its route-awarding authority to achieve other goals, such as the promotion of the survival of weak carriers by allowing them access to lucrative markets. In general, however, the major factors considered by

Passengers Emplaned per Station	Average Passenger Loads	Average Available Seats	Revenues Passenger Miles Flown (000)	Available Seat Miles Flown (000)	Passenger Load Factors (%)	Total Mail Ton-/ miles (000)	Total Freight Ton-/ miles (000)	Number of Stations Operated	Number of Employees End of Year
29,860	10.9	23.7	57,091	123,756	46.1	43	66	14	400
183,054	47.2	88.6	3,304,490	6,203,021	53.3	12,883	19,905	55	7476
41,480	41.5	74.5	1,455,509	2,616,978	55.6	4,630	10,403	91	3657
72,787	46.0	87.2	1,503,725	2,848,516	52.8	2,585	5,865	54	3790
65,436	36.0	75.1	1,071,637	2,234,659	48.0	3,295	8,408	70	3430
68,717	37.8	77.0	983,117	2,003,420	49.1	2,969	6,534	49	2937
71,348	38.4	77.5	1,074,446	2,169,015	49.5	2,810	6,028	50	3058
61,472	38.5	74.7	982,759	1,906,443	51.5	2,153	5,192	51	2639
34,784	36.4	72.9	586,669	1,174,562	49.9	919	3,311	45	2234

the CAB in route awards are the capability of the applicant to serve the route, the effects that adding another carrier will have on the level of competition (including consideration of the effects of diversion of traffic on average load factors) and the extent to which the new route "fits" the applicant's existing route structure. In spite of these guidelines, each case is decided on its own merits.

The CAB can restrict the operating authority of a carrier in a particular market, for example, by specifying compulsory intermediate stops. Carriers may not suspend or abandon service on any route without prior permission from the CAB.

Passenger Fares

All fares charged by air carriers are subject to CAB approval. The CAB can disallow them if they are "unjust or unreasonable, or unjustly discriminatory, or unduly preferential, or unduly prejudicial." In addition to the power of approval, the CAB can prescribe the rate to be charged by a given market or prescribe a maximum or minimum or both. The effect of these exhaustive rate powers of the CAB has been virtually to eliminate price competition between regulated carriers. It should be noted that the CAB also rules on the commissions that may be paid to travel agents (currently 7 percent) for the sale of airplane tickets and thus eliminates price competition in that area. In 1968, travel agents accounted for one-third of airline tickets sold.

Table I-19

Revenue Passenger-miles, by Scheduled Industry Sector[a]

(millions)

	1965[b]	1970	1975
Domestic trunks	48,987	95,900	119,446
Local service	2,621	7,431	10,738
International trunks	16,789	27,563	31,082
Total	68,397	120,894	161,266

Source: Adapted from *Air Transport 1976* (Washington, D.C.: Air Transport Association of America, 1976), pp. 12-16.

[a]Excludes nonscheduled, air taxi, commuter, intrastate, and helicopter operators.

[b]Due to the redefinition of domestic traffic to include operations between the U.S. mainland and Hawaii and Alaska, domestic and international traffic since 1969 is not strictly comparable with previous years.

The CAB's policy with respect to fares has undergone a number of changes since World War II. The pricing of airline services is a complex topic, and the two major investigations of passenger fares conducted since 1950, the General Passenger Fare Investigation (1956-1960) and the Domestic Passenger Fare Investigation, or DPFI (1970-1974), each took four years to complete. The General Passenger Fare Investigation, after some dispute, restricted its attention to the overall level of fares and procedures for setting this level, ignoring the fare

Table I-20

Cargo Ton-miles, by Scheduled Industry Sector, 1965-1975[a]

(millions)

	1965[b]	1970	1975
Domestic combination trunk	1131	2556	2849
Local service	28	86	98
International combination trunk	841	1481	2464
Domestic all cargo	171	259	433
International all cargo	122	573	903
Total	2293	4955	6747

Source: *Air Transport 1976* (Washington, D.C.: Air Transport Association of America, 1976), pp. 12-16.

[a]Excludes nonscheduled, air taxi, commuter, intrastate, and helicopter operators. However, includes nonscheduled operations by scheduled carriers.

[b]See footnote b, Table I-19.

Table I-21

Operating Revenues of Scheduled U.S. Airlines, by Industry Sector and Source of Revenue 1965-1975[a]

($ millions)

	1965[b]	1970	1975
Domestic trunk			
Passenger	2,908	5,536	8,774
Cargo	274	557	775
Other[c]	82	180	762
Subtotal	3,264	6,273	10,311
Local service			
Passenger	203	628	1,162
Cargo	16	45	71
Other[c]	72	64	135
Subtotal	291	737	1,368
International trunk			
Passenger	887	1380	2,230
Cargo	212	301	445
Other[c]	112	233	388
Subtotal	1,211	1,914	3,063
Domestic all cargo			
Cargo	24	39	89
Other[c]	58	10	6
Subtotal	82	49	95
International all cargo			
Cargo	20	89	197
Other[c]	36	107	76
Subtotal	56	196	273
All carriers			
Passenger	3,998	7,544	12,166
Cargo	546	1,031	1,577
Other	360	594	1,367
Total	4,904	9,169	14,110

Source: *Air Transport 1976* (Washington, D.C.: Air Transport Association of America, 1976), pp. 18-21.

[a]Excludes nonscheduled, air taxi, commuter, intrastate, and helicopter carriers.

[b]See footnote b, Table I-19.

[c]Includes charter, public service, excess baggage, foreign mail, incidental, and other transport revenues.

Table I-22
Operating Statement, Trunk Carriers, 1975[a]

($ millions)

	Revenues		Operating Expenses		Operating Profit	
	Domestic Operations	System Operations	Domestic Operations	System Operations	Domestic Operations	System Operations
American	1,580	1,746	1,601	1,756	(21)	(10)
Braniff	433	570	393	517	40	53
Continental	481	492	440	451	41	41
Delta	1,355	1,391	1,263	1,296	92	95
Eastern	1,315	1,586	1,254	1,530	61	55
National	330	350	311	326	19	24
Northwest	582	788	542	731	40	57
Pan American	107	1,623	131	1,799	(25)	(96)
TWA	1,184	1,772	1,231	1,843	(47)	(70)
United	2,255	2,255	2,184	2,184	72	72
Western	454	490	440	474	14	16
Total	10,074	13,063	9,788	12,827	285	236

Source: U.S. Civil Aeronautics Board, *Quarterly Industry Financial Report*, June 1976.

[a]Twelve months ending 20 June 1975.

structure. It introduced the concept of "rate-of-return regulation" into the airline industry by requiring that the fare level should be set so as to give the airline industry a target return on invested capital of 10.5 percent.

Rate-of-return regulation implies that not only must issues of fare levels and fare structures be decided, but also standards must be set and forecasts made about airline costs and financial structure. In consequence, the CAB has had to rule on such matters as the average load factor (percent of available seats filled) to be used as the basis for predicting costs, the treatment of depreciation, the appropriate capital structure of the airline industry, and many other topics. This increased complexity led directly to the second major investigation of airline fares, the Domestic Passenger Fare Investigation.

The DPFI addressed not only the fare level, but also its structure. It was divided into nine phases: (1) treatment of flight equipment depreciation and residual values for rate purposes; (2) treatment of leased aircraft for rate purposes; (3) deferred federal income taxes; (4) joint fares; (5) discount fares; (6) seating configurations and load factors; (7) fare level; (8) rate of return; and (9) fare structure.[2] This investigation led to several significant decisions.

In Phase 1, the CAB determined the depreciation schedules and residual values that were to be used for rate-setting purposes (though not necessarily for airline record-keeping and income-tax purposes). These figures are shown in Table I-23. In Phase 4, the CAB ruled that joint fares (i.e., fares for journeys

Table I-23
CAB Depreciation Standards, 1971

Equipment	Service Life (years)	Residual Value (percent of cost)
Turbofan		
4-engine	14	2
3-engine	14	2
2-engine	14	2
Turbojet		
4-engine	10	5
2-engine	10	5
Turboprop		
4-engine	12	5
2-engine	10	15
Wide-body		
4-engine	14	10
3-engine	16	10

Source: U.S. Civil Aeronautics Board, *Domestic Passenger Fare Investigation*, Phase I, 9 April 1971, p. 3.

involving more than one carrier) must be available and quoted to the public, and it determined rules by which these joint fares could be set and the resulting revenues shared between the carriers.

Phase 5, the investigation of discount fares had an immense impact on air-fare structures. The airlines had constantly experimented with various forms of differential pricing (i.e., offering discounts to certain passengers based on age, size of group traveling, nature of journey, time of travel, and many other factors). Because the costs of aircraft operation were relatively fixed in relation to the number of passengers carried, the airlines attempted to lure people who would not otherwise travel through discount pricing (thus increasing revenues without substantially increasing costs), while maintaining full revenue yield from those who were willing to travel at full fares. In a landmark decision, the CAB ruled that most discount fares existing in the early 1970s (principally the "youth" fares and "family" fares) were unlawful, because they were unjustly discriminatory. These standards were set for lawful discount fares: (1) they must not be unjustly discriminatory; (2) they must improve net profit, even if they do not cover fully allocated costs; and (3) they must contain an expiration date of not more than eighteen months from the effective date. These standards allowed discount fares to be reintroduced; subsequently National Airlines instituted "No Frills" service (which offered lower fares in exchange for fewer cabin services, such as meals).

In Phase 9, the CAB ruled on two other important aspects of the fare structure: distance taper and first-class fares. Prior to the DPFI, airline fares tended to be linearly related to length of journey, as shown in Figure I-3. However, the costs of aircraft operation are such that costs per passenger mile decrease with the length of haul, and thus long-haul operations were more profitable and subsidized the less profitable short hauls. The CAB's decision in Phase 9 changed this structure by increasing the "distance taper" in the rates and thus raising short-haul fares and lowering long-haul fares. The CAB's basis for fare calculation is shown in Table I-24. (Note that the local service carriers were given authority to deviate from this formula by up to 30 percent.)

Prior to the DPFI, first-class fares were set (on average) at 30 percent more than day coach fares (night coach fares were set at 20 percent less than day coach fares). In Phase 9, the CAB found that first-class fares were unjust and unreasonable, because the costs of providing first-class service (primarily the cost of the additional space taken up by first-class seats) were in excess of 30 percent, and it ruled that first-class fares must be based on fully allocated cost. This requirement resulted in first-class fares that were 50 to 65 percent higher than day coach fares. (The problem of night coach fares was not resolved and was deferred to a later investigation.)

Air-Freight Rates

In 1970, the CAB also launched an investigation into air-freight rates known as the Domestic Air Freight Rate Investigation (DAFRI). The last CAB investiga-

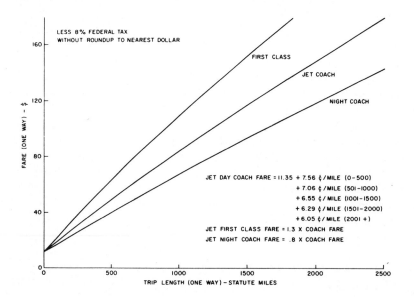

Source: N.K. Taneja, *The Commercial Airline Industry* (Lexington, Mass.: Lexington Books, D.C. Heath and Co., 1976), p. 35.

Figure I-3. U.S. Domestic Passenger Fare Structure, 1974

Table I-24
Domestic-passenger-coach Fare Structure

Terminal Charge	Line-haul Charge (cents per mile)	Mileage
$12.56	7.06	0-500
	5.39	501-1500
	5.18	1501 and over

Source: U.S. Civil Aeronautics Board, *Domestic Passenger Fare Investigation*, Phase 9, 18 March 1974, p. 181.

tion into air-freight rates had taken place in 1948, soon after the creation of the air-freight industry, and it was felt that an investigation of the level and structure of air-freight rates was long overdue.

Air-freight rates fall into three groups: general commodity rates, which apply to all commodities and average 25.69 cents per ton-mile; specific commodity rates, which are quoted for specific commodities over specific routes (primarily northbound and eastbound to correct directional imbalances in traffic); and container rates, which were introduced in an attempt to attract dense commodities in containers in order to make better use of the space available on aircraft. As with freight rates in other modes, air-freight rates are quoted for different shipment weights. Discounts are given for large shipments. In large part this structure results from the high fixed-cost component (relative to shipment size) of ground handling (terminal) operations and documentation procedures.

A large number of issues were addressed in the DAFRI, although a final resolution had not been reached at the time of this writing. (The Administrative Law Judge in charge of the investigation had made his recommendations to the CAB, which had not acted upon them and which was not legally constrained to accept his findings. The findings reported here are therefore not the final decisions.)

Among these issues were the lawfulness of specific commodity rates (most of which were found to be unlawful), weight-related discounts (also found to be unlawful), directional rates (discounts given to traffic moving in opposite directions to predominant traffic flows, which were found to be unlawful) and daylight container rates (based on movement during the day rather than at night, also found to be unlawful).

A central issue in the DAFRI was the conflict between the combination carriers and the all-cargo carriers. The latter naturally wanted rate levels based on the fully allocated costs of freighter aircraft, whereas the former wanted to price air freight on the basis of (marginal) direct costs of carrying freight in passenger aircraft. The administrative law judge ruled in favor of the all-cargo carriers in this matter and used the concept of fully allocated costs to resolve many other issues, such as the allocation of ground costs to traffic of various kinds. He also recommended a rise in the commodity rate to 32.88 cents per ton-mile.

It should be noted that although air-freight-forwarder tariffs must be filed with the CAB, there is no regulation of these rates. In consequence, price competition in the industry is intense and causes many forwarders to maintain unprofitable accounts. Apart from Emery Air Freight, which has used its industry leadership to build a reputation as a premium-service, high-price forwarder, the profitability of individual firms in the industry has been highly erratic.

Mergers

All mergers and takeovers of airlines are subject to CAB approval. Mergers in the airline industry are proposed for a number of reasons. Among the most often given is the desire to raise the profitability of both the merging carriers by creating a more advantageous (combined) route structure or to solve such problems as seasonality and other traffic imbalance problems by combining "complementary" carriers. Most industry analysts believe that there are only small (if any) economies of scale in the airline industry, if scale is measured solely in terms of firm size. However, because larger airlines *tend* to have longer hauls and greater scheduling flexibility because they have more routes (both factors can affect profitability), the desire to reap returns to scale is often given as the motivation for proposed mergers. In addition, a profitable carrier may view an acquisition as a simpler method of expansion than one-by-one route applications. Over the years, the CAB has, at times, actively encouraged some mergers in order to avoid the bankruptcy of certain carriers and the consequent cessation of service. In general, however, the CAB's guidelines in deciding on mergers and acquisitions are "the public interest" and the avoidance of creation of monopolies. However, some critics of the CAB argue that its policies have led to increasing concentration in the industry. Certainly there has been a reduction in the number of carriers through CAB-approved mergers, as shown in Figure I-4.

Intercarrier Agreements

All intercarrier agreements are subject to the approval of the CAB, which is charged with the responsibility of ensuring that these agreements are not adverse to the public interest. Agreements on baggage handling procedures, reservations and ticketing procedures, and interchange of passengers on connecting flights are examples of formal CAB-approved agreements between carriers. The Airline Mutual Aid Agreement, capacity reduction, and "route swapping" between airlines, all three of which have been approved under certain conditions by the CAB, are controversial.

The Mutual Aid agreement is currently under attack by the airline labor

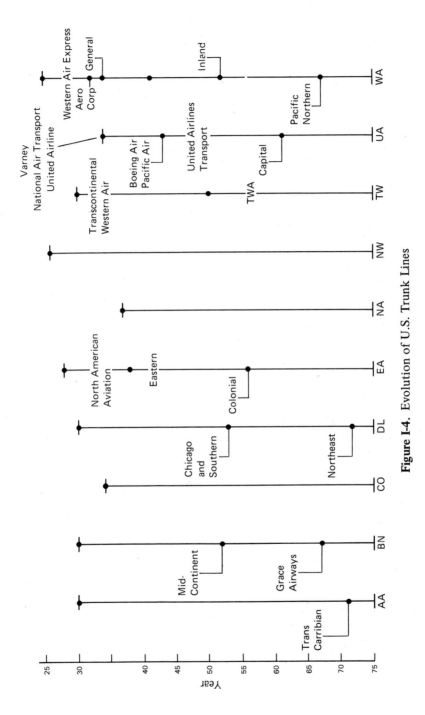

Figure I-4. Evolution of U.S. Trunk Lines

unions, which are sponsoring legislation to bar such agreements. It provides that an airline that has been struck by a union will be partially reimbursed for revenues lost to other carriers as a result of the work stoppage. The Mutual Aid benefits are of two kinds: (1) payments made by competing airlines serving the same routes (payment equals increased revenue gained by the competing airline less the costs of handling the traffic) and (2) additional payments made by all parties to the agreement[3] when the payments described in (1) are insufficient to cover a designated percentage of the struck carrier's normal operating costs. No attempt is made to cover any of the (substantial) poststrike losses incurred by the airline in attempts to regain market share. The Air Transport Association of America estimates that since the agreement went into effect in 1958, the airlines have incurred total strike losses of $909 million, of which only $482 million was covered by Mutual Aid payments. Also, there is strong evidence that a carrier suffers a loss of traffic for a period after a strike. Of course, this loss is not covered by the agreement.

In 1971 the CAB approved a capacity reduction agreement whereby American, TWA, and United agreed collectively to reduce frequency of service in four transcontinental markets. These carriers argued that such an agreement allowed them all to improve their average load factors. Critics of the decision saw it as a loss of desirable competition. A swap of international routes between Pan American and TWA that was also approved in the mid-1970s was an attempt to reduce direct competition between these carriers and raise their profitability.

Service Regulation

The CAB has limited powers over the quality of service offered by the airlines. Above a certain level (to protect against de facto abandonment) the CAB cannot rule on flight frequency, although it does exert some authority in the areas of overbooking (the practice of accepting more reservations than the capacity of the aircraft in order to protect against no-shows), ticket refunds, flight cancellation, liability for loss and damage of baggage and cargo, and other selected aspects of service quality.

Subsidies and Local-Service-Carrier Policy

As noted above, the CAB has the responsibility for promoting the airline industry, and this goal influences its normal decision-making process. The CAB also has the power to issue direct subsidies to the airlines. Prior to 1951, subsidies were treated as payments for transporting the mails, but in 1951 the CAB separated them from airmail payments and began to phase out general subsidy payments. By 1959, subsidies to the trunk carriers had ceased (except for small payments to Northeast in the mid-1960s). A new system of subsidies for local service airlines was created in 1961. Total payments peaked in 1963, when the local service industry received $67.9 million, or 43 percent of commercial revenues.

The CAB's policy with respect to local service carriers has gone through three major phases. Phase I, beginning with the conception of the industry, encouraged rapid route expansion of service in short-haul, low-density markets. The method of subsidy determination was variable so that payments were frequently retroactive to previous years' revenues. Long-range planning and budgeting was nearly impossible in this environment. Phase II, route realignment, began in 1957. It was aimed at giving carriers more flexibility to efficiently serve the cities in their current geographic areas by allowing them to overfly small points to which they provided at least two daily round trips and to criss-cross flights between cities rather than serve them linearly. Average length of haul gradually increased from 75 to 112 miles and the average number of passengers boarded went from 10 to 21 as a result of this policy. In 1961 the CAB introduced a new method of subsidy payment, the Class Rate. It enabled the carriers to determine payments earned for any given volume of service and thus facilitated longer-range planning.

Phase III, route strengthening, was initiated in the midsixties. It was designed to give local service carriers access to longer-haul, higher density routes, a tactic that had helped establish the financial self-sufficiency of the trunk carriers. The new policy meant that rather than carrying passengers to a hub airport and transferring them to trunk carriers for long-haul routes, the local service carriers could fly passengers to their final destination points through the hub or by direct flight. The effect would be to spread the fixed terminal costs of ticketing, baggage checking, landing fees, and physical plant over a larger average ticket price. This policy created two interlocking but operationally very different systems, one subsidy-eligible and the other not.

Not only were the new routes subsidy-ineligible, but they also were anticipated to be sufficiently profitable to allow reduction of payments on subsidy-eligible routes (an effect often referred to as cross-subsidization). Subsidy was reduced as a percent of revenues earned on these new routes. The expected profitability did not materialize, however, primarily due to a softening in the economy and high costs of rapid expansion. In many instances the percent of revenues applicable to subsidy reduction was greater than the margins earned on those routes. The entire industry incurred losses. The CAB finally responded to these growing pains in 1970 with an order eliminating further subsidy reductions based on theoretical profit on any *future* route awards.

To be sure that new routes received adequate service, the CAB gave a carrier ninety days to institute service before revoking the franchise and opening the route to other applicants. This practice became known as the "use-it-or-lose-it" policy.

Criticism of Regulation

Economic regulation of the airline industry by the CAB has been the subject of increasing criticism in recent years, as evidenced by hearings in 1975 before the Subcommittee on Administrative Practice of the United States Senate (known as the "Kennedy Hearings," after the chairman, Senator Edward Kennedy) and the Aviation Act of 1975, a Senate bill that proposed substantial deregulation of the airline industry (the major provisions of this act appear in Appendix IA). These events were part of a general reexamination of regulation of all modes. Similar bills concerned the rail and highway modes. By 1976, only the rail bill, which gave railroads potentially greater freedom from regulation, had become law. In 1977 President Carter stated his support of relaxed regulation.

Critics of regulation argue that CAB restrictions on entry and control of rates have restricted competition in the airline industry and that deregulation would result in lower fares. They also argue that the restrictions on price competition have led the airlines into wasteful service competition. They quote, as a prime example, competition on capacity whereby airlines all attempt to attract passengers by scheduling as many departures as possible (in order to heighten their market exposure), and as close to peak travel times as possible. This practice has resulted, claim the cities, in too many departures with low load factors (percentage of available seats filled), a fact that has led to higher fares; this subject will be discussed in more detail later. Also criticized have been the cross-subsidies built into the rate structure, between long- and short-haul trips, between different types of passengers, and between dense and less-traveled markets. Many of these cross-subsidies have been reduced or removed as a result of the Domestic Passenger Fare Investigation, however.

It is also argued that CAB regulation rewards "pack behavior." For example, if one carrier deviates from the behavior of the other carriers, there is serious doubt whether the potential rewards are worth the potential losses. Assume one carrier elects to purchase a fleet of aircraft that are substantially different from the equipment purchased by the other airlines. If the first carrier makes a poor decision, the CAB will not save the individual carrier. However, if the "pack" makes a poor decision, the CAB will save the industry through rate relief. The single carrier might seem to win under this situation, but it is quite likely that this carrier will not receive favorable consideration with regard to route expansion because it does not need strengthening relative to other carriers. So the risks of being a single errant far outweighs the potential reward for being singularly successful.

Defenders of regulation have argued that complete freedom of entry into and exit from any market would lead to overcompetition on the heavily traveled, most profitable air routes and abandonment or sharply reduced service in other markets. The result, they argue, would be unacceptable instability in the service and fares of many markets. However, even the strongest defenders of continued regulation (which includes most of the regulated airlines) argue that there is room for some improvement in the procedures of the CAB, primarily in speeding up the decision-making process. In addition, most airlines seek a greater degree of management freedom in the setting of rates, as is evident from requests for a "zone of reasonableness," whereby airlines could adjust fares within certain limits (for example, plus or minus 15 percent) without the need for CAB approval.

Airline Cost Structures

In reporting to the CAB, airlines are required to divide their costs into eleven categories: (1) flying operations (which include crew, fuel and oil, insurance, and other expenditures); (2) direct maintenance (maintenance actually performed to operating equipment); (3) maintenance burden (the overhead costs of maintenance facilities); (4) passenger service; (5) aircraft servicing (refueling and other ground services to the aircraft); (6) traffic servicing (costs of terminal operation, baggage handling, and other ground services provided to passengers); (7) service administration; (8) reservations and sales; (9) advertising and publicity; (10) general and administrative; and (11) depreciation and amortization. The relative sizes of these cost categories may be judged from Tables I-25 and I-26.

In all airline categories, a high proportion of costs are incurred in "traffic and aircraft serving," which includes all the terminal functions performed at airports, including check-in procedures, baggage handling, refueling, and handling of cargo through terminals. Given that the basic advantage of the air mode is speed and that a very high proportion of the total travel time for an air journey is spent in obtaining access to the airport and terminal activities (as much as 50 percent for short-haul trips), delays in terminal operations have a profound impact on the attractiveness of the air mode.

Direct Operating Costs (DOC)

In the analysis of airline costs, it has been conventional in the airline industry to regroup the eleven cost elements given above into two categories: direct operating costs (DOC) and indirect operating costs. Direct operating costs usually include some combination of cost categories 1, 2, 3, and 11 above, although many definitions of DOC exist. The intention of the categorization of costs into DOC and indirect cost is to separate the costs of aircraft operation from other cost elements. Aircraft operating expenses (the CAB's definition of DOC, which includes flying operations, flight equipment maintenance, an allocation of maintenance burden, and depreciation and rentals) for various aircraft are given in Table I-27. A more detailed analysis of DOC cost components is provided in Table I-28.

Table I-25
Operating Revenues and Expenses, Total U.S. Scheduled Airlines, 1965-1975[a]
($ millions)

	1965	1970	1975
Operating revenues	4,958	9,290	15,355
Operating expenses			
Flying operations	1,158	2,705	5,094
Maintenance	816	1,402	2,005
Passenger service	382	940	1,408
Aircraft and traffic servicing	735	1,676	2,720
Promotion and sales	551	1,112	1,692
Administrative	212	459	716
Depreciation and amortization	431	952	1,116
Total	4,286	9,247	15,227
Net operating income	672	43	128
Interest on long-term debt	112	318	402
Income taxes	235	(48)	(19)
Net profit (loss)[b]	367	(201)	(84)
Average load factor	50.3	45.6	47.8

Note: Net profit figures shown are after deductions for "special items" and other nonoperating income and expenses not shown.

Source: Adapted from *Air Transport 1976* (Washington, D.C.: Air Transport Association of America, 1976), pp. 17-23.

[a]Includes Intra-Alaska, Intra-Hawaii, and Helicopter operators. Excludes all other intrastate operations.
[b]In the years 1965-1975, 1970 and 1975 were the only two years in which net losses were posted.

Due to the high time-related depreciation charges, the DOC experienced by any aircraft is a function of its utilization, which is usually measured in "block hours" per day (Table I-23). This is the total time that the aircraft is in motion, on the ground or in the air, from "engines on" to "engines off." Utilization and hence DOC, is influenced by the "stage lengths" (length of flight) that the aircraft flies: the longer the stage length, the less proportionate part of the day is spent in the relatively fixed time operations of takeoff and landing, refueling, clearing, and maintenance. Relatively more fuel is also expended in takeoff and landing than in flying at cruising speed (around 550 miles per hour).

Direct operating costs may be expressed as a variety of ratios: per mile, per block hour, per available seat-mile or per revenue passenger-mile. Available seat-miles (ASMs) are calculated by multiplying the seating capacity of the aircraft by the number of miles flown. In cargo operations (and sometimes in

Table I-26

Distribution of Operating Expenses as a Percentage of Revenue, Various Airline Categories, 1975

	Domestic Trunk	Local Service	International Trunk	Domestic All Caro	International All Cargo
Flying operations	32.6	31.9	34.3	47.6	45.8
Maintenance	13.2	15.1	11.9	12.4	10.4
Passenger service	9.9	6.4	9.4	−	1.9
Aircraft and traffic servicing	17.3	22.8	16.6	31.7	20.2
Promotion and sales	10.8	9.5	13.0	4.8	8.4
Administrative	4.2	5.3	4.9	7.1	5.5
Depreciation and amortization	7.8	4.9	6.9	7.8	4.8
Other transportation-related	3.4	1.9	2.9	0.6	0.6
Total	99.2	97.8	99.9	112.0	97.6

Source: Adapted from *Air Transport 1976* (Washington, D.C.: Air Transport Association of America, 1976), pp. 18-21.

passenger operations), an alternate measure of output is used: available ton-miles (ATM), calculated by multiplying the payload of the aircraft (tons that can be carried) by the miles flown. Revenue passenger-miles (RPM) are a standard industry measure of sales calculated by multiplying the number of passengers carried times by the length of the passenger's journey. Revenue ton-miles (RTM) are similarly defined.

Whereas lower cost per aircraft mile is desirable, the key ratio in comparing different aircraft is the cost per ASM, a measure that takes into account the different seating capacities of the aircraft. The relationship between ASM and RPM finds expression in the load factor (percentage of available seats filled, or RPM divided by ASM), a measure that is crucial to an understanding of aircraft economics.

Once an aircraft is scheduled to fly, the major proportion of DOC is fixed; the out-of-pocket cost is not affected greatly by the number of passengers carried. A generally accepted standard is that 10 percent of a passenger's ticket price goes to provide services for that passenger and 90 percent covers costs that would be incurred even if that passenger did not fly. For all-cargo operations, the norm is only 2 percent variable cost (cargo receives no in-flight service, so the only extra cost incurred is due to extra fuel).

Costs, therefore, are mainly related to the number of *seats* rather than the number of passengers flown over a given distance (i.e., dependent upon the number of ASMs). Revenues, however, are directly related to the number of passengers carried, how far they are flown, and how much passengers paid per mile of flight. The product of the first two factors is revenue passenger-miles

Table I-27
Flight Operating Costs, 1973

Aircraft Type	Fleet Size	Cost/Hr. ($)	Seats[a]	Cost/Seat Hr. ($)	Average Stage Length (miles)
Domestic Trunks					
Electra	19	763.60	87.8	8.70	205
B707-100B	102	837.19	120.8	6.93	933
B720	4	673.73	131.0	5.14	699
B720B	53	841.07	115.5	7.28	829
B727-100Q/C	406	671.61	98.0	6.85	556
B737-200	98	559.52	93.6	5.98	306
DC8-20	79	908.07	121.5	7.47	992
DC8-50		839.34	130.5	6.43	841
DC8-61	61	958.45	176.5	5.43	922
DC9-10	42	546.01	68.5	7.97	352
DC9-30	148	517.70	89.9	5.76	335
B747	106	1849.89	328.4	5.63	1858
L-1011	17	1589.81	221.8	7.17	1199
DC10-10	59	1324.81	232.2	5.71	1003
DC10-40		1053.88	238.4	4.42	767
Local Service					
DC9-30	79	534.38	99.7	5.36	258
CV-580	105	369.91	49.4	7.31	123
FH-227	46	315.87	44.5	7.10	104
Helicopters					
S-61	7	419.49	24.8	16.91	13
STOL					
DHC-6	13	163.55	15.0	10.90	90

Source: U.S. Civil Aeronautics Board, *Aircraft Operating Cost and Performance Reports*, June 1974, in N.K. Taneja, *The Commercial Airline Industry* (Lexington, Mass.: Lexington Books, D. C. Heath and Company (1976), p. 47.

[a]Seats are averaged over aircraft miles performed in 1973.

(RPM), and the third term is commonly called the yield per RPM. Hence the load factor, which relates RPM to ASM, is a key indicator of airline profitability. A change in load factor of one point (say, from 55 percent to 56 percent) could mean an increase in profit of approximately 5 percent.

The relationship between DOC and stage length is illustrated in Figure I-5, which also demonstrates the impact of succeeding generations of aircraft. (Due to the rapid changes that have taken place in the prices of factor inputs such as fuel, labor cost, and aircraft prices, data shown in Figure I-5 should not be compared to similar data for other aircraft in succeeding years.)

Table I-28
Average Operating Costs and Performance of Turbofan Aircraft, 1973-1975

Cost or Performance Item	Four-engine Wide Body	Four-engine Regular Body	Three-engine Wide Body	Three-engine Regular Body	Two-engine Regular Body
Costs					
Direct operating costs/block hour					
Crew	$ 411.3	$ 298.0	$ 328.2	$254.2	$225.9
Fuel and oil	959.6	478.9	641.5	355.6	251.3
Other	25.5	5.8	24.2	6.6	4.4
Total flying operating costs	1396.4	782.7	993.9	616.4	481.6
Maintenance costs/block hour					
Airframe	157.1	83.5	113.6	61.4	67.9
Engine	286.4	66.2	186.6	48.6	40.2
Burden	243.5	151.7	157.3	91.9	90.7
Total maintenance costs	687.0	301.4	457.5	201.9	198.8
Depreciation and rentals/block hour	685.9	168.2	496.9	149.6	114.5
Total DOC/block hour	2769.3	1252.3	1948.3	967.9	749.9
Total DOC/ASM (cents)	1.76	2.21	2.03	2.43	2.88
Performance					
Daily utilization (hours)	8.08	7.52	7.26	7.13	6.44
Capacity (average seats)	352.6	144.3	236.3	112.2	89.7
Capacity (average tons)	52.2	19.7	36.6	14.9	1.2
Average stage length (miles)	1796	889	1012	523	335
Average airborne speed (miles/hour)	502	457	473	423	377
Average block speed (miles/hour)	454	404	412	358	311
Average load factor (percent)	51.3	54.6	49.8	57.4	59.9

Costs are in dollars except where noted.

Source: Civil Aeronautics Board, *Aircraft Operating Costs and Performance Report*, July 1976.

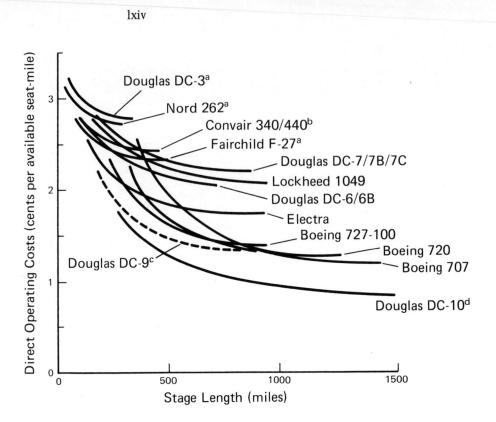

Source: Adapted from M.R. Straszheim, *The International Airline Industry* (Washington, D.C.: The Brookings Institution, 1969), p. 86, and aircraft manufacturers' data.

[a]U.S. local service airlines' costs.

[b]Average of trunk-line and local service airlines' costs.

[c]This curve uses 1966 data.

[d]Based on 1967 data and cost estimates using 238-seat configuration.

Figure I-5. Direct-Operating-Cost Estimates for Selected Aircraft, 1965

The introduction of the wide-body jets posed difficult problems for the airlines. First-generation jets offered reductions in DOC on both a per ASM and a per-mile basis. The wide-body jets, on the other hand, lowered DOC per ASM, but raised DOC per mile 75 to 100 percent higher than the aircraft they were to replace. Consequently, although the Boeing B-747 had a breakeven load factor of approximately 35 percent compared to the B-707's 52 percent, the number of passengers required to achieve breakeven was almost twice that of the B-707. Without a rapid increase in traffic, the B-747 would not be economical on a one-for-one basis, but it would require fewer flights per day for the same level of capacity. Such a change would put an airline at a competitive disadvantage. Nonetheless, wide-body jets were introduced into heavily traveled markets. After the initial introduction period, many airlines discovered that their wide-body jet purchases had led to overcapacity and a number of these aircraft were grounded for a period.

The introduction of wide-body jets into passenger operations had a profound impact on the cargo operations. A B-747 in all-passenger configuration, for example, has approximately 5550 cubic feet of belly space available for cargo. This capacity compared to approximately 7600 cubic feet of space provided by a B-707 in all-cargo configuration. In consequence, the belly load capacity of the airlines as a percentage of total available cargo capacity increased from 66 percent in 1969 to 77 percent in 1972. This vast increase caused the airlines to rethink their cargo strategies. The economics of freighter (all-cargo configuration) aircraft had always been marginal (Table I-29) due to their low yield (rate or fare) compared with passenger operations, and the airlines now had an extra incentive to fill their belly load capacity. Their reaction was to cut back on freighter operations and to introduce new daylight rates for container traffic tendered between 4 A.M. and 4 P.M. These moves were not welcomed by shippers or by air-freight forwarders, whose primary business service is based on next-day delivery for freight tendered at the end of the working day.

The forwarders preferred freighter over passenger aircraft primarily because freighters were scheduled at the prime nighttime hours when freight was available. The freighters also assured that consolidated shipments would be moved intact, provided the best utilization of space, and were more dependable than the passenger flights. The president of Shulman Air Freight, Inc., a leading

Table I-29
Operating Results for Five Largest Freighter Operators, 1967-1975

Twelve Months Ended	Operating Profit or (Loss) ($000)[a]					
	American	Eastern	TWA	United	Flying Tiger	Total
12/31/67	$1354	$(504)	$(4,237)	$1,333	$(1,808)	$(3,862)
12/31/68	339	(2517)	(3484)	782	(3,424)	(8,304)
12/31/69	(5036)	(3053)	(5719)	(6,274)	(2,836)	(22,918)
12/31/70	(6595)	(3828)	(7747)	(99,812)	(1,680)	(39,662)
12/31/71	(7723)	(5014)	(6295)	(11,248)	(1,107)	(31,387)
12/31/72	(7185)	(5123)	(473)	(6,267)	2,569	(16,479)
12/31/73	(163)	(6545)	1148	(2,799)	8,113	(246)
12/31/74	(2293)	(3648)	423	(11,714)	(12,376)	(29,608)
6/30/75	(5446)	(3318)	(7759)	(11,599)	(14,070)	(42,192)

[a]Systemwide results including international and nonscheduled operations, freighter operations only.

air-freight forwarder, testified before a recent Civil Aeronautics Board (CAB) freight rate hearing that:

Prime time freight services provide the standard next-day service demanded by air freight shippers, and enables us to provide the service demanded at the lowest possible cost. While we believe there is a place in the air freight system for belly daylight freight service, it is ancillary to prime time freighter service.[4]

Indirect Costs

Although there is no industrywide standard for computing indirect costs, they tend to approximate 50 percent of total cost (i.e., 100 percent of DOC) for passenger operations and a slightly lower percentage for the all-cargo carriers. For a given flight schedule, indirect costs are largely fixed relative to the volume of traffic.

Labor Costs and Industrial Relations

Labor accounts for approximately 40 percent of airline costs, in contrast to 50 percent for rail and 60 percent for motor carriers. A comparison of labor costs by employee category in the three modes is given in Table I-30. Average labor costs in the airline industry rose steadily from 1958 to 1975 (from less than $7000 per employee to over $22,000 per employee). However, during the early sixties, this rise was offset by a more rapid increase in labor productivity (revenue ton-miles per employee), due mainly to the conversion of the carriers' fleets to jet aircraft. Since 1967, the rise in RTMs per employee has not compensated for rising labor costs, and the average labor cost per revenue ton-mile has risen (Figure I-6).

A major portion of labor costs goes to the salaries of flight crews. Apart from the size of these payments, the basis for calculating pilots' pay is complex. Pilots may not fly more than eighty-five hours in any month or more than eight hours during any consecutive twenty-four hours (unless there is an intervening rest period of at least eight hours or twice the number of hours of duty aloft since the last rest period, whichever is larger). Pilots' pay is based on the mileage flown, the hours flown (which may be substantially less than eighty-five hours in a month), and the type of aircraft flown. In addition to these factors, pilots earn some flying-time credit (towards their maximum flying hours) for time spent on duty or on call on the ground, for "deadheading" (flying as a passenger) back to their domicile, and other activities. Finally, there are certain guarantees given to pilots, such as guarantees of schedule integrity (whereby they are paid even if a flight is cancelled due to bad weather or some other factor).

Table I-30

Distribution of Total Labor Costs, by Employee Category, Various Modes

(percent)

	Domestic Trunk Airlines (1969)	Class I Motor Carriers (1971)	Class I Railroads (1972)
Transportation		54.9	41.7
Pilots and copilots	21.1		
Pursers, cabin attendants	4.8		
Other flight personnel	6.8		
Total	32.7	54.9	41.7
Maintenance			
Garage			
Mechanics	16.8	6.9	32.6
Total	16.8	6.9	32.6
Terminal			
Aircraft and traffic servicing	22.2	29.0	1.9
Total	22.2	29.0	1.9
Other			
Executive		1.4	
Traffic		3.3	
General office	16.0	4.5	
Executive, officials, and staff			4.9
Professional, clerical, and general			18.9
Other	12.3		
Total	28.3	9.2	23.8

Source: D.H. Maister, *An Overview of the U.S. Freight Transportation Industries* (Boston, Mass.: Intercollegiate Case Clearing House, 1973), pp. 55-57.

Since 1936, labor relations in the airline industry have been subject to the Railway Labor Act (the motor-carrier industry is governed by the National Labor Relations Act). Basically, the act provides for five steps in the settling of labor-management disputes: (1) conference and collective bargaining, (2) boards of adjustment or mediation, (3) voluntary arbitration, (4) emergency boards, and (5) presidential action.

The intent of the first step, collective bargaining, is to settle the majority of disputes over contracts, interpretations, and grievances. It has been argued, however, that the mere existence of succeeding steps has jeopardized the success of negotiations at this level.

The next step in the settlement of disputes is the move to one of two

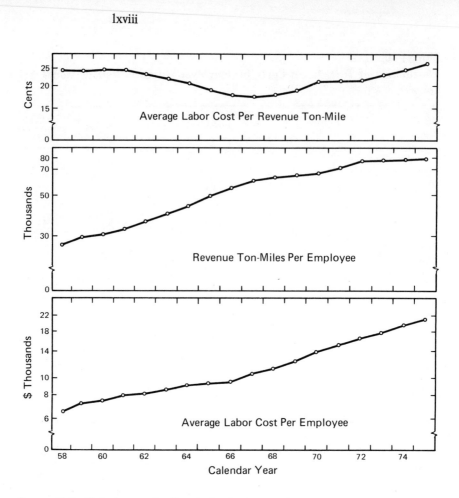

Source: U.S. Civil Aeronautics Board, *Productivity and Cost of Employment: System Trunks; Calendar Years 1974 and 1975*, p. 1.

Figure I-6. Labor Costs and Productivity, 1958-1975

boards. The Board of Adjustment has thirty-six members, eighteen each from the carrier group and the unions, and has jurisdiction over grievances and interpretations of existing contracts. Its four divisions have authority over separate classes of labor. In the case of a deadlock, a neutral referee is selected, and the decisions of the board are binding on both parties. Between 1934 and June 1970, the National Railroad Adjustment Board (NRAB) heard approximately 70,000 cases.

The National Mediation Board's basic jurisdiction is the negotiation of new contracts. The board's three members each serve for three years. They are appointed by the president of the United States with the advice and consent of the Senate. Unlike the NRAB, the Mediation Board does not decide issues, but attempts to help both parties find common ground for contract agreement. Should the Mediation Board fail in this task, the law provides that it should attempt to generate stage three, which is voluntary arbitration. If both sides agree to enter arbitration, they undertake to abide by its results. One-third of the arbitration board is composed of carrier-selected arbitrators, one-third of the members are chosen by the unions, and the remainder are the choices of the carrier-union arbitrators. Should agreement not be reached on this final group, the Mediation Board performs the selection.

Because arbitration may be refused by either side, the Mediation Board has the responsibility of notifying the president, who has the power to create a special emergency board. In the thirty days that this board has to investigate the situation, no change may take place in the conditions that led to the dispute. Emergency board decisions are not binding, but if refused, a second period of thirty days must elapse before any change or action. Between 1934 and June 30, 1970, 176 emergency boards were set up (35 of which heard airline cases).

If all the preceding steps fail, the president of the United States may take personal action.

Airline industry employees have tended to organize by craft rather than on an industrial basis; in 1970 there were sixteen airline unions. Most of the airline unions, especially the Air Line Pilots Association (ALPA), have adopted a policy of carrier-by-carrier negotiations (locals of ALPA are the bargaining units at each of the trunk airlines except American, whose union separated from ALPA several years ago). To some extent, this practice stems from the complexity of pilot compensation, which is based directly on the equipment used and the routes flown. Because these components may vary significantly from carrier to carrier, industrywide agreements can be difficult to achieve.

Fuel Costs

Fuel costs rose dramatically in the 1970s, from an average of 12 cents per gallon in 1973 to over 30 cents in 1976. In that time, fuel costs as a percent of total airline operating costs rose from 12 to approximately 20 percent. The airlines have attempted to lessen the impact of rising fuel costs by substituting energy-efficient aircraft, altering ground and air operating procedures, reducing service levels (i.e., the number of flights), and seeking higher fares. However, in spite of these actions, most airline managers considered the fuel problem to be among the most threatening problems faced in recent years.

Competition and Strategy

It is widely agreed that the major determinants of airline profitability, and hence the principal tools of strategy and competition, are equipment selection, the mix of routes served, scheduling, and, to a lesser extent, various forms of demand stimulation such as promotion and cabin service. Of course, decisions in these areas cannot be taken independently, because the fleet mix affects the scheduling process, the routes served determine the optimum choice of aircraft and the feasible schedules, and so on.

Equipment Cycles and the S Curve

Aircraft selection can be the most crucial management decision in airline operations. Its importance derives not only from the size and long life span of the investment, but also from the impact that fleet mix and capacity levels have on other, shorter-term managerial decisions.

Carriers face two major (interrelated) decisions regarding aircraft selection: the choice of which aircraft to buy (the fleet-mix decision) and the determination of the number of each aircraft to buy (the capacity-level decision). Because profitability is so sensitive to the load factor, it would seem that the industry would be very concerned with profitable load-factor levels through a policy of restraint in adding capacity. This, however, has not been the case. The CAB's target of 10.5 percent return on investment for the airline industry (based on a seat load factor of 55 percent), for example, had been achieved in only two of the ten years prior to 1968.

This industry's below-target performance was due to intense competition between the airlines in a price-regulated industry. Because prices, most amenities, and selling expenses were fixed, the competition took the form of providing excess capacity in order to gain market share. This behavior derived from a widely held industry belief that in a given market, the carriers with the greatest number of departures will normally carry a larger-than-proportionate share of the traffic. Graphically this relationship forms an S-shaped curve (Figure I-7). The effect of this curve on industry thinking and behavior was so pervasive that it had become known as *the* S-curve and was the basis for airline capacity decisions. Because having the largest share of capacity (or departures) in a given market was believed to enable a carrier to capture a large proportion of available traffic, each carrier would attempt to gain an advantage by increasing capacity. However, the ability of other carriers to match capacity increases led to general overcapacity and lower load factors. Such behavior might persist until load factors approached breakeven levels. Although this practice was, in the long run, harmful to the profitability of all carriers, it took only one carrier seeking a short-term advantage to start the "capacity spiral."[5]

Capacity competition is not the only form that service competition takes. Carriers can, and do, compete in the area of cabin services offered. For example, competition has affected the types and quality of food served and, in 1976, the showing of free, inflight movies even on short flights. However, as with capacity

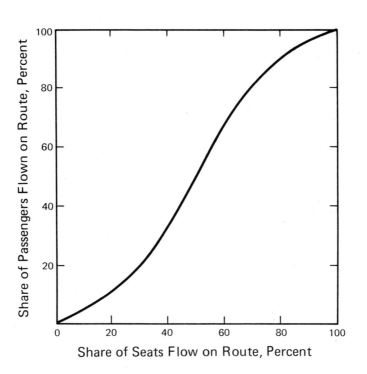

Figure I-7. Market Share vs. ASM Share in a Two-carrier Market

competition, the effect of this kind of competition is usually to raise costs for all carriers without significantly affecting either total traffic or market shares in the long run.

Equipment Selection

Many factors influence the process of equipment selection, that is, choosing the type of aircraft and planning the fleet mix. Although it is described separately here, the choice of type of aircraft, in practice, cannot be separated from the setting of overall capacity levels.

The carriers' "route map" (points served) exerts a strong influence both through the mix of stage lengths (some aircraft being better suited to stages of different lengths) and market densities (which affect the optimum size of aircraft to service a given market). Most carriers believe that, as far as possible, it is desirable to have a fleet composed of as few different types of aircraft as possible, preferably from a single manufacturer. This strategy may not be optimal in relation to the route map, but it brings many advantages in the form of lower maintenance and inventory costs and facilitates scheduling.

Addition of a new type of aircraft to a fleet can have a profound impact on a carrier's ground handling and maintenance procedures and costs. For example, the addition of the B-747 to Pan Am's fleet, apart from the fact that its purchase price was doubled by the cost of spares, forced the company to extensively retrain its maintenance staff. The change in operating patterns induced by the new aircraft led the company to install a completely new maintenance facility at Kennedy Airport in New York, at a cost of $87 million for the basic building and $16 million for tooling.

Aircraft manufacturers have attempted to sell succeeding generations of aircraft on the basis of reduced direct operating costs per ton-mile. However, these potential reductions may be obtained only by substantial initial investment. A DC-8, which cost $8 million in 1970, produced 1000 available seat miles per day, or $8.00 per available seat-mile per day. A B-747 cost $20 million when first introduced and produced 1800 available seat-miles per day, for an average cost of $11.10 per available seat-mile per day.

In addition to purchase cost, direct operating costs are a crucial input to the equipment selection process. Appraisal of the direct operating costs of different aircraft for purposes of equipment selection is a complex process. As noted above, the direct operating cost per available seat-mile varies with the stage length over which the aircraft is operated. Because an aircraft will be operated over a number of stage lengths in the course of a complete routing (few aircraft are simply routed from point A to point B and back to point A), appraisal of its operating costs involves some form of schedule forecast. Furthermore, addition of a new aircraft usually involves rerouting existing aircraft, which may alter the stage lengths over which they are operated and hence their operating cost. In consequence, it is clearly necessary to appraise the operating costs of a new aircraft on a *network* basis, rather than by simply taking a single DOC figure for a typical stage length.

To take these, and other, factors into account, many airlines use computer-based fleet-planning models (which often employ mathematical techniques such as linear programming and heuristic simulation) to aid in the equipment selection decision. The general framework of such models is described in Figure I-8.

In addition to promoting their existing aircraft, aircraft manufacturers tend to work closely with the airlines in the development of new aircraft. Some carriers believe that there is a competitive advantage to be gained in being the first airline to operate a new aircraft (Pan American is an example of such a carrier), but others believe that although there may have been an advantage during the period of transition from propeller-driven to jet aircraft, it no longer exists. Individual carriers do have an effect on the development of individual aircraft as illustrated by Pan American's involvement in development of the Boeing B-747SP (a shorter, long-range version of the B-747 that can transport more than 250 passengers nonstop from New York to Tokyo) and United's influence on production plans for the B-727-300. However, given the extensive development

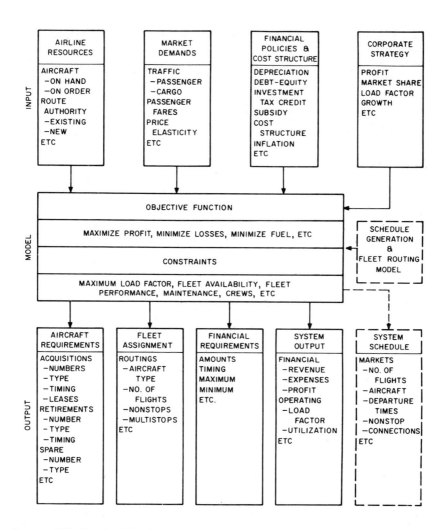

Source: N.K. Taneja, *The Commercial Airline Industry* (Lexington, Mass.: Lexington Books, D.C. Heath and Co., 1976), p. 99.

Figure I-8. General Framework of Fleet-planning Models

costs involved in designing a new aircraft, sales to a single carrier can never be sufficient to achieve breakeven for the aircraft manufacturers. Therefore manufacturers have tended to modify existing aircraft (for example, by "stretching" the aircraft and altering its seating capacity), as evidenced by Boeing's line of aircraft. For the same reason, most aircraft employed as freighters have been cargo versions of passenger aircraft.

A final factor affecting equipment purchase decisions is whether the purchase is part of a general expansion of capacity or whether it is intended as a replacement for old equipment. The market for used aircraft (with proper maintenance aircraft may have extremely long lives: twenty years is normal for a B-707, and there were a number of DC-3 and DC-6 aircraft still flying in 1976) changed significantly during the 1960s. When the trunk airlines were installing their first jet fleets, they found a ready market for their propeller-driven aircraft among domestic local service carriers and foreign airlines. These aircraft could still be economically utilized on the short-haul routes of these airlines. By the late 1960s, however, this market had largely disappeared, due to the introduction of short-haul jet aircraft specifically designed for the needs of local service carriers.

Local service carriers began operations in the late 1940s primarily with nonpressurized, 21-seat, twin-engine Corvair and Martin piston aircraft acquired from the trunk lines. Most of these aircraft were pressurized and operated at an average speed of 380 mph, compared with the 200 mph average of the DC-3s. In 1958 the first twin-engine, turbine-powered, propeller-driven aircraft (turboprop) went into service. Although essentially the same size as the piston aircraft, although slightly faster, the turboprop was considered far superior in quiet and comfort. Coincident with the CAB's route-strengthening program for local service carriers, these carriers acquired twin-engine jet aircraft and converted their twin-engine piston planes to turbine power. The twin-engine jets, the first of which was introduced in 1965, ranged in size from 60 to 100 seats, and flew at an average speed of 570 mph.

Each stage of development required greater capital outlays, but the last phase was of unprecedented proportion. Although the size of the local service fleet had grown slightly over 10 percent between 1962 and 1972, the investment in aircraft and related equipment increased almost sevenfold—from $78.6 million to $523.6 million. A modern twin-engine jet aircraft cost approximately $5 million compared to $500,000 for a used piston-engine aircraft and the $50,000 cost of the old DC-3s. However, each succeeding generation of aircraft had the advantage of being more productive and economical. The DC-3 could provide 4200 ASMs per hour, a twin-engine piston 11,200, and a jet between 33,600 and 56,000. According to one measure of cost of production, a twin-engine piston reduced the cost of providing one ASM per hour by 15 percent compared to the DC-3 and a jet brought about a 45 percent reduction compared to the DC-3. Moreover, improved comfort, speed, and reliability increased passenger appeal and stimulated demand for the local service carriers, thereby increasing revenues.

The 1970s saw the introduction of yet another factor to be considered in equipment selection decisions. The imposition of noise and pollution standards forced airlines to choose between expensive retrofitting of engines on the noisy 707s and DC-8s and replacement of the entire aircraft by the less noisy new generations of aircraft. It was estimated that retrofitting and/or substitution of the entire American fleet of 707s and DC-8s to meet 1980 requirements would involve expenditures of approximately $5 billion.

Expansion of the capacity of an airline's fleet could be achieved not only by purchasing new aircraft, but also by adjusting the seating configuration within each aircraft. A first-class passenger occupied approximately twice the floor space occupied by a coach passenger. First-class passengers paid an average of 20 to 50 percent more per mile than coach passengers, and it was possible for an airline to turn away coach passengers while flying with empty first-class seats. In the mid-1970s, a number of airlines attempted to expand their passenger-carrying capabilities by reducing the number of first-class seats. For example, several airlines converted their aircraft from a mix of 24 percent first class to a mix of 14 percent. In this way, Eastern, for example, increased its passenger capacity by the equivalent of 12 new B-727-200 aircraft, or $120 million.[6]

Route Expansion

Given the existence of the CAB and the consequent restrictions on entry into the airline industry, a carrier's route authorities are among its most important assets, and the route map of an individual carrier is often considered to be a major determinant of the carrier's long-run profitability. As noted previously, the structure of fares that has prevailed in past years has made short-haul routes generally less profitable than long-haul routes, although this disparity might change as a result of the DPFI. In addition to stage length, density of traffic and the number of competing carriers are important determinants of the desirability of individual routes. Over a monopoly route (often taken to mean that one airline carries over 80 percent of the traffic) the density of traffic directly affects the actual load factor and hence profitability. However, the CAB has been vigorous in awarding new authorities to reduce the number of monopoly markets. The average number of effective carriers in the top 100 U.S. domestic markets is given in Table I-31.

Because of the potential impact of new route authorities on their profitability, airlines are constantly looking for and applying to the CAB for certification to operate additional routes, usually those already served directly or indirectly by other carriers. The cities concerned, and in general the CAB, have favored competition, and many such applications are granted each year. However, virtually all such applications are strenuously opposed by existing carriers. The costs (internal, consultant, and legal fees) that can result from litigation range from $10,000 to $3 million and above. The success rate is approximately 25 percent of serious applications. In these applications, it is usually up to the petitioning carrier to demonstrate that there is a need for an additional carrier.

Another way of expanding a route system is by acquisition. Many times carriers whose routes complement those of a financially troubled carrier seek to acquire that carrier. The CAB has usually permitted such acquisitions to avoid

Table I-31
Comparison of Top 100 U.S. Domestic City-pair Markets (12 months ending 30 September 1974)

Market Rank	Average Number of Effective Competitors[a]	Percent of Total U.S. Passengers Enplaned
1-10	2.8	9.28
11-20	2.5	4.47
21-30	2.9	3.29
31-40	2.4	2.74
41-50	2.5	2.35
51-60	2.6	2.05
61-70	2.9	1.91
71-80	2.4	1.70
81-90	2.2	1.56
91-100	2.3	1.39

[a]An effective competitor is defined as one that serves at least 10 percent of the total traffic carried by the largest carrier in the market being considered.

bankruptcy. Individual route purchases between carriers are normally not permitted by the CAB, although some route-swapping agreements in the early 1970s were approved by the CAB in response to the peculiar processes of the fuel crisis.

The selection of routes for application or acquisition is complicated and depends not only on the prime characteristics of the market (density, seasonality, and number of existing carriers, for example), but also on the degree to which the proposed new route matches the existing routes served by the carrier. Route length, location, and compatibility with scheduling requirements are all crucial factors in the decision-making process.

The cost of initiating service on a new route includes both aircraft capacity and station costs, and the level of these costs depends upon whether the carrier already has ground facilities at one or both of the points served, whether it chooses to own or lease new facilities, and whether it plans to provide its own aircraft-servicing capability or purchase it from others. In addition, reservation-system communications must be extended to the new points, advertising and promotion undertaken, and aircraft crews trained for the new route. Training and installation costs at the smallest of airports can run well in excess of $3 million, and promotion expenses in new markets are traditionally high.

There are observable differences in airline strategies that are associated with route features. For example, although the CAB attempts to restrict expenditures to approximately 11 percent, airlines with relatively longer average (passenger) trip length tend to spend a greater portion of operating revenues for promotion and selling, as shown in Figure I-9. Also, as seen in Figure I-10, the portion of operating revenues spent for these activities tends to be lower if a carrier participates in a greater number of markets. The lower percentage appears to be a result of spreading fixed costs over a larger number of markets. The advertising expenditures, a subcategory of the total promotion and selling expenditures, indicate that most of the cost spreading occurs in this one expenditure, as seen in Figures I-11 and I-12.

How does a larger number of competitors influence a carrier's spending? Figure I-13 examines the behavior of carriers facing greater competition. There is an observable trend that carriers in a competitive market do spend a greater portion of their operating revenues on advertising. Figure I-13 suggests that an increase of three in average number of competitors is associated with an increase of approximately two percentage points in the ratio of advertising expenses to operating revenue.

It has been argued that the profitability of a carrier depends on the number of competitors a carrier faces. Figure I-14 suggests that there is no consistent relationship of this type. Figure I-15 does suggest that profitability decreases and is less predictable as the number of markets a carrier participates in increases.

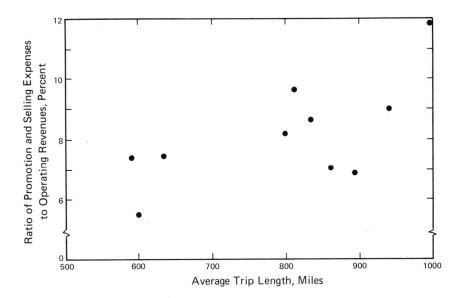

[a]Does not include Pan American.

Figure I-9. Ratio of Promotion and Selling Expenses to Operating Revenues vs. Average Trip Length, 1974[a]

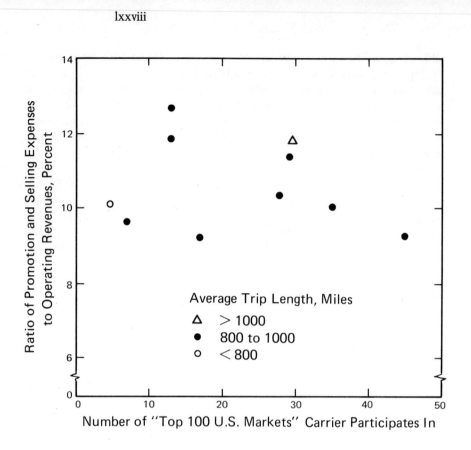

^aDoes not include Pan American.

Figure I-10. Ratio of Promotion and Selling Expenses to Operating Revenues vs. Number of "Top 100 U.S. Markets" Carrier Participates in, 1974[a]

The reasons for this phenomenon are not clear. Possible explanations include an inability to concentrate on a large number of markets and a diverse set of market demands that results in unfocused management.

The pre-DPFI rate structure was believed by most airline managers to favor the long-haul trunk-line carriers. However, Figure I-16 shows, by 1972 there was no consistent evidence that profitability was necessarily related to a carrier's average trip length. The reason may have been fare-structure shifts or variations of load factors. By 1975, there was some evidence to suggest that the long-haul carriers were less profitable (Figure I-17). One of several possible reasons for this occurrence may be. the impact of the DPFI. But it was also a time when long-haul carriers were introducing a large number of wide-body aircraft. The reversal in the profitability of the long-haul carriers is most likely attributable to this series of equipping decisions.

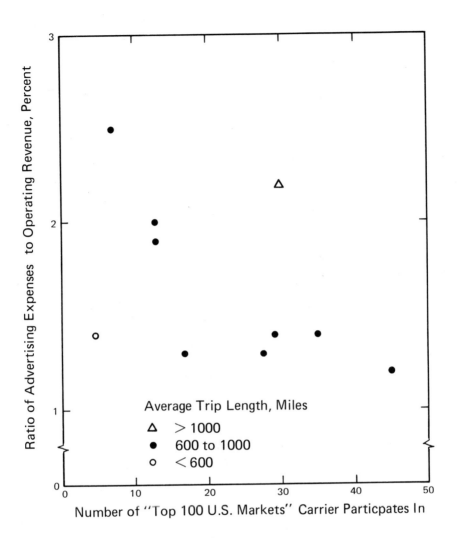

^aDoes not include Pan American.

Figure I-11. Advertising Expenses vs. Number of "Top 100 U.S. Markets" Individual Trunk-line Carrier Participates in, 1974^a

Scheduling

Airline schedules usually change four times a year (April, June, September, and December). Schedule planning is a very long-term process, however, and some carriers compute timetables as much as five years in advance. Specific schedules are planned six to eighteen months ahead, although minor adjustments are made on shorter notice. If business is poorer than expected, flights may be removed

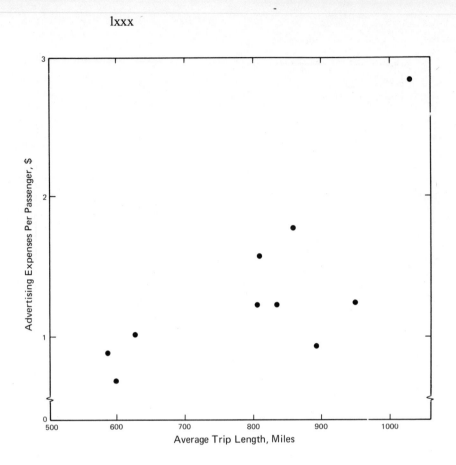

aDoes not include Pan American.

Figure I-12. Advertising Expenses per Passenger vs. Average Trip Length on Individual Trunk-line Carriers, 1974[a]

from a schedule in one month, the lead time required to adjust crew schedules, notify the publisher of the *Official Airline Guide*, and reschedule all other aspects of operations and maintenance.

The first step in the scheduling process is the determination of the general schedule, which gives the frequency of service between each of the city-pairs in the system, and a ship-routing chart, which shows exactly which particular airplane could be used for each flight. These two plans are determined by an iterative process.

The process of scheduling aircraft requires many compromises, because, given a limited number of aircraft, it is impossible to provide prime-time departures in all markets. Therefore, airline schedules must consider not only the

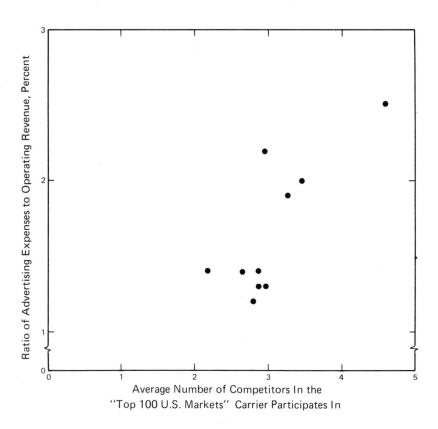

^aDoes not include Pan American.

Figure I-13. Ratio of Advertising Expenses to Revenues vs. Average Number of
Competitors in the "Top 100 U.S. Markets" Carrier Participates in,
1974[a]

utilization and cost impacts of their schedules, but also the revenue implications.
Obviously a choice must be made between a strategy of serving as many markets
as possible and a strategy that concentrates on providing frequent departures in
selected major markets.

Apart from the cost and demand data, airplane schedules are based on a
large number of other inputs. Noise standards, night curfews, route restrictions,
quotas on the number of flights at certain airports in a given time, ground
handling and terminal congestion, the need to synchronize flights to facilitate
connections are all important variables. The varying needs of business travelers,
vacationers, freight shippers, the U.S. Post Office, travel agents, and others all
must be recognized. Another important factor is the need to recognize the

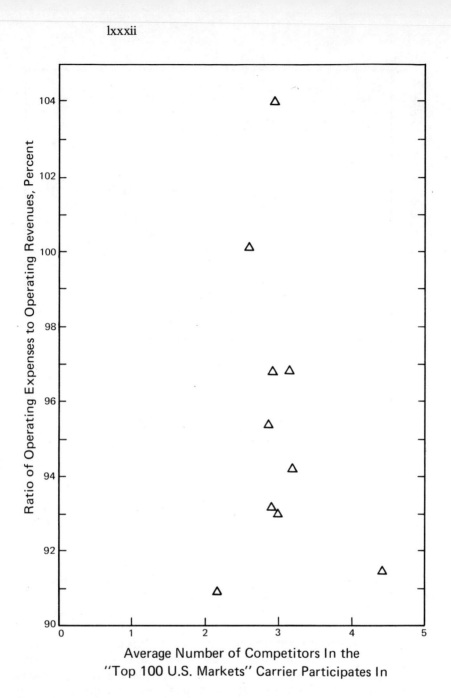

aDomestic operations. Does not include Pan American.

Figure I-14. Ratio of Operating Expenses to Revenues vs. Average Number of Competitors in the "Top 100 U.S. Markets" Individual Trunk-line Carrier Participates in, 1974-1975[a]

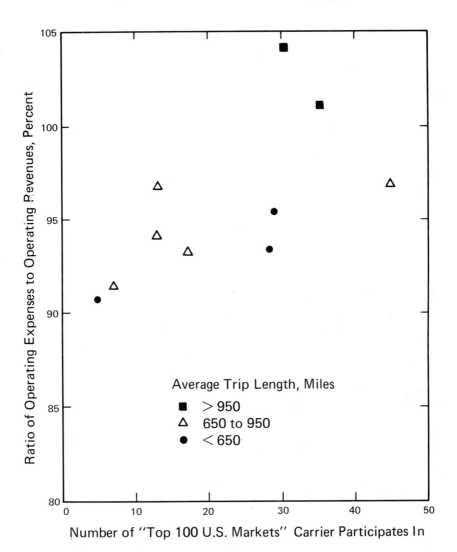

aDomestic operations. Does not include Pan American.

Figure I-15. Ratio of Operating Expenses to Revenues vs. Number of "Top 100 U.S. Markets" Individual Trunk-line Carrier Participates in, 1974-1975[a]

routine maintenance requirements of individual aircraft and build these into the schedule, not only considering the amount of maintenance required, but also taking care to route the aircraft to a base where the maintenance is available.

Another set of compromises involves making aircraft schedules compatible with flight-crew schedules. A given pilot normally is allowed to fly only one type

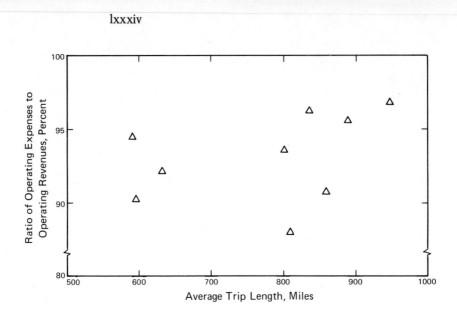

aDomestic operations. Does not include Pan American.

Figure I-16. Ratio of Operating Expenses to Revenues vs. Average Trip Length on Individual Trunk-line Carrier, 1974[a]

of aircraft unless he or she undergoes a period of retraining (even if the pilot has been previously trained for the aircraft). In addition, at most airlines, pilots are allowed to "bid" for certain routes (conflicts are resolved on a seniority basis). Given the size and complexity of pilots' pay, the airlines must attempt in scheduling to maximize utilization not only of aircraft but also of flight crews.

Because of the evident complexity of the scheduling process, airlines are increasingly turning to computers to assist in making schedule decisions. However, human judgment remains the predominant determinant.

Finance

The airline industry has experienced—and continues to experience—a great need for funds as the investment in aircraft and ground equipment has grown (Tables I-32 and I-33). The introduction of jet aircraft in the early 1960s and the introduction of wide-body aircraft in the early 1970s both involved the airlines in significant fleet readjustments and changes in ground handling facilities (Table I-34). Since 1962, the airlines have employed both debt and equity financing and have relied increasingly on the latter. In part, the strain on the capacities of the traditional sources of debt financing to the industry—banks and the major

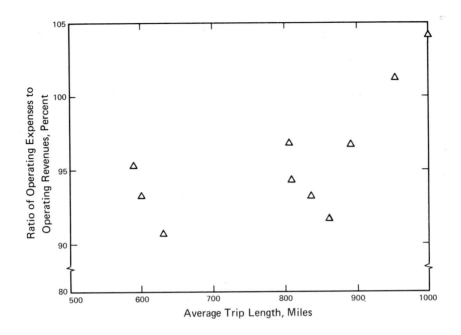

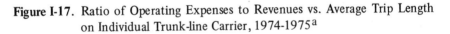

aDomestic Operations. Does not include Pan American.

Figure I-17. Ratio of Operating Expenses to Revenues vs. Average Trip Length on Individual Trunk-line Carrier, 1974-1975[a]

insurance companies—was responsible for this turn of events. In 1967, these institutions held 25 percent and 50 percent, respectively, of all airline debt.

The stock market has been highly variable in its attitude toward airline stocks since 1962. Braniff International, for example, experienced a swing in its price/earnings ratio from 6 to 104 in the period 1962-1972. In general, however, the airlines have been able to increase their equity funding by judicious timing. Internal sources of funds for the airlines have been dominated by depreciation and amortization, due to the poor earnings performance in recent years (Tables I-35 and I-36).

The air carriers have also made extensive use of the investment tax credit, which, prior to 1969, allowed a company to subtract 7 percent of the initial cost of an investment from its income tax, provided that the tax liability was equal to at least twice the amount of credit. Accrued credits could be carried forward for seven years. Because of this provision, the airlines also became significant users of what were termed income tax credit leases. Under this arrangement, a financial intermediary having a high marginal tax rate could purchase an aircraft

Table I-32
Total Balance Sheet, All U.S. Scheduled Airlines, 1965-1975
($ millions)

	As of December 31		
	1965	1970	1975
Assets			
Current assets	3,736	2,448	3,941
Investments and special funds	1,118	1,283	893
Flight equipment	13,541	10,946	14,034
Reserve for depreciation	(5,095)	(3,485)	(5,554)
Ground property and equipment	2,352	1,598	2,465
Reserve for depreciation	(1,158)	(632)	(1,266)
Other property	364	428	239
Deferred charges	342	325	312
Total assets	15,200	12,911	15,064
Liabilities			
Current liabilities	3,419	2,344	3,520
Long-term debt	5,598	6,094	5,535
Other noncurrent liabilities	283	315	247
Deferred credit	1,444	1,063	1,422
Stockholder's equity	4,456	3,094	4,340
Total liabilities	15,200	12,911	15,064

Source: Adapted from *Air Transport 1976* (Washington, D.C.: Air Transport Association of America, 1976), p. 24.

and simultaneously lease it on a long-term basis to an air carrier. The intermediary gained the benefit of the tax credit and was able to pass back to the air carrier a lease rate that carried a lower effective financing cost than other debt alternatives.

Although the Civil Aeronautics Board has ruled that a healthy airline industry requires a rate of return on investment of 12 percent, this level has not been attained for many years (Table I-37). In spite of its performance, the airline industry, according to an estimate by the Air Transport Association of America, will require approximately $6 billion to finance new flight equipment and related ground support equipment required to meet demands in the years 1976 through 1980.

In the early 1970s, a number of airlines (primarily United and Flying Tiger Line) underwent corporate restructuring in order to facilitate diversification. The CAB has not prevented these activities, but it has advised the industry that it will monitor such activities to ensure that the interests of the airline industry are not adversely affected by corporate restructuring and diversification.

Table I-33

Comparative Balance Sheets, Various Airline Categories, 31 December 1975

($ millions)

	International and Domestic Trunk	Local Service	International and Domestic All Cargo	Total U.S. Scheduled
Assets				
Current	3,473	302	110	3,941
Flight Equipment[a]	7,738	522	131	8,480
Ground Property and Equipment[a]	1,089	50	43	1,199
Other	1,101	200	107	1,444
Total assets	13,401	1074	391	15,064
Liabilities				
Current	3,094	305	64	3,520
Long-term debt	4,908	447	102	5,535
Equity	3,823	305	159	4,340
Other	1,576	17	66	1,669
Total liabilities	13,401	1074	391	15,064

Source: Adapted from *Air Transport 1976* (Washington, D.C.: Air Transport Association of America, 1976), pp. 24-25.

[a]Net of depreciation.

Case Synopses

The cases presented in Chapters 1 through 10 illustrate the types of decisions faced by managers in the domestic airline industry. Each case contains several issues. Decisions must be made in the context of the firm and the industry. Individual cases should be examined with reference to all of the previous cases and the material presented in the Introduction. Each case was selected for this book with the following specific issues in mind.

Position Within the Industry

Southwest Airlines (Chapter 1). This company is attempting to establish itself as a Texas intrastate carrier in competition with well-established interstate carriers. The largest established carrier sees Texas as its domain and considers the Texas operation as a feeder system to its network. Southwest must determine how to position itself to compete against one of America's most profitable trunk-line carriers.

Table I-34
Aircraft in Service, U.S. Scheduled Airlines, 1965-1975

	1965	*1970*	*1975*
Boeing			
707	187	399	264
720	121	115	23
727	168	631	765
737	–	133	133
747	–	79	97
McDonnell-Douglas			
DC-8	130	257	177
DC-9	4	327	337
DC-10	–	–	121
Lockheed			
L-1011	–	–	75
Other jets	102	100	30
Total jets	712	2041	2022
Turboprop	288	300	193
Piston	875	80	45
Helicopters	21	16	7
Total	1896	2437	2267

Source: Adapted from *Air Transport 1976* (Washington, D.C.: Air Transport Association of America, 1976), p. 29.

United Air Freight (Chapter 2). This airline was a pioneer in the use of all-cargo aircraft by a combination passenger and freight carrier. Shippers and the air-freight forwarders were anxious for freighter operations to continue, but the airline was operating daytime flights with excess belly capacity on its recently acquired wide-body aircraft. United found itself caught between the desires of the shippers and forwarders, the CAB, and the economics of the situation.

Technology Selection

Braniff International (Chapter 3). This case describes the equipment selection and capacity decisions of the very aggressive domestic operation of a trunk-line carrier. Braniff was attempting to identify a "break-out strategy" to change its competitive position and accommodate its growth. The airframe manufacturers had just introduced wide-body aircraft. Braniff's competitors were already committed to the new technology. The question was: What did Braniff see as its equipment needs for the next ten to twenty years of operation?

Table I-35
Net Operating Income as a Percentage of Revenue,[a] Various Airline Categories,
1965-1975

	Total U.S. Scheduled	Domestic Trunk	Local Service	International Trunk	Domestic All Cargo	International All Cargo
1965	13.6	12.8	8.3	17.3	10.4	18.5
1966	13.5	12.4	6.9	17.2	21.6	20.5
1967	10.3	9.3	0.0	15.4	10.9	12.3
1968	6.5	6.4	(1.8)	10.4	(15.7)	7.2
1969	4.4	5.6	(2.8)	3.0	(2.0)	8.5
1970	0.5	0.3	(1.2)	1.0	(7.9)	12.8
1971	3.3	3.4	3.5	1.4	(2.1)	19.8
1972	5.2	5.8	5.7	2.2	3.1	18.1
1973	4.7	5.0	6.0	2.7	5.9	11.7
1974	4.9	6.8	7.7	(2.5)	(14.4)	5.1
1975	0.8	0.8	2.2	0.1	(12.1)	2.2

Note: If data in the table are deducted from 100, the resulting figure is known as the
operating ratio (operating expenses as a percentage of operating revenues).

Source: Adapted from *Air Transport 1976* (Washington, D.C.: Air Transport Association of
America, 1976), pp. 22-23.

[a]Figures in parentheses indicate operating loss.

Table I-36
Pretax Profits[a] as a Percentage of Revenue, Various Airline Categories, 1965-
1975

	Total U.S. Scheduled	Domestic Trunk	Local Service	International Trunk	Domestic All Cargo	International All Cargo
1965	11.3	10.5	6.5	15.2	5.8	13.3
1966	11.3	10.2	4.5	15.1	18.5	17.7
1967	8.1	7.3	(4.3)	13.4	8.6	9.5
1968	3.6	3.8	(8.1)	7.8	(20.4)	4.4
1969	1.2	2.9	(9.6)	0.0	(11.8)	2.1
1970	(3.0)	(2.5)	(7.2)	(2.9)	(16.6)	4.7
1971	0.0	0.6	(1.0)	(2.6)	(8.3)	13.8
1972	2.5	3.4	2.2	(1.4)	(0.3)	13.8
1973	1.7	2.3	2.7	(1.2)	3.7	7.6
1974	2.1	4.2	4.6	(5.9)	(16.6)	2.1
1975	(1.8)	(1.7)	(0.4)	(2.9)	(15.7)	0.0

Source: Adapted from *Air Transport 1976* (Washington, D.C.: Air Transport Association of
America, 1976), pp. 22-23.

[a]Figures shown are net operating income less interest on long-term debt, divided by total
operating revenues (times 100). Figures in parentheses indicate losses.

Table I-37
Rate of Return on Investment,[a] Various Airline Categories, 1965-1975

	Domestic Trunk	Local Service	International Trunk	Domestic All Cargo	International All Cargo	Total U.S. Scheduled
1965	11.2	10.4	15.0	7.2	21.7	12.0
1966	9.7	7.2	14.6	17.1	33.0	11.0
1967	6.9	2.4	11.1	5.3	13.6	7.6
1968	4.9	(0.4)	7.5	(4.9)	6.2	4.9
1969	4.3	(4.2)	3.2	(0.9)	6.2	3.3
1970	1.4	(3.9)	2.4	(8.3)	5.9	1.2
1971	3.3	3.7	3.2	(3.6)	11.9	3.5
1972	5.1	5.5	3.0	4.2	14.8	4.9
1973	4.7	8.9	4.5	7.9	12.9	5.1
1974	7.8	10.9	0.6	(4.8)	9.3	6.4
1975	2.2	3.5	2.2	(2.7)	7.8	2.5

Source: Adapted from *Air Transport 1976* (Washington, D.C.: Air Transport Association of America, 1976), pp. 22-23.

[a]Calculated as net profit plus interest paid on the noncurrent portion of long-term debt as a percentage of total investment. Total investment is a five-year quarter average of total net worth plus long-term debt. Does not reflect tax adjustments resulting from the investment tax credit.

Flying Tiger Line (Chapter 4). Flying Tiger had settled on one standard aircraft that was very well-suited for its operations. Because of the shift in technology, the airframe manufacturer had stopped producing the aircraft in favor of a more advanced aircraft. Flying Tiger had purchased a large number of the existing aircraft of this model. Should Flying Tiger persist in using this aircraft or should the company accept the new model, even though it might be less appropriate for the company's operations?

Operating Policy

Eastern Airlines December Schedule (Chapter 5). Eastern had decided to level its supply of pilots. The decision implied a possible stock-out of available pilot flying-time hours in the heavy-schedule seasons. As December (typically a heavy-schedule month) approached there was an indication that there would be a stock-out if bad weather occurred. Should Eastern cancel selected flights in anticipation of bad weather or "tough it out" and run some risk of having to cancel flights if pilots run out of hours?

Southern Airways (Chapter 6). This case examines a proposed aircraft acquisition by Southern from a competitor. The acquisition of new aircraft, coupled with new schedules that avoided Atlanta, the traditional hub of the competitor, offered an innovative competitive operating strategy. What implications would the "avoid Atlanta" operation have on Atlanta-based Southern Airways? What competitive reaction would this operation set off?

Federal Express Corporation, Part 1 (Chapter 7). This case describes the start of an innovative small-package air carrier. Federal Express proposed using Memphis as the hub of a radial network of executive jet flights throughout the United States. Was the hub concept feasible? Could a new operation be started in the face of well-established competition? How would the Memphis hub be managed in the middle of the night when all the aircraft arrived for freight transfer? How should the aircraft capacity be managed?

Manning the Boeing B-737 (Chapter 8). How many crew members are required to properly operate a jet aircraft? The B-737 was designed to operate with a cockpit crew of two persons. However, the pilots and others began to argue for the addition of a third person to the crew. The case examines safety, economics, operations, and labor relations arguments of the situation.

Control

CP Air Passenger Reservations (Chapter 9). This company faces the problem of whether, and when, to computerize its passenger reservations system. It must also choose between alternative computer systems. The company must determine how any computerization is to be justified, developed, implemented, and managed.

Managing Change

Federal Express Corporation, Part 2 (Chapter 10). This part of the Federal Express case describes events after the start-up phase of the company. As the concept becomes more generally accepted by the shipping public, the firm must manage its operations differently. Management is considering several innovations that will substantially change the cost structure, management task, and service offering.

Notes

1. "Air Freight as the Shippers See It," *Distribution Worldwide*, January 1976, p. 33.

2. For a comprehensive review of each phase of the DPFI, see N.K. Taneja, *The Commercial Airline Industry* (Lexington, Mass.: Lexington Books, D.C. Heath and Company, 1976).

3. The following carriers are parties to the Mutual Aid Agreement: American, Braniff, Continental, Eastern, Frontier, Hughes Airwest, National, North Central, Northwest Orient, Ozark, Piedmont, Texas International, TWA, United, and Western.

4. Domestic Air Freight Rate Investigation, Docket 22859, *Initial Decision of the Administrative Law Judge*, (15 April 1975), p. 38.

5. For a comprehensive description of the capacity spiral, the S-curve and industry behavior, see W. Fruhan, *The Fight for Competitive Advantage* (Boston, Mass.: Division of Research, Harvard Business School, 1973).

6. "Money-short Airlines Jam More into Coach and Strip First Class," *Wall Street Journal*, 19 February 1976, p. 1.

Appendix IA
Major Provisions of the
Aviation Act of 1975

1. Policy Changes

   The Declaration of Policy, enacted in 1938 . . . is revised to stress the desirability of competition rather than the protection of established carriers. . . . [D]irects the Board to encourage the entry of new firms into air transportation.

2. Pricing Flexibility

   . . . substantially increases airline pricing flexibility over a three year period. During the first year . . . airlines may lower as much as 40 percent. . . . By the third year fare decreases may be disallowed only if they are below the direct cost of the service. Fares may be increased by up to 10 percent per year.

3. Entry

   The Act directs the Board to eliminate all existing operating restrictions within five years. . . . [A]llows each carrier to increase route mileage by about five percent per year. After January 1, 1978, a carrier may sell, transfer or lease any portion of its operating authority to any air carrier found by the CAB to be fit, willing, and able to provide air service. The Act allows supplemental airlines to apply for authority to provide scheduled service. The Act requires the CAB to permit entry by qualified applicants for nonstop service between cities not receiving such service from certificated carriers . . . [reduces] the strict limitations on charter services . . . allows commuter airlines to increase the size of aircraft they operate from 30 to 35 seats.

4. Abandonment of Service

   Carriers will be permitted to exit upon 90 days notice if alternative schedules air service is provided by another carrier. Where alternative scheduled air service is not provided, carriers will be permitted to exit whenever, taking subsidies into account, they could not cover fully allocated costs for one year or they could not cover DOC for three months. The Board may require continued service if the community or another public body were willing to defray the carrier's losses.

5. Subsidies

   No change. Secretary of Transport to study the current system and report to Congress within one year.

6. Mergers

   The Act brings airline merger standards more in line with antitrust laws. The Board could not approve a merger which would tend to create a monopoly

Taken from U.S. Department of Transportation, *Aviation Act of 1975.*

or substantially lessen competition, unless it found that the anticompetitive effects were outweighed by the probable benefits to the communities concerned and that no less anticompetitive alternatives were available.

7. Anticompetitive Agreements

The Act prohibits the Board from approving agreements to control levels of capacity, equipment or schedules, or which relate to pooling or apportioning of earnings or of fixing of rates.

8. Procedural Changes

The Act requires the Board to hear and decide cases speedily ... [W] ill end the practice of dismissing applications on procedural grounds, leaving the applicants with no recourse to court review.

1
Southwest Airlines

Introduction

"Y'all buckle that seat belt," said the hostess over the public address system, "because we're fixin' to take off right now. Soon as we get up in the air, we want you to kick off your shoes, loosen your tie, an' let Southwest put a little love in your life on our way from Big D to Houston." The passengers settled back comfortably in their seats as the brightly colored Boeing 737 taxied toward the takeoff point at Dallas's Love Field. Moments later, it accelerated down the runway and climbed steeply into the Texas sky on the 240-mile flight to Houston.

On the other side of Love Field away from the airport terminal, executives of Southwest Airlines ignored the noise of the departing aircraft, although it was clearly audible in the company's modest but comfortable second-floor offices next to the North American-Rockwell hangar. They were about to begin an important meeting with representatives from their advertising agency to discuss the alternative strategies open to them in response to an announcement by their major competitor, Braniff International Airways. Braniff had announced that it was introducing a sixty-day, half-price "sale" on Southwest's major route effective that same day, 1 February 1973.

History

Southwest Airlines Co., a Texas corporation, was organized in March 1967. The founder, Rollin W. King, had graduated from the Harvard Business School in 1962 and had been an investment counselor with a San Antonio firm. Since 1964, King (who held an airline transport pilot's license) had also been president of an air taxi service operating between San Antonio and various smaller South Texas communities.

From the middle 1960s onward, Rollin King and his associates became increasingly convinced there was an unmet need for improved air service within Texas between the major metropolitan areas of Houston, Dallas/Fort Worth, and San Antonio. These four cities were among the fastest growing in the nation. By 1968 the Houston standard metropolitan statistical area had a population of 1,867,000. Dallas's population was 1,459,000, San Antonio's 850,000, and Forth Worth's 680,000. The cities of Dallas and Fort Worth are located thirty

1

miles apart in northeastern Texas, but they were generally thought of as a single market area. Dallas and Fort Worth each had its own airport (Dallas's Love Field was the busier of the two and the only one served by the airlines), but construction had recently begun on the huge new Dallas/Fort Worth Regional Airport, located midway between the two cities and intended to serve both.

Air service between these market areas was provided primarily by Braniff International Airways and Texas International Airlines. In 1967, Braniff operated a fleet of sixty-nine jet and turboprop aircraft on an extensive route network, with a predominantly north-south emphasis, serving major U.S. cities, Mexico, and South America. Total Braniff revenues in that year were $256 million and it carried 5.6 million passengers. Texas International (TI) Airlines (then known as Trans-Texas Airways) was a regional carrier serving Southern and Southwestern states and Mexico. In 1967, it operated a fleet of forty-five jet, turboprop, and piston-engined aircraft mostly on short-haul routes. TI carried 1.5 million passengers and generated total revenues of $32 million. Both Braniff and TI were headquartered in Texas.

Service by these two carriers within Texas represented legs of much longer, interstate flights, so that travelers flying from Dallas to San Antonio, for example, might find themselves boarding a Braniff flight which had just arrived from New York and was calling at Dallas on its way to San Antonio. Local travel between Dallas and Houston (the most important route) averaged 483 passengers daily in each direction in 1967. Braniff carried 86 percent of this traffic (Table 1-1).[1] Looking back at the factors that first stimulated his interest in developing a new airline to service these markets, King recalled:

The more we talked to people, the more we looked at figures of how big the market was and the more we realized the degree of consumer dissatisfaction with the services of existing carriers, the more apparent the opportunities became to us. We thought that these were substantial markets, and while they weren't nearly as large as the Los Angeles-San Francisco market, they had a lot in common with it. We knew the history of what PSA had been able to do in California with the same kind of service we were contemplating.[2]

But the main reason Southwest ever got into the business was the lousy job that Braniff and TI were doing. When you went into somebody's office, from whom you were trying to raise money, you weren't faced with telling them *why* there ought to be another airline serving these markets. Because they all hated Braniff—and to a less extent, TI. So you didn't have the problem of convincing people that there was a need for good air service. The only problem we had was convincing them that we were going to do a first class job, so that there was a chance of having some success financially.

On 20 February 1968, the company was granted a Certificate of Public Convenience and Necessity by the Texas Aeronautics Commission, permitting it

Table 1-1

Southwest Airlines and Competitors: Average Daily Local Passengers Carried in Each Direction, Dallas-Houston Market

	Braniff[a]		Texas Int.[a]		Southwest		Total Market
	Passengers	% of Market	Passengers	% of Market	Passengers	% of Market	Passengers
1967	416	86.1	67	13.9			483
1968	381	70.2	162	29.8			543
1969	427	75.4	139	24.6			566
1970							
1st half	449	79.0	119	21.0			568
2nd half	380	76.0	120	24.0			500
Year	414	77.5	120	22.5			534
1971							
1st half	402	74.7	126	23.4	10	1.9	538
2nd half	338	50.7	120	18.0	209	31.3	667
Year	370	61.4	123	20.4	110	18.2	603
January 1972	341	48.3	105	14.9	260	36.8	706
February	343	47.6	100	13.9	277	38.5	720
March	357	47.5	100	13.3	295	39.2	752
April	367	48.3	97	12.8	296	38.9	560
May	362	48.5	84	11.3	300	40.2	746
June	362	46.8	81	10.5	330	42.7	773
1st half	356	48.0	93	12.5	293	39.5	742
July	332	48.1	74	10.7	284	41.2	690
August	432	53.7	56	6.9	317	39.4	805
September	422	54.9	55	7.2	291	37.9	768
October	443	53.1	56	6.7	335	40.2	834
November	439	50.6	55	6.3	374	43.1	868
December	396	52.1	56	7.4	308	40.5	760
2nd half	411	52.1	59	7.5	318	40.4	788
Year	384	50.1	77	10.0	306	39.9	767
January 1973[b]	443	51.5	62	7.3	354	41.2	859

[a]These figures were calculated by Muse from passenger data that Braniff and TI were required to supply to the Civil Aeronautics Board. He multiplied the original figures by a correction factor to eliminate interline traffic and arrive at net totals for local traffic.

[b]Projected figures from terminal counts by Southwest personnel.

to provide intrastate air service between Dallas/Fort Worth, Houston and San Antonio, a triangular route structure in which each leg ranged in length from roughly 190 to 250 miles. Because the new airline proposed to confine its operations to the state of Texas, its executives maintained that it did not need certification from the federal Civil Aeronautics Board.

The following day, Braniff and TI initiated a lawsuit in the Texas courts, seeking to enjoin issuance of the Texas certificate. These two airlines already offered service on the proposed routes and considered the market insufficiently large to support entry of another airline. More than three years of legal maneuvering followed, including a refusal by the United States Supreme Court to review the case (thus upholding the issuance of the Texas certificate to Southwest). Failing in their efforts, Braniff and TI then went before the Civil Aeronautics Board and argued that Southwest should be regulated by that Board. Without CAB regulation, Southwest would have a great deal more freedom of operation than its competitors and could set fares without CAB approval. The CAB turned the complainants down, stating that it had no jurisdiction over an intrastate carrier. These legal battles cost the new airline $530,000 before its first flight ever left the ground. Reportedly it cost Braniff more than twice as much.

Although this extensive litigation delayed the start of Southwest operations by several years, management felt that the net effect had been beneficial in terms of the equipment finally purchased and the makeup of the management team.

During the summer of 1970, Rollin King was approached by M. Lamar Muse, an independent financial consultant who had resigned the previous fall as president of Universal Airlines—a Detroit-based supplemental carrier—over a disagreement with the major stockholders on their planned purchase of Boeing 747 jumbo jets. Muse had read of Southwest's legal battles and told King and his fellow directors that he would be interested in helping them transform the company from "a piece of paper" into an operating airline.

The wealth of experience that Lamar Muse could bring to the new airline was quickly recognized. Before assuming the presidency of Universal in September 1967, he had served for three years as president of Central Airlines, a Dallas-based regional air carrier. Prior to 1965, Muse had served as secretary-treasurer of Trans-Texas Airways, as Assistant Vice President-Corporate Planning of American Airlines, and as Vice President-Finance of Southern Airways. After working informally with Southwest for a couple of months, Muse became an employee of the company in October 1970 and was elected president, treasurer, and a director on 26 January 1971. King was named Executive Vice·President-Operations at the same time.

One of the reasons he was attracted to Southwest, Lamar Muse explained, was that:

I felt the interstate carriers just weren't doing the job in this market. Every one of their flights was completely full—it was very difficult to get reservations. There were a lot of cancelled flights; Dallas being Braniff's base and Houston TI's base, every time they had a mechanical problem it seemed like they always took it out on the Dallas-Houston service. From Dallas south to San Antonio and Houston is the tag end of Braniff's system, everything was turning around and going back north to Chicago or New York or wherever. There was so much interline traffic that most of the seats were occupied by those people. While Braniff had hourly service, there really weren't many seats available for local passengers. People just avoided flying in this market—they only went by air when they had to.

In discussing the characteristics of Braniff and TI, Muse stated that the former's reputation for punctuality was so poor that it was popularly referred to by many travelers as the "World's Largest Unscheduled Airline."

Optimistic about the outcome of Southwest's legal battles and content to leave such matters to the company's lawyers, Muse and King spent many weeks on the West Coast in late 1970 and early 1971 prospecting for new aircraft. There was a recession in the airline industry at the time and prospective aircraft purchasers were being courted assiduously. High-pressure negotiations were initiated by Southwest with representatives of McDonnell-Douglas, Boeing, and several airlines for the purchase of new or used jet aircraft.

These negotiations included detailed discussions with Pacific Southwest Airlines (PSA), which was interested in selling Southwest not only aircraft, but also crew training, manuals, technical advice, and consulting services. PSA had revolutionized commuter air service in California in the early 1960s. Aggressive promotion campaigns, including cartoonlike ads that emphasize convenience and provide amusement at the same time (slogans included "PSA gives you a lift" and "PSA routes for your home town"), and reduced fares quickly obtained for PSA a significant market share in the face of entrenched competition from United and Western. Although nothing eventually came of the PSA negotiations, Muse and King felt that the understanding they had gained of that carrier's activities would prove extremely useful in designing Southwest's own, smaller but not dissimilar operations. Finally, the Boeing Company, which had overproduced its Boeing 737 twin jet (in a speculative assessment of future orders that had failed to materialize), offered both a substantial price reduction and very favorable financing terms. In March 1971, the Southwest executives signed a contract for three Boeing 737-200 aircraft (some months later they increased their order to four). The total purchase price for the four 737s was $16.2 million, compared with a previous asking price for this aircraft of approximately $4.6 million each.

Muse and King were delighted to have obtained such attractive terms on the 737s, which they regarded as a better aircraft for their purposes than the

McDonnell-Douglas DC-9 or other alternatives. The Boeing 737 was a more modern aircraft than the DC-9, having first been introduced into airline services in 1968. It was specially designed for short-distance routes and had been developed by Boeing from their successful long-range, four-engine 707 and intermediate-range, trijet 727 airliners. The new model 737-200 had a seating capacity of 112 and incorporated a number of refinements and improvements to the basic design. Nicknamed "Fat Albert" by pilots because of its short, stocky fuselage, the 737 offered the same spacious cabin interior as the larger Boeing 727 (six-abreast seating versus five-abreast in the DC-9), but it required a smaller crew.

Preparing for Takeoff

Returning to Texas from their successful negotiations in Seattle, Muse and King faced some urgent problems and an extremely tight deadline. The start of scheduled operations had been tentatively set for 18 June, a little over four months away. During this period, Southwest had to raise additional capital to finance both start-up expenses and what might prove to be a prolonged period of deficit operations. The existing skeleton management team had to be expanded by recruiting several new specialist executives. Personnel had to be hired and trained for both flight and ground operations. Numerous marketing problems had to be resolved and an introductory advertising campaign developed to launch the new airline. Finally, Braniff and TI continued their legal efforts to stifle Southwest.

Southwest's initial proposal called for the use of fully depreciated, turbo-prop Lockheed Electra aircraft and the schedules proposed in the original application before the Texas Aeronautics Commission (TAC) reflected this fact. The airline's purchase of the Boeing 737 gave Braniff and TI (which operated 727s and DC-9s, respectively, on most of their Texas schedules) an excuse for a last effort to stop Southwest. Arguing that the purchase of jets was never contemplated in the original application, they jointly obtained a court order enjoining the TAC from allowing Southwest to provide any service other than that originally proposed in 1967—with old equipment and relatively slow schedules. However, on appeal, the injunction was stayed by the Texas Supreme Court and Southwest was permitted to initiate operations with the new fleet and schedules.

Once again legal matters were left to the company's lawyers while the Southwest executives moved quickly to attend to financial, personnel, and marketing problems. It was urgent to improve the airline's financial position; at year's end 1970 the company had a mere $183 in its bank account (Table 1-2). Between March and June 1971, Southwest raised almost $8 million through the sale of convertible promissory notes and common stock. The cover of the stock prospectus, issued on 8 June, carried the warning, in heavy black type: "These securities involve a high degree of risk."

Vacancies on the existing management team were soon filled. The man selected as vice president of maintenance, John A. Vidal, had previously been manager of line maintenance for Braniff International and had experience in airline maintenance with four different airlines, dating back to 1946. Recruited as vice president of ground operations was William W. Franklin, a veteran of twenty-three years' service with Texas International whose most recent assignment had been seven years as TI's vice president of customer service. The position of vice president of flight operations was filled by Captain Donald G. Ogden, a thirty-four-year veteran of American Airlines, whose management experience included positions as chief pilot and manager of flying at American's bases in Dallas/Fort Worth, Memphis, Tulsa, and Nashville, in addition to his latest position as director of flight standards. To fill the position of vice president of marketing, Southwest succeeded in hiring Richard Elliott, a hard-driving marketing manager formerly with Braniff who had also held marketing positions with Mohawk Airlines and Central Airlines. Vidal, Elliott, and Franklin had all been recently fired by their former employers, Braniff and TI—a fact that Muse considered one of their strongest recommendations for employment with Southwest.

Considerable marketing planning had taken place while the new staff members were being recruited and initiated into their new jobs. Some decisions, such as route structure and schedules, had been made earlier. Initially, two of the three Boeing 737s would be placed in service on the busy Dallas-Houston run and the third would fly between Dallas and San Antonio. For the time being, Southwest did not plan to exercise its rights to operate service on the third leg of the triangle between Houston and San Antonio.

Schedule frequency was constrained by aircraft availability. To allow time to turn the aircraft around at each end it was concluded that flights could be offered in each direction between Dallas and Houston at seventy-five-minute intervals, and between Dallas and San Antonio at intervals of every two and a half hours. Both services were scheduled for fifty minutes. The Monday-Friday schedule called for twelve round trips daily between Dallas and Houston and six round trips daily between Dallas and San Antonio. Saturday and Sunday schedules were limited to reflect both the lower travel demand at weekends and the need for downtime to service the aircraft.

The pricing decision had been arrived at during the Southwest executives' visit to PSA. Rollin King recalled:

What Andy Andrews [president of PSA] said to Lamar and me one day was the key to our initial pricing decision. Andy told us that the way you ought to figure your price is not on how much you can get, or what the other carriers were charging or anything, but that you had to sort of go back and forth. He said, "Pick a price at which you can break even with a reasonable load factor, and a

Table 1-2
Balance Sheet at 31 December 1970, 1971, and 1972

	1970	1971	1972
Assets			
Current assets			
Cash	$ 183	$ 231,530	$ 133,839
Certificates of deposit	–	2,850,000	1,250,000
Accounts receivable			
Trade	–	300,545	397,664
Interest	–	35,013	14,691
Other	100	32,569	67,086
	100	368,127	479,441
Less allowance for doubtful accounts	–	30,283	86,363
	100	337,844	393,078
Inventories of parts and supplies, at cost	–	171,665	154,121
Prepaid insurance and other	31	156,494	75,625
Total current assets	314	3,747,533	2,006,663
Property and equipment, at cost			
Boeing 737-200 jet aircraft	–	16,263,250	12,409,772
Support flight equipment	–	2,378,581	2,423,480
Ground equipment	9,249	313,072	346,377
	9,249	18,954,903	15,179,629
Less accumulated depreciation and overhaul allowance	–	1,096,177	2,521,646
	9,249	17,858,726	12,657,983
Deferred certification costs less amortization	530,136	477,122	371,095
	$539,699	$22,083,381	$15,035,741
Liabilities and stockholders' equity			
Current liabilities			
Notes payable to banks (secured)	$ –	$ –	$ 950,000
Accounts payable	30,819	355,539	124,890
Accrued salaries and wages	79,000	54,713	55,293
Other accrued liabilities	–	301,244	136,437
Long-term debt due within one year	–	1,500,000	1,226,457
Total current liabilities	109,819	2,211,496	2,493,077

Table 1-2 (cont.)

	1970	1971	1972
Long-term debt due after one year			
7% convertible promissory notes	–	1,250,000	–
Conditional purchase agreements– Boeing Financial Corporation (1½% over prime rate)	–	16,803,645	11,942,056
	–	18,053,645	11,942,056
Less amounts due within one year	–	1,500,000	1,226,457
	–	16,553,645	10,715,599
Contingencies			
Stockholders' equity			
Common stock, $1.00 par value, 2,000,000 shares authorized, 1,108,758 issued (1,058,758 at 31 December 1971)	372,404	1,058,758	1,108,758
Capital in excess of par value	57,476	6,012,105	6,062,105
Deficit	–	(3,752,623)	(5,343,798)
	429,880	3,318,240	1,827,065
	$539,699	$22,083,381	$15,035,741

Notes to financial statement not shown here.

load factor that you have a reasonable expectation of being able to get within a given period of time, and that ought to be your price. It ought to be as low as you can get it without leading yourself down the primrose path and running out of money."

After estimating the amount of money required for preoperating expenditures and then carefully assessing both operating costs and market potential, Muse and King settled on a $20 fare for both routes, with a breakeven point of thirty-nine passengers per flight. This compared with existing Braniff and TI coach fares of $27 on the Dallas-Houston run and $28 on the Dallas-San Antonio service. The two executives felt that an average of thirty-nine passengers per flight was a reasonable expectation in light of the market's potential for growth and the frequency of flights Southwest planned to offer, although they projected a period of deficit operations before this breakeven point would be reached. They anticipated that although Braniff and TI would probably reduce their own fares eventually, Southwest could expect an initial price advantage.

Immediately after returning from Seattle, Lamar Muse met with the marketing vice president, Dick Elliott, to select an advertising agency (the company already employed a public relations agency to handle publicity). Several advertising agencies were invited to make presentations for the airline's account, among them the Bloom Agency, which had come to the Southwest executives' attention as a result of a beer advertising campaign which they liked. Muse and Elliott were highly impressed by the Bloom Agency's presentation and gave them the account. The assignment was to come up with a complete communications program (other than publicity) within four months. "We have no hostesses, uniforms, airplanes, design, nor money," Muse told the agency people, "but we're going to have an airline flying in 120 days!"

Bloom, a large regional advertising agency conveniently headquartered in Dallas, immediately set to work assigning personnel to the account. As account group supervisor, they selected Raymond J. Trapp, an MBA graduate of Northwestern University who had previously worked for the Ogilvy & Mather agency in New York on Lever Brothers and General Foods accounts.

The account group approached Southwest Airlines, in Ray Trapp's words, "as though it were a packaged goods account." Their first task was to evaluate the characteristics of all American carriers competing in the Texas markets. To facilitate comparisons, Trapp prepared a two-dimensional positioning diagram rating each airline's image on "conservative-fun" and "obvious-subtle" dimensions (Figure 1-1). The diagram was based primarily on a content analysis of recent airline advertising, with a view to determining the image conveyed by each carrier.

Texas International was immediately dismissed as dull and conservative with a bland image. In 1970-1971, for example, their understated ads billed TI as an "intelligent airline" and announced, "We don't run big expensive ads. We run big expensive jets instead." and "If we listed all the 66 cities in the 9 states and Mexico that we jet to it would take up this entire costly page. We'd rather spend the money getting you there on time." Braniff's advertising, however, presented an interesting contrast in styles. From 1965 to 1968, Braniff had employed the New York agency of Wells, Rich, Greene, which had developed an innovative marketing and advertising strategy for their client on a budget that exceeded $10 million in 1967. Instead of the traditional, rather conservative, aircraft color schemes (typically white and silver with thin, colored stripes along the fuselage), the agency president, Mary Wells, had Braniff's entire fleet of nearly six dozen aircraft painted a variety of brilliant colors. Braniff hostesses were outfitted in couture costumes created by the Italian fashion designer Emilio Pucci. The advertising sought to make flying by Braniff seem a glamorous and exciting experience. This strategy proved extremely successful and was believed by many observers to have been an important factor in Braniff's rapid growth during the second half of the 1960s. The airline enjoyed a fruitful relationship with Wells, Rich, Greene until 1968 when the agency resigned the account following Wells's marriage to Harding Lawrence, president of Braniff International. (Immediately

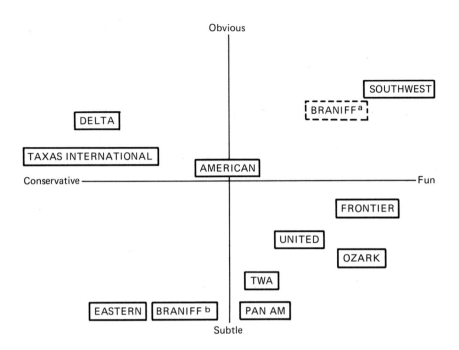

[a]Former advertising by Wells, Rich, Green ("The End of the Plain Plane," "The Air Strip").
[b]Clinton Frank advertising.

Figure 1-1. Advertising Agency's Positioning Diagram of Advertising by U.S. Airlines Competing in Texas Markets

thereafter, Mary Wells Lawrence and her agency obtained the even larger TWA account.) From 1968 to 1970, the Braniff account was held by Lois Holland Gallaway. When Clinton E. Frank, Inc. took the account in 1970 the budget had been reduced to approximately $4 million. The Frank agency retained the brightly colored aircraft and Pucci uniforms but adopted a subtler, more conservative style for the advertising messages. (One 1970 press ad presents Braniff as a staid but exclusive kind of club.) The Bloom executives concluded that Braniff's image was changing; the airline had abandoned its fun image in favor of chic. There was a vacuum that Southwest Airlines could fill. The agency decided to position Southwest even further out on the "fun"/"obvious" side of the old Braniff image.

The account group developed what they termed "an entire personality description model" for the new airline. The objective was to provide the agency's creative specialists with a clear understanding of the image that Southwest should project, so that this might be reflected consistently in every facet of the communications campaign they had to design. This personality statement, which was also used as a guideline in staff recruiting, saw Southwest as "young and vital . . . exciting . . . friendly . . . efficient . . . dynamic."

While the copywriters busied themselves developing appropriate advertising themes, other specialists at the Bloom Agency worked feverishly on research, overall marketing plans, media evaluation, and a variety of other tasks. Personnel from the firm of Ernest G. Mantz & Associates, industrial designers, flew to Seattle to work with Boeing on the design for the aircraft interior. Mantz, who had been retained to develop the exterior color scheme and all related corporate image collateral material, worked closely with the agency people. The same colors were used inside and outside the aircraft and gave a bright, cheerful appearance to the cabin. Meantime, fashion specialists at Bloom worked to design uniforms for the airline personnel. Straightforward, navy blue suits and uniform caps were selected for the flight crew, but eye-catching colors and patterns were chosen for the hostesses and counter staff; the hostess uniform consisted of an orange knit top, red hotpants, and high, bone-colored boots.

At one point, as many as thirty different people at Bloom were working on the Southwest account, which had a first-year budget of $700,000. An office was found at the agency for Dick Elliott, the airline's marketing vice president. He, Lamar Muse, and other Southwest personnel were constantly in and out of the agency during this preoperating period. Looking back, one member of the Bloom account group observed, "It was almost as if we were an arm of the airline."

One constraint on marketing activities in the months and weeks prior to passenger operations was the planned issue of over $6 million worth of Southwest stock on 8 June. The company's lawyers had advised that a media campaign promoting the airline prior to the stock issue might violate Securities and Exchange Commission regulations against promotion of stock. Virtually the only advertising conducted prior to this date, therefore, was for personnel.

Recruitment advertising in one area proved outstandingly effective. Over 1200 young women responded to advertisements placed in national media for positions as air hostesses with Southwest. Forty applicants were selected for training, and although airline officials made no secret that the successful candidates were chosen partly for their attractiveness, they also pointed out that the average scores on the required FAA proficiency test placed the Southwest hostesses among the highest ranked in the nation.

The prohibition on advertising did not entirely keep Southwest out of the news. The airline's continuing legal battles with Braniff and TI received wide press coverage in the mass media, and Southwest's public relations agency distributed a number of press releases that subsequently appeared as news or feature stories.

Inauguration of Service: The First Six Months

On 10 June 1971, the Bloom Agency's advertising campaign for Southwest finally broke. It began modestly with small "teaser" advertisements in the newspapers, containing provocative headlines such as "the 48-minute love affair," "at last a $20 ticket you won't mind getting," "love can change your ways," and "a fare to remember." The ads were unsigned, but contained a telephone number for the reader to call. On phoning, a caller in Dallas would hear the following message:

Hi. It's us. Southwest Airlines. Us with our brand new, candy-colored, rainbow-powered Boeing 737 jets. The most reliable plane flying today. And we start flying June 18, to Houston or San Antonio. You choose—only 45 minutes non-stop. In that time, we'll be sharing a lot of big little things with you that mean a lot. Like love potions, a lot of attention and a new low fare. Just $20. Join us June 18. Southwest Airlines. There is somebody up there who loves you.

There were approximately 25,000 telephone calls as a result of these teaser ads.

On Sunday, 13 June, all newspapers in the three market areas ran a four-color double-truck[3] advertisement for Southwest (see Figure 1-2). On each succeeding day for the next two weeks, full-page newspaper ads were run in all markets. Each one focused on the various advantages Southwest Airlines offered the traveler, including new aircraft, attractive hostesses, low fares, fast ticketing, and inexpensive, exotically named drinks. Television advertising was also heavy and included thirty-second spots featuring the Boeing 737, the hostesses, and an automatic ticketing device nicknamed the "love machine." Whereas the competition used traditional, handwritten airline tickets, Southwest counter staff accelerated the ticketing process by using a machine to print out tickets and a pedal-operated tape recorder to record the passengers' names for the aircraft manifest as they checked in—both ideas having been copied from PSA. Rounding

1. Modern aircraft and experienced pilots.
2. "Love stamps" for free drinks if a passenger experiences difficulty.
3. Frequent departures.
4. Inexpensive drinks ($1 rather than $1.50 charged by the competition).
5. Fast check-in.
6. $20 fare (a savings of $14 to $16 per round trip on the competition).
7. "Trying to Please."

Figure 1-2. Themes of Southwest Airlines' Advertisement

out the advertising campaign were strategically located billboards at entrances to all three airports served by Southwest, which contained painted displays. Nearly half the year's promotional budget was spent in the first month of operations (Table 1-3 shows a media breakdown of expenditures in 1971 and 1972).

Scheduled revenue operations were inaugurated in a blaze of publicity on Friday, 18 June, but it soon became evident that the competition was not about to take matters lying down. In half-truck and full-page newspaper ads, Braniff and TI announced $20 fares on both routes. The CAB had disclaimed authority over intrastate fares and Texas law barred jurisdiction by TAC over carriers holding federal Certificates of Public Convenience and Necessity. Thus, the CAB carriers were free to charge any fare they wanted. Braniff's advertising stressed frequent, convenient service ("every hour on the hour," hot and cold towels "to freshen up with," beverage discount coupons, and "peace of mind" phone calls at the boarding gate); it also announced an increase in frequency of service between Dallas and San Antonio, effective 1 July. TI, meantime, announced that on 1 July it would inaugurate hourly service on the Dallas-Houston route, leaving Dallas at thirty minutes past each hour. TI also introduced a "flirty thirties" theme with "extras" such as free beer, free newspapers, and $1 drinks on those routes competing with Southwest. Southwest countered with advertising headlined "the other airlines may have met our price but you can't buy love."

Initial results for Southwest were hardly spectacular; between 18-30 June, there were an average of 13.1 passengers per flight on the Dallas-Houston service and 12.9 passengers on the Dallas-San Antonio route (Table 1-4). Passenger loads during the month of July showed only a marginal improvement. Southwest management concluded that it was essential to improve schedule frequencies to

Table 1-3
Advertising and Promotional Expenditures, 1971 and 1972

	1971			1972
	Preoperating	*Operating*	*Total*	
Advertising				
Newspaper	$139,831	$131,675	$271,506	$ 60,518
Television	36,340	761	37,101	127,005
Radio	5,021	60,080	65,101	95,758
Billboards	26,537	11,670	38,207	90,376
Other publications	710	20,446	21,156	28,139
Production costs	52,484	43,483	95,967	83,272
Other promotion and publicity	19,694	27,200	56,894	48,366
	$290,617	$295,315	$585,932	$533,434

compete more effectively with those of Braniff and TI. This change became possible with the delivery of the company's fourth Boeing 737 in late September 1971. On 1 October, hourly service was introduced between Dallas and Houston and flights between Dallas and San Antonio took off every two hours.

Regular television advertising and frequent publicity events, usually featuring Southwest hostesses, continued. A direct-mail campaign was targeted at 36,000 influential business executives living in Southwest's service areas. Each of these individuals received a personalized letter from Lamar Muse describing Southwest's service and enclosing a voucher good for half the cost of a round-trip ticket; about 1700 of these vouchers were subsequently redeemed.

Surveys of Southwest passengers departing from Houston showed that a substantial percentage would have preferred service from the William P. Hobby Airport, twelve miles southeast of downtown Houston, rather than from the new Houston Intercontinental Airport, twenty-six miles north of the city. Accordingly, arrangements were completed in mid-November for seven of Southwest's fourteen round-trip flights between Dallas and Houston to be transferred to Hobby Airport (thus reopening this old airport to scheduled commercial passenger traffic). Additional schedule revisions made at the same time included a reduction in the number of Dallas-San Antonio flights to four round trips each weekday, inauguration of three round trips daily on the third leg of the route triangle between Houston (Hobby) and San Antonio, and elimination of the extremely unprofitable Saturday operation on all routes. These actions contributed to an increase in transportation revenues in the final quarter of 1971 over those achieved in the third quarter, but Southwest's operating losses in the fourth quarter fell only slightly, from $1,006,000 to $921,000 (Table 1-5). At year's end 1971, Southwest's accumulated deficit stood at $3.75 million.

Second Six Months

In February 1972, Southwest initiated a second phase of the advertising campaign, hired a new marketing vice president and terminated its public relations agency (hiring away the agency's publicity director to fill a newly created position as public relations director at Southwest).

The objective of this new phase was to sustain Southwest's presence in the marketplace after eight months of service. Heavy-frequency advertising, employing a wide variety of messages, was directed at the airline's primary target, the regular business commuter. Surveys had shown that 89 percent of Southwest's traffic at that time was accounted for by such travelers. Extensive use was made of television in this campaign, which featured many of Southwest's hostesses.

Elliott, whom the president described as having performed a "Herculean task" in getting Southwest off the ground, resigned to take a position with a national advertising agency. The new marketing vice president, Jess R. Coker,

Table 1-4
Monthly Flights and Passenger Counts on Each Route, by Type of Fare
(000 of passengers)

| | Dallas-Houston | | | | Dallas-San Antonio | | | | San Antonio-Houston | | | | Grand Totals | |
| | Full Fare | | Discount | | Full Fare | | Discount | | Full Fare | | Discount | | | |
	Passengers	Flights	Passengers	Flights	Passengers	Flights	Passengers	Flights	Passengers	Flights	Passengers	Flights	Passengers	Flights
June 1971[a]	3.6	276			1.9	148							5.5	424
July	10.3	642			5.2	346							15.5	988
August	11.3	672			4.8	354							16.1	1026
September	11.7	612			4.8	327							16.4	939
October	14.6	764			6.5	382							21.0	1146
November	14.0	651	0.1	3	4.2	240			0.9	72			19.1	966
December	14.5	682	0.2	5	4.0	165			1.7	134			20.4	986
1971 Total	80.0	4299	0.3	8	31.4	1962			2.6	206			114.0	6475
January 1972	16.0	630	0.2	4	2.8	141			2.0	128			20.9	903
February	15.9	636	0.2	4	2.8	142			2.1	134			20.9	916
March	17.9	664	0.4	5	3.9	204	0.3	5	2.8	146			25.4	1024
April	17.4	601	0.3	4	4.3	185	0.3	4	2.3	130			24.7	924
May	17.1	554	1.5	30	3.5	177	0.7	21	2.5	138			25.3	1020
June	16.5	474	3.3	47	3.8	170	1.4	31	2.6	140			27.6	862
July	13.6	447	4.0	47	3.3	162	1.8	31	2.1	131			24.7	818
August	15.7	496	4.0	50	3.2	177	1.8	31	2.4	146			27.0	900
September	13.7	436	3.8	53	3.1	154	1.6	30	2.2	127			24.4	800
October	16.0	474	4.8	71	3.4	173	1.8	27	2.5	139			28.5	884

November	15.1	403	7.4	104	2.4	122	4.2	77	2.3	123	0.5	16	32.0	845
December	12.8	377	6.3	91	2.4	117	3.9	69	2.0	110	0.5	16	27.8	780
1972 Total	187.7	6192	36.2	510	38.9	1924	17.8	326	27.8	1592	1.0	32	309.2	10676
January 1973[b]	15.1	404	6.8	101	1.4	75	6.3	122	2.4	120	0.5	16	32.5	838

[a]Part-month only.
[b]Estimated figures.

Table 1-5
Quarterly Income Statements, 1971-1972

Income Statements ($000)	1971		1972			
	Q3	Q4	Q1	Q2	Q3	Q4
Transportation revenues[a]	887	1138	1273	1401	1493	1745
Operating expenses						
Operations & maintenance	1211	1280	1192	1145	1153	1156
Marketing & gen. admin.	371	368	334	366	313	351
Depreciation & amortiz.	311	411	333	334	335	335
Total	1893	2059	1859	1845	1801	1842
Operating profit (loss)	(1006)	(921)	(586)	(444)	(308)	(97)
Net interest revenues (costs)	(254)	(253)	(218)	(220)	(194)	(204)
Net income (loss) before extraordinary items	(1260)	(1174)	(804)	(664)	(502)	(301)
Extraordinary items	(571)[c]	(469)[c]	–	533[d]	–	–
Net income (loss)	(1831)	(1643)	(804)	(131)	(502)	(301)

[a]Includes both passenger and freight business. Freight sales represented 2 percent of revenues in 1972.

[b]Incremental costs per flight were $226 during the second half of 1971, $231 in the first half of 1972, $245 in the second half of 1972. Management estimated that variable costs per passenger carried during the second half of 1972 amounted to $2.80.

[c]Write-off of preoperating costs.

[d]Capital gain on sale of one aircraft.

had spent ten years in the outdoor advertising business after graduating from the University of Texas. His most recent assignment before joining the airline, had been as vice president of Southern Outdoor Markets, a company that represented 85 percent of all outdoor advertising facilities in the fourteen southern and southeastern states. As marketing vice president at Southwest, Coker became responsible for all marketing functions of the airline, including advertising, sales, and public relations. Jess Coker typically met weekly with the account executive from the Bloom Agency to discuss not only media advertising, but also the numerous other small activities handled by the agency. These included preparation and execution of pocket timetables, point-of-sales materials for travel agents, and promotional brochures.

Although the majority of ticket sales were made over the counter at the airport terminals, sales were also made to travel agents and corporate accounts (Table 1-6 shows the monthly breakdown of ticket sales for each of these three categories). Travel agents, who received a 7 percent commission on credit-card sales and 10 percent on cash sales, would often arrange package deals such as a weekend in San Antonio, including airfare, hotel, and meals. Corporate accounts—companies whose personnel made regular use of Southwest Airlines—received no discount, but benefited from the convenience of having their own

Table 1-6
Ticket Sales by Outlets, July 1971-January 1973

Month	Counter	Travel Agents	Corporate Accounts	Total
July 1971	$245,177	$28,193		$273,370
August	238,780	48,111		286,891
September	260,511	40,105		300,616
October	328,578	46,828		375,406
November	293,507	54,432		347,939
December	308,510	57,902		366,412
January 1972	325,495	$46,923	$16,020	388,438
February	318,604	43,211	16,335	378,150
March	378,508	53,520	17,005	449,033
April	375,120	49,434	17,560	442,114
May	364,327	55,240	20,125	439,692
June	399,235	52,337	16,110	467,682
July	384,336	44,590	14,390	443,316
August	439,712	49,423	19,477	508,612
September	409,743	45,263	11,746	466,752
October	467,847	64,303	22,399	554,549
November	491,227	80,086	22,111	593,424
December	461,751	50,516	14,472	511,739
January 1973 (est.)	516,355	63,317	16,013	595,685

supply of ticket stock (which they issued themselves) and of receiving a single monthly billing. Jess Coker was responsible for a force of six sales representatives whose job was to develop and service both travel agents and corporate accounts and to encourage maximum use of Southwest through distribution of point-of-sale materials, development of package arrangements, distribution of pocket timetables, and so on. Sales representatives also promoted the availability of Southwest's air-freight business, which featured a special rush delivery service for packages. Each representative, like most company officers, drove an AMC Gremlin car, strikingly painted in the same color scheme as Southwest's aircraft.

Also reporting to Coker was Southwest's new public relations director, Camille Keith, former publicity director of Read-Poland, Inc., the public relations agency that had handled the airline's account. Keith, a graduate of Texas Christian University, had joined WFAA television in spring 1967 while still in college. After four years with this Dallas-based station as promotion assistant and then publicity director, she had joined Read-Poland and there spent much of her time working on the Southwest account. Keith's responsibilities focused on obtaining media coverage for the airline and included publication of Southwest's in-flight magazine and development of certain promotions jointly with the advertising agency.

Figure 1-3, a partial organization chart, summarizes the organization of the marketing staff at Southwest and its relationship to other areas of management.

Between October 1971 and April 1972, average passenger loads systemwide increased from 18.4 passengers per flight to 26.7 passengers. However, this number was still substantially below the number necessary to cover total costs per trip flown, which had been tending to rise. It had become evident that the volume of traffic during the late morning and early afternoon could not realistically support flights at hourly intervals. It was also clear that most Houston passengers preferred Hobby Airport to Houston Intercontinental. Over time, the number of Southwest flights to Hobby had been steadily increased and the decision was now taken to abandon Houston Intercontinental altogether.

On 14 May, a new schedule reduced the total number of daily flights between Dallas and Houston from twenty-nine to twenty-two, primarily by reducing service in the 9:30 a.m. to 3:30 p.m. period from hourly to bi-hourly. Eleven flights daily continued to be offered on the Dallas-San Antonio route and six between San Antonio and Houston, with some minor schedule modifications. Hobby Airport was to be used exclusively for all flights to and from Houston.

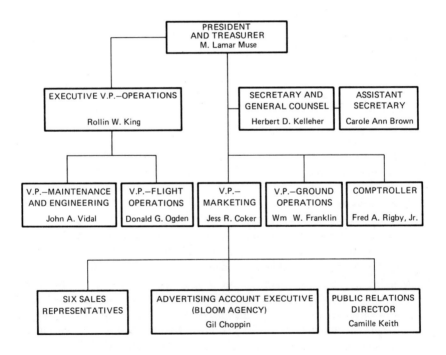

Source: Company records.

Figure 1-3. Partial Organization Chart, 1972-1973

Braniff quickly retaliated by introducing its own service from Dallas to Hobby and undertaking an extensive publicity program to promote this airport.

From a financial viewpoint, the most significant aspect of Southwest's actions was that the new schedule made it possible for the company to dispose of its fourth Boeing 737. Experience had shown that the 737s could be turned around (i.e., loaded and unloaded) at the gate in as little as ten minutes. Consequently, an hourly schedule on the Dallas-Houston run could be maintained with two aircraft, instead of three. With the slack provided by the reduced midday frequencies and a schedule that involved periodically flying an aircraft around all three legs of the route triangle, management concluded that a total of three aircraft would suffice and that the fourth could be sold. By mid-1972, the airline industry had recovered from its 1970-1971 slump, and aircraft manufacturers had waiting lists for their more popular models. Southwest had no trouble finding a ready buyer for its now-surplus 737 and made a profit of $533,000 by reselling it. The combination of this capital gain, lower operating costs and a continued increase in revenues resulted in a reduction of the quarterly net loss from $804,000 to $131,000 between the first and second quarters of 1972.

For some months, Southwest had been experimenting with a $10 fare on Friday evening flights after 9:00 p.m. In May, this reduced fare was extended to post-9:00 p.m. flights on a daily basis. The result was sharply higher load factors on this discount flights relative to the average achieved on standard price flights (Table 1-7).

June 1972 saw Southwest Airlines celebrating its first birthday. This occasion provided Keith with an opportunity for some more of the publicity stunts for which the airline was already becoming renowned. Posters were hung inside the aircraft and in the waiting lounges, the aircraft cabins were decorated and there was an on-board party everyday for a week, with birthday cake for the passengers and balloons one day for the children. This activity, promoted by newspaper advertising, generated considerable publicity for the airline and, in management's view, reinforced Southwest's image as the plucky, friendly little underdog that had survived an entire year against powerful, entrenched competition. Discussing her job, Keith observed:

One good point was that Mr. Coker and I didn't have airline backgrounds. Our backgrounds were in the areas that we're serving—public relations and marketing and sales. Nobody had ever told me "You can't have a flying birthday party" and I didn't know you're not supposed to have Easter bunnies on airplanes. So we did things that other people who'd been brought up in the [airplane] business never did. We went out and tried things, and if they didn't work, we tried something else. We had more flexibility in that area to do it. We were new; we knew all our employees, and everybody knew that if the company went under we were all out of a job. Our really great bunch of hostesses has made it easy. How many airline stewardesses would dress up in Halloween costumes on a flight and pass out trick-or-treat candy? Or wear bunny costumes at Easter or reindeer horns at Christmas?

Table 1-7
Number of Discount and Regular Fare Flights, All Routes, 1971-1972

Month	Regular Flights		Discount Flights[a]		Price Changes
	Passengers	Flights	Passengers	Flights	
June 1971[b]	5,530	424			
July	15,459	988			
August	16,121	1,026			
September	16,440	939			
October	21,044	1,146			
November	19,042	963	73	3	←$10 fares on some evening
December	20,178	981	198	5	weekend flights
1971 total	113,814	6,467	271	8	
January 1972	20,694	899	170	4	
February	20,696	912	216	4	
March	24,656	1,014	702	10	
April	24,077	916	573	8	
May	23,112	869	2,189	51	←$10 fare on all flights after
June	22,972	784	4,636	78	9 p.m.
July	18,994	740	5,720	78	←Basic fare raised to $26
August	21,257	819	5,739	81	
September	19,020	717	5,358	83	
October	21,894	786	6,599	98	
November	19,825	648	12,141	197	←Half-price fares weekdays after
December	17,142	604	10,617	176	8 p.m. and on all weekend
1972 total	254,339	9,708	54,660	868	flights
January 1973[c]	18,893	599	13,635	239	←Half-price fares on all Dallas-San Antonio flights

[a]Includes flights on which gifts were offered.
[b]Part-month only.
[c]Estimated figures.

Not all public relations activity was just hoopla, Keith stressed, mentioning that she worked quite closely with the advertising agency to coordinate the airline's mass communication strategy.

I keep them informed and I sit in on their meetings and they sit in on some of our brainstorming sessions, because it has to go together. I can't do one kind of PR campaign if they're doing an opposite advertising campaign. Neither can we have advertising running that I'm unaware of, in case the media should ask me about it.

One example of a specialized promotional campaign involving input from both Keith and Bloom was the Southwest Sweetheart's Club. Based on a specialized mailing list, a direct-mail piece was sent to executive secretaries in Southwest's market area, offering them membership in this club. For each reservation on Southwest she made for her boss, the secretary received a "sweetheart stamp," and for each 15 stamps, she obtained a free ride on Southwest. Additional bonuses for members included a twice-yearly drawing for a big Mexico City vacation.

Recognizing that interesting, well-written press releases could generate publicity, Keith believed nevertheless that for Southwest to get far more than its fair share of media coverage, the airline had to be constantly alert to opportunities for newsworthy stories or incidental coverage.

The unusual is what's going to get covered. The standard thing that we flew everyday on time (which is what we're supposed to do), and that we didn't lose any bags (which is an obligation under our certificate), and that the passengers were happy (which is our responsibility to them), is *not* news. It's supposed to happen. The news is that Senator Bentsen flew on Thursday afternoon and the girls knew him and spoke to him, and that I was in Houston when he landed and had a nice talk with him. . . . Lots of times, PR is getting the TV people to pan your airplane when someone like this gets off, instead of just taking his picture inside the terminal building.

On several occasions, Southwest had been featured in articles appearing in such national media as *Business Week*. Keith stressed that typically these articles did not just "happen," but were often the result of a long-term selling effort on her part to interest the editors of a particular publication.

Introduction of New Pricing Strategies

After a year of operation, Southwest's management decided it was time to take a hard look at the fare structure and its relationship to costs and revenues. They soon concluded that the airline could no longer afford a $20 fare on daytime flights. New tariffs were therefore filed with the Texas Aeronautics Commission, effective 9 July 1972, that raised Southwest's basic one-way fare from $20 to $26, provided for a round-trip fare of $50, and offered a $225 Commuter Club Card providing unlimited transportation for the purchaser on all routes for a thirty-day period.

One problem was how to break news of the increased fares to the public. A strategy session was held between management and representatives of the Bloom Agency at which Camille Keith suggested that Southwest announce a new "executive-class" service on all full-fare flights. The idea was quickly refined: two rows of seats would be removed from the aircraft, reducing its capacity from 112 to 104 seats but increasing legroom; additionally, passengers would be offered free drinks (it was felt that the hostesses would not have time to serve more than two drinks per passenger on such short flights). Full-page newspaper advertisements announced Southwest Airlines' new executive-class service, with first-class legroom for everyone and free cocktails at a price of $26, which also absorbed the security-check charges introduced the previous month.

The key consideration was how the competition would react. "For a few days," admitted Jess Coker, "we were really sweating." Braniff's initial response was to devote an additional aircraft to its Dallas-Hobby Airport flights on 11 July, thus permitting them to offer on-the-hour service most hours of the business day. However, on 17 July, Texas International increased fares to the same level as Southwest's; then on 21 July, Braniff met all aspects of the fare and on-board service changes and added a $10 "Sundowner" flight to Hobby at 7:30 p.m. As a result of Braniff's increased service and the higher fares, Southwest's patronage fell back by 2 percent in the third quarter of 1972, compared with that in the second quarter, but transportation revenues increased.

In September, a third phase of the advertising campaign was launched, based on the slogan "remember what it was like before Southwest Airlines?" which the agency saw as a war cry to rally consumers. The principal media used in this campaign were billboards and television. A particularly dramatic TV commercial featured a Southwest hostess standing at the end of a runway, citing the advantages of flying Southwest while a Boeing 737 accelerated down the runway towards her, took off, and roared low over her head.

At the end of October, another major change was made in pricing strategies. The $10 discount fares, which had never been advertised, were replaced by half-fare flights ($13 one-way, $25 round-trip) in both directions on the two major routes each weekday night after 8 p.m. Saturday flights were reintroduced and *all* weekend flights were offered at half-fare. An intensive, three-week advertising campaign accompanied this new schedule and pricing-policy change. It included one-minute radio commercials on country and western, top-forty, and similar types of stations.[4] (Figure 1-4 shows the script for one of these commercials.) The response was immediate and November 1972 traffic levels were 12 percent higher than those in October—historically the best month of the year in Southwest's commuter markets.

In the new year, management turned its attention to its largest single remaining problem. The company was actually making money on its Dallas-Houston flights but incurring substantial losses in the Dallas-San Antonio market. Southwest offered only eight flights a day on this route, versus thirty-three by its major competitor, and it was averaging a mere seventeen passengers on each full-fare flight. Southwest management concluded that unless a dramatic improvement in patronage was quickly achieved on this route, they would have to abandon it. They decided to make one last attempt to obtain the needed increase and on 22 January 1973 announced a "60-Day Half-Price Sale"

NUMBER: 98-23-2 LENGTH: 60 secs. (Dallas version) DATE: 10/13/72

MUSIC: Fanfare

ANNCR: Southwest Airlines introduces the Half-Fare Frivolity flights.

HOSTESS: Now you can afford to fly for the fun of it.

SFX: LAUGHTER OF ONE PERSON BUILDING FROM UNDER, WITH MUSIC

ANNCR: Now you can take any Southwest Airlines flights any week night at eight o'clock and all flights on Saturday or Sunday for half-fare. Just $13 or $25 round trip.

SFX: LAUGHTER, MUSIC OUT. STREET SOUNDS UNDER.

MAN: You mean I can visit my uncle in Houston for only $13?

ANNCR: Right.

MAN: That's weird. My uncle lives in St. Louis.

MUSIC: MEXICAN FIESTA SOUND

CHICANO: Take your wife or lover on a Southwest Airlines Half-Fare Frivolity Flight to San Antonio this weekend. Float down the river while lovely senoritas strum their enchiladas and sing the beautiful, traditional guacomoles.

SFX: ROCKET BLASTING OFF

ANNCR: Take a Southwest Airlines Half-Fare Frivolity Flight to Houston and watch Astronauts mow their lawns.

SFX: FOOTBALL CROWD NOISES

ANNCR: Take a Southwest Airlines Frivolity Flight to Dallas and watch Cowboys hurt themselves.

SXF: OTHERS OUT. RINKY-TINK MUSIC UP.

HOSTESS: Half-Fare Frivolity Flights, every week night at eight o'clock and *all* weekend flights. Only $13. Almost as cheap as the bus. Cheaper than your own car. So relax with me, and stop driving yourself.

ANNCR: Southwest Airlines' Half-Fare Frivolity Flights.

HOSTESS: Fly for the fun of it.

Figure 1-4. Radio Advertising for Half-fare (Off-peak) Flights, Fall 1972

on *all* Southwest Airlines flights between Dallas and San Antonio. This sale was announced by advertising on TV and radio (see Figure 1-5 for sample radio scripts). If the sale was successful, it was Lamar Muse's intention to make this reduced fare permanent, but he felt that announcing it as a limited-period offer would stimulate consumer interest more effectively and also reduce the likelihood of competitive response.

The impact of these half-price fares was faster and more dramatic than the results of the evening and weekend half-price fares introduced the previous fall. By the end of the first week, average loads on Southwest's Dallas-San Antonio service had risen to forty-eight passengers per flight and continued to rise sharply at the beginning of the following week.

On Thursday, 1 February, however, Braniff employed full-page newspaper advertisements to announce a half-price "Get Acquainted Sale" between Dallas and Hobby on all flights, lasting until April 1 (Figure 1-6). Lamar Muse immediately called a meeting of the management team, including Rollin King, the marketing VP, the public relations director, the company's attorneys, and the account people from the Bloom Agency, to decide what action Southwest should take in response to Braniff's move.

NUMBER:	118-23-2 LENGTH: 60 secs. (Dallas version) DATE: 12/21/72
WOMAN:	Harold, this is your mother in San Antonio talking to you from the radio, Harold. I want you to know that Southwest Airlines is having a half-price sale, Harold. For 60 days you can fly between San Antonio and Dallas for half price. Only $13, Harold. I expect to see a lot of you for those 60 days. Are you listening, Harold? Harold! (STATION WIND) I'm talking to you!
MUSIC:	LIGHT, HAPPY
HOSTESS:	Southwest Airlines half-fare flights. Every flight between San Antonio and Dallas every day. Only $13.
SFX:	STREET NOISES
IRATE MALE VOICE:	Hey! You people fly Southwest Airlines during this half-price sale, you're gonna have a lonely bus driver on your conscience. Take the bus. It only costs a little more, but it's four hours longer! You'll have a lot more time with me, won't you? (FADE) Well, won't you?
SFX:	STREET NOISES
MAN:	There is a cheaper way than Southwest Airlines. Put on roller skates, tie yourself to a trailer truck . . .
MUSIC:	LIGHT, HAPPY
HOSTESSES:	Fly Southwest Airlines. Half price between Dallas and San Antonio on every flight every day. Why pay more?
VOICE:	Half price? Can they do that?
SECOND VOICE:	They did it!

Figure 1-5. Radio Advertising for All San Antonio Half-Fare Flights, January 1973

NUMBER:	118-23-2 LENGTH: 60 secs. DATE: 12/21/72, revised 12/29/72
MUSIC:	CLINKY PIANO
ANNCR:	It's time for Captain Moneysaver, the man who knows how to save your dough!
CAPTAIN MONEYSAVER:	Hello, money-savers! Since Southwest Airlines introduced its half-price sale on all flights every day between Dallas and San Antonio, many listeners have asked that age-old question: Can I get there cheaper? Cheaper than $13? Sure! You can strap five thousand pigeons to your arm and fly yourself. Or propel your body with a giant rubber band. Put a small motor on a ten-speed bike . . .
MUSIC:	LIGHT, HAPPY
HOSTESS:	Southwest Airlines announces the 60-day half-price sale between Dallas and San Antonio. It's good on all flights every day. Just $13 one way. 25 round trip. So what are you waiting for?
SFX:	STREET
COWBOY:	You mean I kin fly between San Antonio and Dallas on a real jet airplane fer only $13?
ANNCR:	That's right! On any Southwest Airlines flight, every day.
COWBOY:	They still gonna have them pretty girls and all?
ANNCR:	Same Southwest Airlines love service. And it's cheaper than the best bus service.
COWBOY:	Howzit compare to my pickup?
MUSIC:	LIGHT, HAPPY
HOSTESS:	Fly now while it's half fare on every Southwest Airlines flight every day between Dallas and San Antonio. All our love at half the price.
VOICE:	Half price? Can they do that?
SECOND VOICE:	They did it!

Figure 1-5. (cont.)

BRANIFF'S "GET ACQUAINTED SALE"

Half-Price to Houston's Hobby Airport

$13 Coach $17 First Class

(schedule showing 7 nonstop departures)

Sale lasts 'til April 1

From now to April 1, Braniff International Flights to Houston's Hobby Airport are priced to go. Half-price to be exact. 50% off.

A one-way ticket in coach is $13.00. Round-trip is an even better bargain at $25.00. And in first class, $17.00 one-way, $34.00 round-trip.

We believe we have the best service to Hobby Airport. But not enough people know about it. So. we're offering you a chance to sample our big 727 Wide-Body jets to Houston's Hobby at half the regular price. We call it our "Get Acquainted Sale."

Figure 1-6. Braniff Newspaper Advertising for Dallas-Hobby Half-price Sale, Dallas Newspapers, February 1973

Notes

1. Local travel figures excluded passengers who were traveling between these cities as part of a longer journey.

2. Pacific Southwest Airlines had built up a substantial market share on the lucrative Los Angeles-San Francisco route, as well as on other intrastate operations within California.

3. "Double-truck" is a printer's term used to describe material printed across two full pages. A "half-truck" ad is one printed across two half-pages.

4. A "top-forty" station is one that specializes in currently popular rock-music recordings.

United Air Freight

Introduction

As summer 1975 approached, United Air Lines was becoming increasingly concerned over the continuing losses of its all-cargo operations (that is, the operation of freight-only aircraft). The last all-cargo profit had been $406,000 in 1968. During the previous year, operating costs had increased faster than freight rates so that there was no improvement in the all-cargo losses. United's management wondered whether sufficient rate increases could be secured to reverse the losses of its existing operation.

United had many shippers who depended on the all-cargo service and were willing to pay more for it. In fact, several large shippers had publicly supported freight-rate increases because they feared the service might be discontinued if the airlines continued to incur losses. United's objective was to realign its all-cargo operations to provide the services demanded by shippers but, at the same time, to be profitable.

Company History

United was the largest of the ten U.S. domestic trunk-line carriers providing both passenger and cargo service to 113 cities throughout the continental United States and Hawaii. This service was provided by a fleet of 362 aircraft over a coast-to-coast network of more than 12,000 certified route miles (see Figure 2-1).

United's history began with the first scheduled commercial air transportation in the country. In 1926 Varney Air Lines, a predecessor of United, started the service. In 1930 four pioneer airlines (Varney, National Air Transport, Boeing Air Transport, and Pacific Air Transport) combined to form United Air Lines. Although they maintained their separate identities until 1934, the combination made possible the first coast-to-coast mail route. United's role as a pioneer continued. It was the first airline to employ stewardesses, the first to offer Douglas DC-3 service, the first to fly nonstop flights between New York and San Francisco, and the first domestic airline to order jetliners (thirty Douglas DC-8's on 25 October 1955).

In 1968, United began to diversify by forming UAL, Inc. as a holding company for the airline. The acquisition of Western International Hotels, Inc. in

29

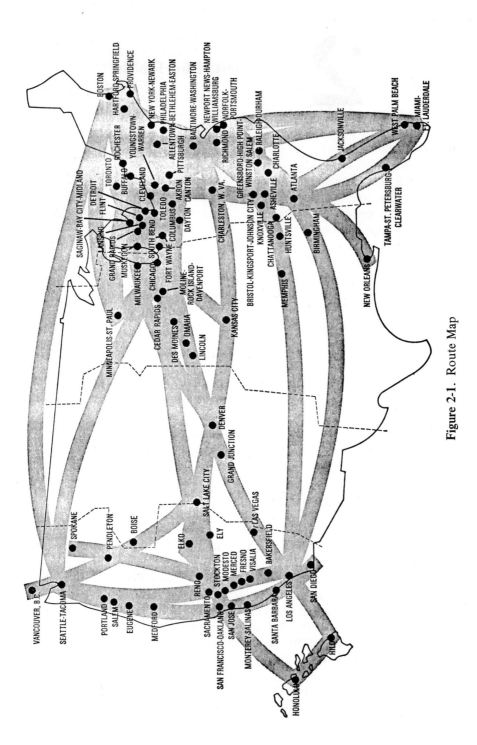

Figure 2-1. Route Map

the following year became the first UAL, Inc. expansion. In 1970, UAL, Inc. recorded a $40 million loss, which was the worst in the airline's history. The loss precipitated the selection of Edward Carlson, Chairman of UAL, Inc.'s Western International Hotels Division, as president. His immediate response to the economic crisis was to regroup the airline into a profit center organization. The new organization divided the airline's operations into an eastern, a central, and a western division. Each division was accountable for its own share of revenues and expenses (see Figure 2-2).

For the fiscal year ending 31 December 1974, UAL, Inc. recorded net earnings of $101 million (see Table 2-1). Although United ranked first in number of domestic freight ton-miles carried and total domestic freight revenue for 1974, the all-cargo operation recorded a loss of $5.8 million (see Table 2-2).

United's Freighter Fleet

United's jet freighter service began in March 1964 when two McDonnell-Douglas DC-8F freighters went into operation. In 1966 the Boeing B-727-QC (quick change) aircraft were added to the growing freighter fleet. The maximum number of freighters in scheduled service reached fifteen DC-8F's and thirty-six B-727-QC's during 1971-1972 (Table 2-3).

The DC-8F was a windowless all-cargo version of the DC-8 passenger jet. It had a maximum trans-Atlantic cargo payload capacity of about 92,000 pounds

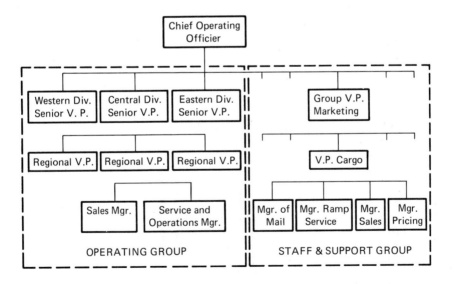

Figure 2-2. United Air Lines Cargo Organization

Table 2-1
Financial and Operating Statistics, 1970-1974
(thousands of dollars)

For Year ending 31 December	1970	1971	1972	1973	1974
Operating revenues					
Airline					
Passenger	$1,354,106	$1,348,605	$1,549,285	$1,749,389	$1,989,657
Cargo	155,420	157,496	172,126	189,229	193,915
Other revenue, net	(7,927)	20,955	4,965	7,085	35,679
Hotels	88,471	90,514	101,981	114,565	145,816
Total	$1,590,070	$1,617,570	$1,828,357	$2,060,268	$2,365,067
Operating expenses exclusive of income taxes	$1,603,111	$1,575,099	$1,743,817	$1,898,092	$2,167,593
Earnings (loss) from operations	$(13,041)	$42,471	$84,540	$162,176	$197,474
Other deductions (income), net:					
Interest on long-term debt	$56,983	$59,015	$60,768	$61,541	$61,296
Interest income	(3,087)	(3,334)	(5,262)	(17,668)	(66,739)
Gain on debenture repurchase	–	–	–	–	(20,603)
Nonoperating aircraft expense	–	–	6,066	15,211	–
Other, net	(16,680)	(7,287)	(11,310)	895	(526)
Total	$37,216	$48,394	$50,262	$59,979	$(26,572)
Earnings (loss) before income taxes	$(50,257)	$(5,923)	$34,278	$102,197	$224,046
Income taxes	(9,380)	(852)	13,902	51,069	123,044
Net earnings (loss)	$(40,877)	$5,071	$20,376	$51,128	$101,002
Dividends on preferred stocks	2,127	2,100	2,100	2,012	1,131
Earnings (loss) applicable to common stock	$(43,004)	$(7,171)	$18,276	$49,116	$99,871
Earnings (loss) per common and common equivalent share	$(2.33)	$(.36)	$.80	$2.03	$4.04[a]

Cash dividends declared on common stock	$.65	—	—	—	$.75
Shares used in computing earnings (loss) per common and common equivalent share	24,899,119[a]	24,899,119	24,882,064	19,770,111	18,424,059
Financial					
Net working capital at 12/31 (000)	$369,029	$166,658	$23,334	$69,680	$36,595
Capital expenditures (000)	253,553	127,646	308,534	151,261	262,909
Per common share					
Earnings (loss) per common and common equivalent share	$4.04	$2.03	$.80	$(.36)	$(2.33)
Earnings (loss) per common share assuming issuance of all dilutive contingent shares	4.01	2.03	.80	(.36)	(2.33)
Cash dividends paid	.65	—	—	—	.75
Stockholders' equity at 12/31	31.75	28.34	26.59	25.79	25.15
Shares outstanding at 12/31					
Preferred	733,555	3,803,142	3,907,488	3,900,403	3,901,232
Common	24,237,266	21,177,679	21,097,041	20,923,865	18,424,065
Number of common stockholders	51,720	51,231	48,123	51,940	60,561
Operating earnings (loss) as % of revenues	8.3%	7.9%	4.6%	2.6%	(0.8%)
Revenue as % of invested capital	134.3%	121.0%	106.7%	97.3%	97.1%
Return on investment[b]	7.9%	6.3%	4.7%	3.5%	1.2%
Operating[c]					
Airline					
Revenue airplane-miles flown	359,707	403,267	406,184	411,352	439,462
Revenue passenger-miles	29,295,938	29,121,456	26,952,153	23,602,146	25,280,807
Revenue passengers	31,510	31,176	29,591	26,048	28,527

Table 2-1 (cont.)

For Year ending 31 December	1970	1971	1972	1973	1974
Available seat-miles	48,734,160	47,324,513	49,359,145	52,150,319	49,147,146
Available ton-miles	7,337,114	7,188,377	7,487,478	7,813,084	7,269,638
Revenue ton-miles	3,284,986	3,129,068	3,499,732	3,747,063	3,734,110
Passenger ton-miles	2,528,046	2,360,140	2,695,125	2,912,101	2,929,551
Freight ton-miles	545,102	582,220	616,346	650,297	628,309
Mail ton-miles	188,645	170,022	170,651	164,524	161,283
Express ton-miles	23,193	16,686	17,610	20,141	14,967
Percent of scheduled miles flown	96.7%	98.6%	98.5%	98.8%	99.1%
Passenger load factor	51.9%	49.9%	54.6%	55.8%	59.6%
Payload factor	44.8%	43.5%	46.7%	48.0%	51.4%
Passenger revenue per passenger-mile	$.054	$.057	$.057	$.060	$.068
Revenue per ton-mile of payload					
Passenger	$.536	$.571	$.575	$.601	$.679
Freight	.203	.199	.211	.216	.239
Mail	.211	.206	.211	.222	.236
Express	.328	.351	.340	.335	.375
Average	.460	.481	.493	.516	.585
Operating expenses					
Per revenue ton-mile	$.464	$.478	$.472	$.479	$.546
Per available ton-mile	.208	.208	.220	.230	.280
Number of aircraft in fleet at 12/31	376	381	363	369	376
Hotels					
Occupancy	75.2%	71.8%	73.9%	76.3%	77.5%
Average daily rate	$26.69	$27.51	$28.02	$30.34	$32.88

Personnel

Airline

Average number of employees	52,079	48,213	48,230	49,009	49,650
Employee wages and benefits (000)	$738,301	$725,995	$797,059	$832,660	$930,382
Investment in assets per employee	$39,362	$42,966	$45,058	$44,556	$46,577
Hotel employees	5,514	4,948	5,459	6,999	9,533

Source: United Air Lines, Inc., 1974 Annual Report.

[a]Earnings per common share assuming issuance of all dilutive contingent shares were $4.01. The average number of shares used in the computation was 25,702,628. The assumed conversion of outstanding convertible debentures did not have a dilutive effect on per-share results in prior years.
[b]Pertains only to the airline.
[c]Mileage, passenger- and ton-mile figures shown in thousands.

Table 2-2
Operating Results for United's Scheduled Domestic All-cargo Operations, 1965-1974

Year ending 31 December	1965	1966	1967	1968	1969	1970	1971	1972	1973	1974
DC-8F										
Revenue[a]										
Freight	$10,130	$17,211	$24,051	$26,029	$34,945	$40,152	$40,514	$46,435	$55,252	$59,031
Mail, Express & Other	2,502	4,624	4,161	5,548	5,977	5,278	8,316	8,567	9,142	9,941
	12,632	21,835	28,212	31,577	40,922	45,430	48,830	55,002	64,394	68,972
Operating Expense										
Flying operations	2,825	4,387	6,579	9,767	13,854	17,407	17,064	17,360	19,394	26,595
Maintenance	1,989	2,656	3,713	4,303	6,085	7,439	6,373	6,789	7,930	10,345
Other	6,478	11,056	14,835	16,452	23,268	30,761	31,028	32,797	36,753	41,410
Total	11,292	18,099	25,127	30,522	43,207	55,607	54,465	56,946	64,077	78,350
Operating profit (loss)	1,340	3,736	3,085	1,055	(2,285)	(10,178)	(5,634)	(1,944)	317	(9,378)
Income tax	643	1,793	1,481	506	(1,120)	(4,885)	(2,704)	(933)	152	(4,689)
Profit (loss) after tax	$697	$1,943	$1,604	$548	$(1,165)	$(5,292)	$(2,930)	$1,011	$165	$(4,689)
Revenue tons enplaned	40,718	67,863	95,634	126,933	156,206	179,333	171,829	185,806	208,467	204,824
Total–RTM (000)	70,843	195,946	150,787	192,183	244,741	281,166	287,349	304,386	344,373	296,229
Revenue departures	2,844	4,938	6,877	9,640	12,937	14,379	13,068	12,725	13,122	13,179
B-727-QC										
Revenue[a]										
Freight		$1,169	$10,383	$18,763	$23,289	$24,948	$21,688	$21,251	$18,771	$11,694
		$1,169	$10,383	$18,763	$23,289	$24,948	$21,688	$21,251	$18,771	$11,694
Mail, express, other		561	3,837	5,700	6,080	5,811	7,359	6,532	4,985	3,136
Total		1,730	14,220	24,513	29,369	30,759	29,047	27,783	23,756	14,830

Operating expense									
Flying operations	380	3,562	7,690	10,691	13,042	11,266	10.092	8,605	6,695
Maintenance	268	2,300	4,261	5,469	6,205	4,616	4,254	3,563	2,160
Other	1,021	8,091	12,501	16,989	20,872	18,494	17,164	13,794	7,905
Total	1,669	13,953	24,452	33,149	40,119	34,376	31,510	25,962	16,760
Operating profit (loss)	61	267	61	(3,780)	(9,360)	(5,329)	(3,727)	(2,206)	(1,930)
Income tax	29	128	29	(1,928)	(4,867)	(2,771)	(1,938)	(1,059)	(965)
Profit (loss) after tax	32	139	32	$(1,928)	$(4,867)	$(2,771)	$(1,938)	$(1,147)	$(965)
Revenue tons enplaned	8,228	69,230	137,230	161,715	161,180	136,508	125,806	99,593	50,330
Total–RTM (000)	6,673	61,155	110,170	130,608	138,979	123,143	115,802	94,503	53,673
Revenue departures	780	7,062	14,534	17,808	17,999	13,551	11,599	8,805	4,207

Source: *CAB Form 242.*

aThousands of dollars.

Table 2-3
Growth of United's Freighter Fleet, 1964-1974

	Number of Aircraft in Service	
Year Ending December 31	*DC-8F*	*B-727-QC*
1964	3	–
1965	5	–
1966	7	7
1967	9	19
1968	12	29
1969	13	29
1970	14	27
1971	15	36
1972	15	36
1973	15	15
1974	15	15

and space for thirteen freight pallets. The DC-8F was essentially a long-haul freighter with an average haul length of approximately 1185 miles.

The short-haul B-727-QC was attractive because of its dual role. In less than thirty minutes, with the use of advanced cargo-loading techniques the cargo configuration could be changed into a passenger layout by inserting the palletized passenger seats and galleys. The maximum all-cargo payload was about 35,000 pounds with an average haul length of approximately 1020 miles.

Although the quick-change configuration allowed the jet to be used for passenger flights during the day and cargo at night, this advantage was somewhat offset by the increased maintenance cost. Significant also was the fact that the B-727-QC exceeded its weight maximum before the cargo space was filled (i.e., weight rather than volume limited), whereas the opposite occurred in the DC-8F. The decrease in the number of B-727-QC's in all-cargo operations between 1972 and 1975 was primarily because of the weight-limiting characteristic.

The operating expenses of the freighters were predominately independent of the mileage flown. Expenses such as landing and take-off fees, real-estate rentals, ground services, and flight planning were essentially the same for long or short flights. Also, the fuel consumption rate was much higher for the takeoff than it was during the airborne segment of the flight. The only major operating costs that varied with the length of the flight were the crew expenses and fuel consumed after reaching cruising altitude. This front-end loading of operating cost was known as the "short-haul phenomenon."

Because of the short-haul phenomenon, United estimated that its air-freight rates were below the fully allocated operating cost by 55 percent for short hauls (less than 500 miles), 25 percent for medium hauls (500-1000 miles), and 17 percent for long hauls (greater than 1000 miles).

United's jet aircraft had an economic life of twenty years. After that time the increasing maintenance cost made the aircraft unprofitable to operate. Often aircraft operated for less than twenty years because of technological obsolescence, a need to replace early to accommodate the market or congressional mandate (such as noise abatement). The DC-8F's were owned by United, but the B-727-QC's were leased for fifteen years with an option to purchase at the expiration of the lease. United had no alternative uses for the DC-8F, but the B-727-QC could be permanently converted to the passenger configuration if the freighter service was no longer needed. United's invested capital in its all-cargo operations is shown in Table 2-4.

United's Air-Freight Market

United had determined that 80 percent of its freight shipments were the "emergency" (time-sensitive and price-inelastic) type that moved on prime-time freighters. This market was extremely time/service quality sensitive and price inelastic. The remaining 20 percent was price elastic and was shipped air freight instead of by a competing surface carrier because of the delivery speed advantage and the overall distribution cost savings. Table 2-5 compares air-freight and truck rates.

United offered two basic types of freight service: priority service and regular air freight (see Appendix 2A). Its priority service was divided into small package dispatch (SPD) and first freight. First freight was a United service begun in May 1975. The SPD was for packages less than fifty pounds, whereas the first freight had no limit. Regular freight was shipped either on the nighttime freighters or

Table 2-4
Invested Capital in Domestic Scheduled All-cargo Service, 1974
(000)

Year ending 31 December 1974		
Working capital		$10,889
Fixed capital (net)		64,835
Flight equipment	53,785	
Ground property and equipment	11,050	
Investments and special funds		1,629
Long-term prepayments		54
Unamortized discount and expense on debt		91
Total investment		$77,498
Leased flight equipment		7,511
Total investment plus leased equipment		$85,009

Source: *CAB Form 242*, December 1974.

Table 2-5
Truck-Air-freight Rate Comparisons Between Boston and Cleveland

		Commodity Rate per 100 lbs.		
	Shipment Size	Auto Parts	Electrical Machinery	Printed Matter
United Air Freight	100 lbs.	$19.75[a]	$19.75	$19.75
(24 hr. delivery)	1000 lbs.	17.80	17.80	17.80
Consolidated Freightways[b]	100 lbs.	9.28[c]	10.77	8.41
(3rd morning delivery)	1000 lbs.	7.09	7.68	6.49

[a]All three commodity groups are classified under United's general commodity rate.
[b]Based on less-than-truckload (LTL) rates.
[c]Truck rates for auto parts based on density of 10 lbs. per cubic foot or greater.

with a daytime belly load. About 4 percent of United's sales for May 1975 were priority service and 96 percent were regular air freight. Freight forwarders originated 40 percent, interline shipments (from other carriers) 10 percent, and commercial sales (direct shipment) 50 percent.

Daylight Belly Freight

With the introduction of the Boeing B-747 and McDonnell-Douglas DC-10, United's combination aircraft belly freight capacity was certainly increased considerably (see Table 2-6). The increase, however, was during the daytime passenger flights, not the prime-time freight hours. The airline's response was to begin thinking in terms of daylight freight market as an addition to the traditional overnight service.

The primary policy guiding the marketing of the daylight wide-body belly space was to keep the heavy-volume shippers on the nighttime freighters and seek new customers for the wide-body space from shippers using motor trucks. The air-freight salesmen believed that the advantages of air-freight, such as greater security and lower packaging and inventory costs, would enable them to attract the LTL-size truck shippers.

One item that concerned the airline officials was that any program to lower the freight rates in order to fill the wide-body bellies would subvert the already shaky economics of the all-cargo aircraft fleet by dragging down the freight rate structure. The airlines had generally experienced losses in their freighter services and the profitability of belly freight was much disputed. The dispute centered around the allocation of cost between the passenger and cargo services on the combination flights. Several airlines contended that because the passenger flight

Table 2-6
Growth of United's Aircraft Fleet, 1971-1975

Type Aircraft	Passenger Capacity	Payload[a] Capacity (lbs)	Number by Year[b]				
			1971	1972	1973	1974	1975
B-747	325	172,400	9	13	14	18	18
DC-10	270	101,700	0	5	16	18	31
DC-8-61	259	66,665	30	30	30	30	30
DC-8-62	189	47,335	10	10	10	9	9
DC-8	105	34,360	59	57	57	57	56
B-727 (elong.)	163	39,000	28	28	28	28	28
B-727	94	25,000	86	86	86	92	107
B-727-QC	103	39,000	36	36	36	30	15
B-737	103	29,400	74	73	68	66	67
DC-8F		95,282	15	15	15	15	15
B-720			29	29	0	0	0
Total			376	382	360	363	376

Sources: Adapted from *Moody's Transportation Manual; Jane's—All the World's Aircraft.*

[a]Payload capacity includes both freight and passenger load—each passenger and baggage was an estimated 200 pounds.

[b]Fleet size on January 31 for each year.

would be flying anyway, the belly space was essentially a "free load." The all-cargo carriers argued that this method of allocating cost would drive freight rates below the level at which they could profitably operate.

Although the forwarders firmly believed that the shippers would continue to demand freighter flights, Delta Air Lines disagreed. Delta had discontinued its all-cargo service and achieved next-day delivery through its extensive use of night-coach flights. Delta's cargo manager testified in the CAB Air Freight Rate Investigation that the overnight feature of air service "is not an absolute requirement for much of our air freight traffic, and I believe that this aspect of our service will have less and less prominence in the years ahead."[1]

Freight Rates

Air-freight rates have historically been below the fully allocated cost of the all-cargo freight service. The collective operating loss of the five largest domestic scheduled all-cargo carriers for the fiscal year ended 30 June 1975 amounted to a record $42,192,000. In no single year had there been a collective operating profit. The continuing losses had led Continental, Delta, and Western to discontinue their all-cargo services by 1975.

In April 1975, the CAB released the findings of its preliminary investigation of air-freight rates. In the investigation, the administrative law judge concluded that the all-cargo aircraft should be the basis for determining cost of air freight. In the investigation, freight transportation costs were developed based on the fully allocated cost of freight service. Average costs were calculated for the industry using information from the domestic trunk-line carriers, Airlift International, Inc. and the Flying Tiger Line, Inc. Costs were divided into capacity and noncapacity. The former included the direct operations of the aircraft and the latter included the ground operation.

The results of the cost calculations were stated as follows:

Costs are developed for the base year 1972 and then updated to the twelve months ended September, 1974. On that basis, freight rates were unjust and unreasonable because the total economic cost of the freight service, 32.88 cents per freight revenue ton-mile, is 38.8 percent greater than the yield of 23.69 cents per freight revenue ton-mile.[2]

The report then stated that "in view of the substantial increase in freight rates which is required, the higher rates should be phased in over a period of years with no overall annual increase exceeding 12 percent."

Although the preliminary CAB hearing found that air-freight rates were unreasonable and should be increased by 38.8 percent, the rapid inflation and rising fuel cost acted to keep United from decreasing the all-cargo losses. Between September 1974 and September 1975, United filed general freight rate increases that had compounded revenue impact of 14.5 percent. As shown in Table 2-7, the total unit operating cost for all-cargo aircraft increased 21.3 percent over this same period. The corresponding increase in cargo yield was only 13.9 percent. The unit cost increase was primarily due to a 37.0 percent increase in the cost of United's flying operations. The 2.68 cents per revenue ton-mile increase for this category, which was heavily influenced by rising fuel cost, represented 57.3 percent of the total 4.68 cents cost increase.

The forwarders were concerned that if faced with continued losses the remaining all-cargo freighter flights would be discontinued. For this reason, they urged the CAB to grant freight rate increases sufficient to insure that the airlines would have a profitable all-cargo operation. In a *Distribution Worldwide* interview, John Emery, president of the world's largest air-freight forwarding company, Emery Air Freight, expressed his views on air freight rates:

Recently, we supported a United Airlines request for a rate increase of up to 15% on short-haul segments. Actually, I think it should have been more like 40%. Because, unless the airlines get a reasonable return for operating freighters in short-haul routes, it just won't be economically feasible to continue these operations. We think there's a value-added factor. If the airlines provide the service, the shippers will be willing to pay for it.[3]

Table 2-7
United's All-cargo Cost per Revenue Ton-mile

	Year Ending 30 June		Change	
	1974	1975	Cents	Percent
Freight RTMs as % of total[a]	87.2%	86.9%	–	(0.3) pts.
Average cargo length of haul	1476.9 mi.	1530.4 mi.	–	3.6
Cargo load factor	56.2%	52.6%	–	(3.6) pts.
Operating expense per RTM				
Flying operations	7.25¢	9.93¢	2.68	37.0
Flight equip. maintenance	2.89	3.43	0.54	18.7
Gr. property and equipment	0.50	0.64	0.14	28.0
A/C servicing	1.68	2.02	0.34	20.2
Traffic servicing	4.53	4.87	0.34	7.5
Reservations and sales	0.67	0.81	0.14	20.9
Advertising and publicity	0.08	0.17	0.09	112.5
General and administrative	1.38	1.57	0.19	13.8
Flight equip. depreciation	2.51	2.68	0.17	6.8
Ground equip. depreciation	0.51	0.56	0.05	9.8
Total	21.99¢	26.67¢	4.68	21.3
Average cargo yield	20.28¢	23.09¢	2.81	13.9
Breakeven deficit	(1.71)¢	(3.58)¢	–	–
Percent deficit	(7.8)%	(13.4)%	–	–
Economic cost deficit[b]	(5.36)¢	(8.00)¢	–	–
Percent deficit	(24.4)%	(30.0)%	–	–

Note: ( ) denotes negative figure.

[a]Includes mail, express, and freight.

[b]Based on a required average tax and return markup of 16.59% per Initial Decision, Domestic Air Freight Rate Investigation, Docket 22859, Appendix G, p. 1.

Notes

1. *Domestic Air Freight Rate Investigation*, p. 38.

2. Ibid., p. 18.

3. "Forwarding Spells Service," *Distribution Worldwide*, January 1974, p. 36.

**Appendix 2A
The Shipper's Guide to
United Airlines Cargo
Service**

	Speed	Service to	Fleet	Cost	Size/Container	Pickup and Delivery	United Handling	Transfers	Shipper's Control	Shipper's Action
Priority Services "SPD" (small package dispatch)	Guaranteed on specified flight. Cross-country TODAY!	All 113 United cities.	All 362 United jets.	Flat charge airport-to-airport. (Examples: New York City to Los Angeles: $35. Denver to Chicago: $25. These rates effective 1-1-76, subject to change.)	50 pounds maximum. 90 inches maximum total dimensions single package or our bag.	Shipper's vehicle or local messenger service or courier service. (Costs vary by city.)	Package identified as SPD. Guaranteed boarding. Priority handling. (Hazardous materials not accepted at passenger terminal.)	Connecting flights to all United cities.	Prepaid receipt and flight number. (Phone addressee this information plus arrival time.)	Get package to SPD center in passenger terminal at least 30 minutes before your flight. Addressee picks up at baggage delivery area within 30 minutes of arrival (except Canadian cities).
"First freight"	Guaranteed on specified flight. Reservation assures planned arrival.	All 113 United cities	All 362 United jets.	Regular General and Specific commodity rates plus 30%. (Container, discount not applicable.)	No limit to pieces or weight. Individual pieces or your container or ours.	Your truck or United's truck or cartage agent. (Costs vary by city.) (8200 communities linked by United's Air Cargo Service.)	Each piece distinctly labeled. Segregated in freight terminals. Guaranteed boarding. Priority handling. Expedited recovery. (Over 2000 air freight specialists.)	Connecting flights to all United cities. Call United for specifics.	Each shipment computer-monitored by United's A.F.I.S. (Air Freight Information System).	Call United 6 hrs. before flight time to reserve space. Get your shipment to United's freight terminal at least 90 minutes before your flight departs. Or call your freight forwarder.
Regular air freight Jet Freighters	Prime time overnight speed. Early morning arrivals.	21 major cities with connecting trucks to even more markets.	15 freighters. 15 DC-8Fs.	Regular General and Specific commodity rates. Container discounts apply. Call United for specifics.	Containerized freight: 12,500 lbs., 440 cu. ft.; 12,500 lbs., 393 cu. ft.; 2000 lbs., 57 cu. ft.; 500 lbs., 16 cu. ft. or large shipments as individual pieces.	Your truck or United's truck or cartage agent. (Costs vary by city.) (8200 communities linked by United's Air Cargo service.)	Freight terminal handling. At major stations: —Terminal bypass systems for large containers (A-1, A-2) —Cold-temp rooms —In-bond rooms. (Over 2000 air freight specialists.)	Connecting flights to all United cities. United also connects with all U.S. airlines. And all international airlines serving the U.S. Plus over-the-road trucks.	Each shipment computer-monitored by United's A.F.I.S. (Air Freight Information System).	One call to United for any details—Then direct your shipment (with instructions) to our freight terminal.
Widebody Passenger Jets	Daily scheduled flights. (United flies over 1400 flights a day—and every one carries freight.)	27 major cities with connecting trucks to even more markets.	55 widebodies (world's largest widebody fleet): 18 B-747s, 37 DC-10s.	Save big on big planes with United's "Daylight Savings." Air speed at surface rates. Call United for specifics.	Containerized freight: 6450 lbs., 241 cu. ft.; 3160 lbs., 150 cu. ft.; 3160 lbs., 91 cu. ft.; 10,200 lbs., 370 cu. ft.	Your truck or United's truck or cartage agent. (Costs vary by city.) (8200 communities linked by United's Air Cargo service.)	All-container service: Weather-safe. Secure. Entire shipment stays together. (Over 2000 air freight specialists.)	Connecting flights to all United cities. United also makes widebody container connections with most U.S. and international airlines with widebody equipment. Plus over-the-road trucks.	Each shipment computer-monitored by United's A.F.I.S. (Air Freight Information System).	Get containers to us between 4 a.m. and 4 p.m. and save big. Call United for specifics.
Other Passenger Jets	Daily scheduled flights. (United flies over 1400 flights a day—and every one carries freight.)	All 113 United cities.	292 jets: 150 B-727s, 85 DC-8s, and 57 B-737s.	Regular General and Specific commodity rates. Container discounts apply. Call United for specifics.	Small Containers: 500 lbs., 16 cu. ft. or small shipments as individual pieces.	Your truck or United's truck or cartage agent. (Costs vary by city.) (8200 communities linked by United's Air Cargo service.)	Systems designed to expedite your shipments. Extra care all the way. (Over 2000 air freight specialists.)	Connecting flights to all United cities. United also connects with all U.S. airlines. And all international airlines serving the U.S. Plus over-the-road trucks.	Each shipment computer-monitored by United's A.F.I.S. (Air Freight Information System).	One call to United for any details—Then direct your shipment (with instructions) to our freight terminal.

Braniff International

Introduction

In early 1969, Harding Lawrence, chief executive officer and chairman of the board of Braniff International Airways (BI), in a meeting with his corporate staff stated:

There is no question that the wide-body look is the airline look of the '70s. Every trunk airline will have to determine its own approach to securing the wide-body look while maintaining and improving service to every city it serves, primarily in terms of frequent and convenient flight schedules.

BI had recently finished an examination of its equipment strategy in the Latin American Division and was now considering the strategy to be used for domestic operations during the next several years. The company planned to purchase an average of 1400 seats of aircraft capacity each year for the next six years.

Since coming to Braniff, Lawrence had stressed the policy of aircraft "communality", that is, the minimization of the number of types of aircraft operated to promote increased economies in maintenance, crew training, and space-parts inventories. At the time, BI operated a number of aircraft types, but it had been suggested that the company might take the opportunity of the recent introduction of wide-bodied aircraft to take steps to create a more uniform fleet for domestic operations.

The questions Lawrence asked his corporate staff were:

(1) Are wide-bodies inherently more economic than our present aircraft types?
(2) Can they be developed on our domestic route structure profitably?
(3) How will they affect our competitive situation in terms of market share and frequency of service?

Company Background

BI was one of eleven major American domestic trunk-line carriers providing passenger and cargo services to points throughout the continental United States. BI also served Hawaii, Mexico, and South America from gateways on the East, Gulf, and West Coast.

The airline, founded in 1928 by T. E. Braniff, had grown to a route structure of 30,000 miles in the United States and Latin America, and was carrying over 6 million passengers annually in 1968.

BI grew through internal development, but a major expansion in 1952 was accomplished in a merger with Mid-Continental Airlines. Through the merger BI acquired 6241 additional route miles from the Dakotas to Louisiana. In 1967, BI purchased Pan American Grace Airways and its routes throughout Latin America (see Figure 3-1).

Braniff had a reputation for innovation in the industry, particularly under Harding Lawrence, who took over direction of the airline in 1965. For example, in 1967 Braniff was the first airline to retire its piston-engine aircraft. This move left the Lockheed Electra as the only remaining nonjet aircraft in service (see Table 3-1). BI was the first airline to utilize jet-assist takeoff systems at high-altitude airports and a pioneer in airborne weather radar. On 1 August 1966, Braniff inaugurated the world's first Boeing B-727 "Quick Change" convertible trijet. The B-727-QC can be converted from a passenger to an all-cargo or combination passenger/cargo configuration in thirty minutes. This change greatly improved aircraft utilization, because it allowed use of the plane to transport passengers by day and cargo by night. Other innovations included the substitution of Pucci fashions for more conventional hostess uniforms and brightly colored aircraft for conservative "plain planes."

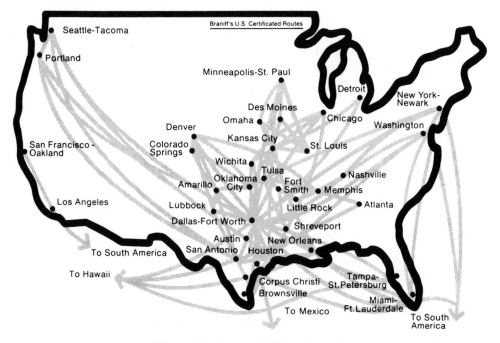

Figure 3-1. Domestic Route Structure

Table 3-1
Comparative Fleet Mix and Domestic Capacity, 1968

Aircraft Type	Industry Fleet Mix (percent)	Braniff Fleet Mix (percent)	Braniff Fleet Mix (number of aircraft)	Braniff ASM Production per Aircraft Type (000,000)	Domestic Operations	
					Braniff ASM Production per Unit–Aircraft Type (000,000)	Braniff Average Domestic Stage Length per Type
Electra 188	1.4	11.4	8	595	74.4	210
BAC-111	1.6	18.6	13	757	58.0	236
B-707	17.4	18.6	13[a]	752	188.0	661
B-720	11.8	7.1	5	820	164.0	441
B-727	33.8	34.3	24[b]	2972	124.0	479
B-737	1.8					
CV-880	3.9					
CV-990	0.1					
DC-8	15.7	10.0	7[c]			
DC-9	9.2					
Caravelle	0.5					
Fairchild 227	0.1					
Viscount 700	0.2					
Total	100.	100.	70	5896	N/A	364.3

[a]Two flown in Latin American division, seven flown under Military Air Command operations.
[b]All B-727-110s; the annual ASM capacity of the B-727-200 is estimated at 160 million ASM/year.
[c]All used in Latin American division operations.

BI was considered to be a financially healthy member of the airline industry with an above-average return on investment during a period of substantial growth. See Table 3-2 for 1964 to 1968 financial statements and Table 3-3 for BI operating performance over the same period.

Aircraft Selection

A prominent industry trend had been toward faster and larger aircraft. For example, the average terminal-to-terminal speed in domestic service increased from 314 mph in 1962 to 413 mph in 1968. Each aircraft type had its own particular optimization in terms of cost per ASM over a specific range limitation. Generally speaking, total cost per ASM included fixed and variable elements and decreased on a per-unit basis as distance increased. The terminology used in the industry to describe these inherent aircraft costs/ASM were couched in terms of "assignability." This transition was a delicate one because direct operating cost (DOC) should not be confused with "variable costs"; they are not all variable with the amount of ASMs flown. For example, some vary with flight hours, others per departure, and some are arbitrarily assigned (e.g., overhead was estimated to be 40 percent of DOC). Similarly, indirect operating costs (IOC) were not considered "fixed" because the industry's estimate of them was simply 100 percent of the DOC.

In early 1969, the "era of wide-bodies" was imminent. The Boeing B-747 was to be available by the end of 1969. McDonnell-Douglas and Lockheed were taking orders for the DC-10 and L-1011 to be introduced in 1970 and 1971, respectively. Taken as a group, wide-bodies were expected to have decided economic advantages over aircraft types then in service. They were designed to have longer flight ranges with direct operating costs 20 percent below the B-727-200 and 14 percent below the DC-8, assuming comparable load factors. They offered unsurpassed luxury, comfort, and passenger appeal with extras such as lounges, piano bars, and increased leg room (pitch between seats). In fact, it was strongly suspected that their introduction into commercial use would stimulate demand by as much as 30 percent in some city-pair markets.

The industry expected the B-747 to be used mainly over transcontinental and intercontinental routes where frequency of service played less of a role in capturing market share. The initial reaction to test flights brought many excited comments from pilots. One said "I thought they would never build a better airplane after having flown the 707—but they've done it with the 747!"

The DC-10 and L-1011 were commonly referred to as "airbuses" due to their favorable economics over quite short routes. These wide-body trijets combined the maneuverability and ease of operation of the 747 with the ability to fly in and out of small airports at a lower noise and smoke level than existing aircraft. Terminal expansion was being contemplated at many large airports to handle the increased concentration of passengers, although flight congestion was expected to decline as the number of flights decreased.

American and United Airlines had ordered more than 50 DC-10s and expected to purchase at least 150 more in the next few years. They were planning to utilize these aircraft primarily on stage lengths ranging from 1000 to 1800 miles.

Because of the resulting back-order situation at Douglas, other trunks were opting for priority delivery of the similar Lockheed L-1011 (Table 3-4). Delta and Eastern thought the L-1011 to be more suited to medium- and short-range hauls. However, L-1011 deliveries were still somewhat uncertain due to the tenuous financial position of Rolls-Royce, the maker of the aircraft's RB-211 jet engines.

Arguments for Wide-bodies

A staff engineer suggested that the "airbus" glamour was an important consideration. Also, the wide-bodies not only were likely to stimulate primary demand due to greater flying comfort, but also operated at lower cost per ASM (even on shorter routes) and, therefore, they had greater profit potential. He admitted that they used more fuel, but fuel consumed per ASM was actually slightly lower than that used by smaller aircraft. "All in all, they are technologically a better aircraft." The BI pilots who had had occasion to test fly the wide-body aircraft agreed with this last point. They felt that for its size, it had as much maneuverability as any aircraft in the market, and they were very impressed by the consumer benefits of more space and comfort.

The scheduling and operations group noted that fewer wide-body aircraft would be needed to fill the ASM gap, and fewer operations would facilitate computerized scheduling. However, they felt that large aircraft would be less flexible to meet short-term fluctuations in specific city-pair markets. At the same time, these aircraft would help to reduce airport congestion.

Finally, it was mentioned that wide-body aircraft could best provide for BI's faster-than-industry growth. BI was experiencing growth in primary demand and market share in most of the markets it served. Thus it was desirable to operate larger aircraft if they were most profitable on dense routes.

Argument Against Wide-bodies

The marketing department argued against introducing the wide-bodies to the Braniff route structure at this point in time. Russ Thayer noted that "in terms of density and length of haul, Braniff cannot economically apply a wide-body." He pointed out the BI's densest route was ranked 28 on the list of the densest

Table 3-2
Financial Statements, 1964-1968
(thousands)

Profit and Loss Statement	1964	1965	1966	1967	1968
Operating Revenues					
Passenger	$ 96,857	$114,730	$156,771	$188,487	$211,208
Military contract services	–	–	140,041	38,851	48,207
Express and freight	7,090	8,297	9,973	16,707	17,998
Mail	2,942	3,563	4,492	6,661	8,548
Other	2,808	2,675	2,550	5,671	6,688
	109,697	129,265	187,827	256,377	292,649
Operating Expenses					
Flying and ground operations	55,325	63,124	89,175	133,751	155,603
Maintenance	18,377	21,760	28,502	39,459	41,855
Sales and advertising	12,022	15,545	23,383	30,759	32,157
Depreciation and amortization less amounts charged to other accounts	8,376	10,014	15,079	26,393	24,992
General and administrative	4,300	5,059	7,265	11,553	12,673
	98,400	115,502	163,404	241,915	267,280
Operating income	11,297	13,763	24,423	14,462	25,369
Nonoperating expenses—net	938	718	3,538	9,711	11,971
Income (loss) before provision for income taxes	10,359	13,045	20,885	4,751	13,398

Provision (Credits) for Income Taxes

Federal					
Current–before investment tax credit	4,182	5,424	4,816	1,245	7,317
Current–investment tax credit	(731)	(1470)	(207)	–	(3,697)
Deferred	876	–	2,305	–	(806)
Other	61	148	217	–	168
	4,388	4,102	7,131	1,245	2,982
Income (loss) before extraordinary items	5,971	8,943	13,754	3,506	10,416
Extraordinary items	–	505	4,062	1,245	–
Net income (loss)	5,971	9,448	17,816	4,751	10,416
Selected Balance Sheet Items					
Cash dividends paid	295	295	1,474	1,474	1,155
Stock dividends paid	–	–	–	–	5,441
Current assets	24,131	29,406	60,441	68,658	78,292
Current liabilities	13,164	13,971	20,972	86,411	56,594
Net working capital	10,967	15,435	39,469	(17,753)	21,698
Property and equipment—net	65,072	95,795	190,844	287,655	270,724
Total assets	98,806	130,336	309,678	378,082	372,526
Long-term debt	29,600	51,105	204,753	199,000	213,927
Shareholders' equity					
Special stock, Class A	–	–	–	–	7,428
Common stock	7,370	7,370	7,370	7,370	1,561
Capital surplus	18,355	18,355	18,355	18,355	22,208
Retained earnings	19,997	29,151	45,494	48,787	52,607
Total shareholders' equity	45,722	54,876	71,219	74,512	83,804

Table 3-3
Operating Performance, 1964-1968

	1964	1965	1966	1967	1968
Revenue Passenger-miles (000)					
Mainland	1,342,394	1,580,988	2,236,434	2,499,004	2,846,595
Hawaii	–	–	–	–	–
Mexico	36,461	44,282	91,874	95,163	121,075
South America	136,732	179,092	249,705	562,916	633,223
Total scheduled	1,515,587	1,804,362	2,578,013	3,157,083	3,600,893
Charter	28,338	14,339	481,561	1,608,628	1,996,954
Total	1,543,925	1,818,701	3,059,574	4,765,711	5,597,847
Available seat-miles (000)					
Mainland	2,455,523	2,891,069	3,835,376	4,878,538	5,325,356
Hawaii	–	–	–	–	–
Mexico	58,412	68,041	184,466	193,979	240,407
South America	328,048	385,181	575,745	1,147,201	1,474,634
Total scheduled	2,841,983	3,344,291	4,595,587	6,219,718	7,040,397
Charter	40,331	20,176	554,485	1,773,510	2,269,668
Total	2,882,314	3,364,467	5,150,072	7,993,228	9,310,065
Revenue passengers carried (000)					
Scheduled	2,854	3,372	4,585	5,283	5,749
Charter	22	13	105	312	386
Total	2,876	3,385	4,690	5,595	6,135
System scheduled passenger load factor (%)	53.3	54.0	56.1	50.8	51.1
Breakeven passenger load factor on before tax expense (%)	47.6	47.5	48.5	49.2	47.6
Revenue plane-miles (000)					
Scheduled	35,847	40,303	53,331	67,862	71,908
Charter	568	280	4,846	13,428	17,233
Total	36,415	40,583	58,177	81,290	89,141
Revenue block hours flown	146,558	154,903	191,628	231,822	242,329
Average segment length in scheduled service (miles)	282	289	317	376	409

Table 3-4
Comparison of DC-10 and L-1011 with B-727-200

	B-727-200	L-1011/DC-10
Investment (including spareparts)	$7,969,000	$17,503,000
Seats (low-density seating configuration)	125	300
Effective maximum economic range (miles)	1700	2800
Direct Cost per takeoff and landing	$90	$300

routes served by the domestic airline industry. Also, Thayer continued, "In my opinion, people don't ask what aircraft you're flying. When they call reservations, they ask for departure times. A transportation company serves the consumer by proper scheduling. That's what I've stressed in my advertising program." Jack Reagan, vice president of marketing planning, favored the greater flexibility of scheduling allowed by the smaller-capacity B-727-200.

A Need for Hard Numbers

Harding Lawrence felt that the Dallas-Chicago market was typical of the BI situation. The industry demand was approximately 350,000 passengers per year, of which BI served 144,000. BI expected the industry demand to grow at the rate of approximately 10 to 15 percent per year over the next decade. At the time, BI flew five flights in each direction daily over the 811-mile route, whereas American Airlines operated eight flights to provide approximately half of the ASMs in the market.

Lawrence believed that it would be possible to finance the investment in new equipment. He asked his staff to calculate the approximate return on investment that might be expected for the B-727-200 and DC-10 or L-1011 for a variety of passenger levels and stage lengths. The conventional practice in industry was to estimate total cost as 200 percent of the direct operating costs (which include crew, fuel, maintenance, depreciation, and insurance).

There was some argument that this rule of thumb had been developed for smaller aircraft. Because a significant portion of the indirect costs was related to the number of flights rather than the number of passengers, it might be more appropriate to estimate total costs for wide-body aircraft as 150 percent of estimated direct costs. A return-on-investment calculation based on average fare yield of 6 cents per revenue passenger-mile is summarized in Table 3-5. Table 3-6 summarizes the city-pair markets served by BI in 1969.

Table 3-5
Return on Investment (ROI) as a Function of Passengers Carried and Stage Length[a]
(percent)

Stage Length (miles)	Number of Passengers				
	50	75	125	200	300
DC-10 or L-1011 (300 seats)[b]					
500	−31.7	−22.8	−4.9	21.7	57.3
1000	−28.7	−16.8	6.9	42.5	89.9
1500	−26.9	−13.6	13.1	53.1	106.5
2000	−26.4	−12.3	17.7	62.7	122.6
DC-10 or L-1011 (300 seats)[c]					
500	−19.3	−10.4	7.4	34.1	69.7
1000	−15.6	−3.7	20.0	55.6	103.0
1500	−13.4	−0.2	26.6	66.5	119.9
2000	−13.0	2.0	32.0	77.0	136.9
Boeing 727 (125 seats)[d]					
500	−19.8	6.9	45.6	26.2	26.2
1000	1.1	24.7	76.2	50.5	50.5
1500	4.8	33.8	91.8	62.8	62.8
2000	(maximum range = 1700 miles)				

Source: Casewriter's estimate based on engineering data.

[a]Assumptions: Revenue = six cents per passenger-mile. Utilization = 3285 block hours per year. Block speed is approximately equal for 727s and wide-bodies and 500-mile stage length consumes 1.6 block hours; 1000-mile stage length consumes 2.4 block hours; 1500-mile stage length consumes 3.2 block hours; 2000-mile stage length consumes 3.8 block hours.

[b]Total operating cost = 200 percent of direct operating cost.

[c]Total operating cost = 150 percent of direct operating cost.

[d]Total operating cost = 200 percent of direct operating cost.

Table 3-6
Analysis of Markets: Sixty-five Top BI City-pair Markets, 1969

Estimated BI Market Share <50%

Stage Length (miles)	Average Number Passengers Carried by BI/Day				
	0-100	*101-200*	*201-400*	*401-800*	*>800*
<750	7	4	1	0	0
750-1249	3	0	2	0	0
1250-1750	1	0	1	0	0
>1750	0	0	0	0	0

Estimated BI Market Share >50%

Stage Length (miles)	Average Number Passengers Carried by BI/Day				
	0-100	*101-200*	*201-400*	*401-800*	*>800*
<750	14	17	4	1	1
750-1249	2	2	2	0	0
1250-1750	0	1	1	1	0
>1750	0	0	1[a]	0	0

[a]Dallas-Honolulu.

Flying Tiger Line

Introduction

In September 1973, the Flying Tiger Line, the largest of the three American all-cargo airlines, operated a fleet consisting solely of the DC-8-63Fs (the "stretch" DC-8), as it had done since 1970. By 1972, however, McDonnell-Douglas, the manufacturer of the aircraft, had ceased production of all versions of the DC-8, after a total run of sixty DC-8-63Fs. Tiger owned or leased twenty of these aircraft. Tiger was thus faced with deciding when to move to a different type of aircraft and what that aircraft should be.

Early History

The Flying Tiger Line (Tiger) was incorporated on 25 June 1945 as National Skyway Freight Corporation to furnish air-freight service on a contract carrier basis. Contract air-freight service proved unprofitable, and on 6 August 1946, an application for a Certificate of Public Convenience and Necessity authorizing common carriage of cargo was filed with the Civil Aeronautics Board. The routes sought generally paralleled those operated by the transcontinental scheduled airlines. In May 1947 the CAB temporarily granted the company and several other contract operators authority to provide common carrier service until it could reach a decision on the application.

Because of heavy air-freight losses, due in part at least to rate wars, operations were curtailed until establishment of minimum rate levels by the CAB in June 1948. In July 1949, the CAB authorized common carrier service for a five-year period over certain domestic routes.

Following certification, Tiger gradually expanded regularly scheduled services by adding more flights and opening new stations. Traffic grew at an accelerated pace after the start of the Korean War. To some extent, growth was aided by the withdrawal of the C-54 cargo aircraft, which were operated by major trunk lines for service on the Pacific Airlift. In May 1952 the company activated its certificated routes into the Pacific Northwest (Figure 4-1).

Faced with a business slowdown after the Korean War and the return of intense competition in cargo transport, Flying Tiger and Slick Airways decided to merge. Following conditional approval by the CAB, the all-cargo competitors combined many operations early in 1954 as the first step toward complete

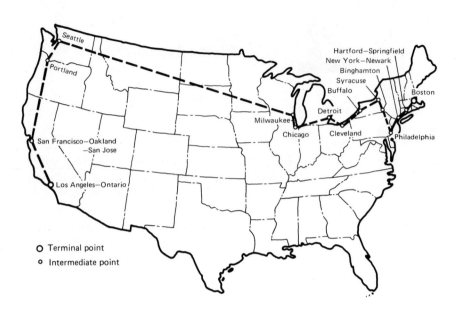

Figure 4-1. Domestic Points Served

integration. The merger had to be abandoned, however, when at the behest of the unions, the CAB attached conditions governing integration of personnel and severance pay that appeared too costly. The prospective cost of retaining unneeded employees would have defeated one main purpose of the merger and threatened the financial solvency of the surviving carrier.

During the late fifties and early sixties, Flying Tiger continued to struggle, reporting operating losses in 1956 and 1960 and a net loss from all activities in 1961. Scheduled air-freight service proved continually unprofitable, and the company supported itself through charters, outside maintenance work, sales for Lear aircraft, and sales of its own aircraft. Military Airlift Contract (MAC) consistently provided over 50 percent of revenues throughout the 1960s (Table 4-1). The company also was allowed to carry mail at "service rates," which brought in a good deal more revenue per ton-mile than freight, but its plea for a subsidy was unsuccessful.

In the meantime, a battle over traffic and rates continued unabated. Although Flying Tiger had been instrumental in persuading the CAB to establish minimum rates, thereby forcing combination carriers to raise their rates, it devised special reduced tariffs from time to time designed to benefit the all-cargo lines primarily. One was the so-called "block space" tariff, which the CAB barred the combination carriers from offering. This tariff allowed forwarders and other customers to reserve space at low rates on scheduled flights. Despite this and other moves, such as use of more economical aircraft (e.g., Canadair CL-44D), profits remained elusive; the company paid no dividends between 1960 and 1966.

The Vietnam War, which required long-distance handling of vast quantities of men and materials, provided Flying Tiger (and other carriers) with substantial charter revenues, and gave the company considerable experience operating across the Pacific. In 1969 the CAB certificated a sweeping increase in scheduled route authorities over the Pacific, based largely on the assumption that the rapid growth of traffic stimulated by the war would continue. Three new lines received international routes. One of the three, Tiger, received a great-circle route to Japan, Korea, Okinawa, Taiwan, Hong Kong, the Philippines, South Vietnam, and Thailand. The new route, known as Route 163, increased Tiger's scheduled route authority from 3906 to 17,537 miles (Figure 4-2).

Tiger's route essentially duplicated those operated by Northwest and Pan American. As might be expected, Tiger diverted substantial business from these carriers, especially mail, which produced high unit revenues. Because of the large number of American troops in Vietnam, military mail was exceptionally heavy. It accounted for 71 percent of international scheduled operations in 1969. In the first year of operation, the new route produced over 13 percent of Tiger's revenue and contributed to the turnaround in profitability after the loss-making year of 1968.

Recent History

During 1970, the Chairman of the Board Wayne Hoffman (Figure 4-3), initiated a program of improving the company's financial base by expanding in directions that would provide steady revenue to offset the cyclic nature of the air-freight business. He also wanted to find other low labor-intensive activities to offset the high proportion of labor costs inherent in the airline business. Correspondingly, Flying Tiger formed a holding company. It was the second major airline, after United, to do so. Approval was granted by the CAB, with the proviso that the actions of the holding company would be carefully scrutinized by the CAB. In July 1970, Tiger began acquiring stock in North American Car Corporation, which leased rail cars in the United States and Canada (Hoffman had come to Tiger in 1967 from the New York Central Railroad). After gaining control of North American Car in January 1971, Tiger acquired control of National Equipment Rental in October 1971. This company leased airplanes, computers,

Table 4-1
Financial and Operating Statistics, 1962-1970
(thousands)

	1962	1963	1964	1965	1966	1967	1968	1969	1970
Consolidated income statements									
Operating Revenues									
Scheduled cargo operations									
Domestic	$ 10,259	$ 10,919	$ 13,707	$ 17,087	$ 23,483	$ 21,689	$ 21,430	$ 22,467	$ 30,497
International	—	—	—	—	—	—	—	13,102	50,183
Military Airlift Command	38,395	27,466	23,151	30,237	48,074	53,413	43,255	49,386	30,629
Charters, services sales, etc.	3,609	3,825	8,610	8,832	14,462	11,929	12,014	11,938	12,063
	52,263	42,210	45,468	86,156	86,019	87,031	76,699	96,893	123,372
Operating expenses									
Depreciation and amortization	5,767	5,860	5,345	5,909	6,592	6,577	6,572	8,008	7,780
All other	39,991	34,259	35,792	42,208	59,531	67,754	72,198	76,080	93,726
	46,688	40,119	41,137	48,117	66,123	74,331	78,770	84,038	101,506
Operating income (loss)	7,235	2,091	4,331	8,039	19,896	12,700	(2,071)	12,805	21,866
Other (income) and expenses									
Interest expense	2,792	2,425	2,120	2,423	2,302	1,775	3,087	8,676	7,875
Miscellaneous (net)	85	(234)	(355)	(345)	(1,727)	(903)	(530)	(1,783)	(2,802)
	2,877	2,191	1,765	2,078	575	872	2,557	6,893	5,073
Income (loss) before deferred income taxes and extraordinary items	4,359	(100)	2,566	5,961	19,321	11,828	(4,628)	5,912	16,793
Deferred income taxes	2,266	(52)	1,075	2,740	7,439	3,958	(2,226)	1,601	6,322
Income (loss) before extraordinary items	2,092	(48)	1,491	3,221	11,882	7,870	(2,402)	4,311	10,471
Extraordinary items less income taxes	478	317	200	—	—	(801)	(4,249)	—	57
Net income (loss)	$ 2,570	$ 269	$ 1,691	$ 3,221	$ 11,882	$ 7,069	$ (6,651)	$ 4,311	$ 10,528

Primary Earnings Per Common Share									
Income (loss) before extraordinary items	$ .63	$ (.01)	$ .44	$ .94	$ 2.87	$ 1.66	$ (.50)	$ .90	$ 2.19
Extraordinary items	.15	.09	.06	—	—	(.17)	(.89)	—	.01
Net income (loss)	$ .78	$ .08	$ .50	$ .94	$ 2.87	$ 1.49	$ (1.39)	$ .90	$ 2.20
Other financial information									
Shares outstanding at end of year									
Preferred	99,112	99,112	99,112	99,112	—	—	—	—	—
Common	3,299,208	3,371,277	3,372,159	3,376,790	4,661,332	4,765,045	4,767,070	4,771,870	4,791,770
Stockholders' equity	$ 13,795	$ 14,507	$ 15,996	$ 18,993	$ 40,259	$ 46,021	$ 38,966	$ 42,903	$ 53,811
Book value per common share	$ 4.18	$ 4.30	$ 4.74	$ 5.63	$ 8.64	$ 9.66	$ 8.17	$ 8.99	$ 11.23
Current assets	$ 18,591	$ 16,717	$ 20,506	$ 21,556	$ 39,688	$ 37,497	$ 41,761	$ 53,478	$ 43,769
Current liabilities	$ 10,993	$ 10,681	$ 12,709	$ 12,411	$ 19,892	$ 17,590	$ 27,059	$ 21,693	$ 19,512
Working capital	$ 7,598	$ 6,036	$ 7,707	$ 9,145	$ 19,796	$ 19,907	$ 14,702	$ 31,785	$ 24,257
Flight equipment at cost	$ 71,354	$ 70,825	$ 69,837	$ 92,247	$ 88,995	$ 89,501	$ 96,965	$ 116,852	$ 117,139
Long-term debt	$ 42,785	$ 36,018	$ 29,283	$ 48,154	$ 34,867	$ 79,967	$ 102,536	$ 118,133	$ 114,471
Scheduled Cargo Statistics									
Domestic									
Available ton-miles (000)	103,245	117,354	135,642	172,570	226,700	246,415	263,223	309,813	376,906
Revenue ton-miles (000)	74,197	77,832	99,489	127,611	169,811	163,250	166,041	174,353	213,062
Load factor	71.9%	66.3%	73.3%	73.9%	74.9%	66.2%	63.1%	56.3%	56.5%
Revenue per ton mile (cents)	13.83	14.03	13.78	13.39	13.83	13.29	12.91	12.89	14.31
International									
Available ton-miles (000)								138,688	449,448
Revenue ton-miles (000)								78,030	290,126
Load factor								56.7%	64.6%
Revenues per ton-mile (cents)								16.66	17.30
Number of Airline Employees	1,430	1,234	1,359	1,666	2,089	2,096	2,475	2,241	2,781

64

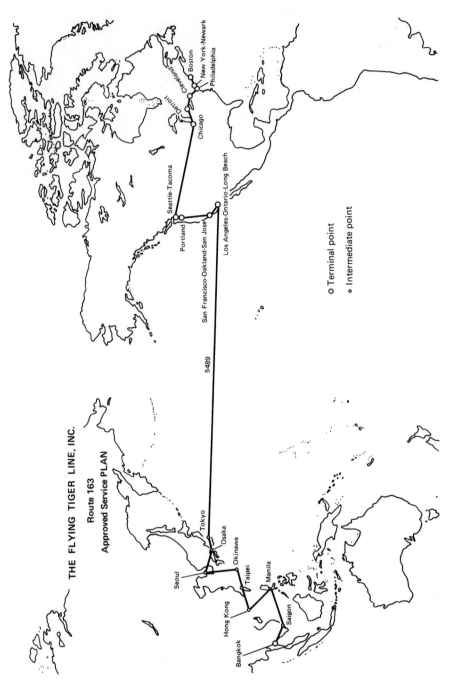

Figure 4-2. Route 163

65

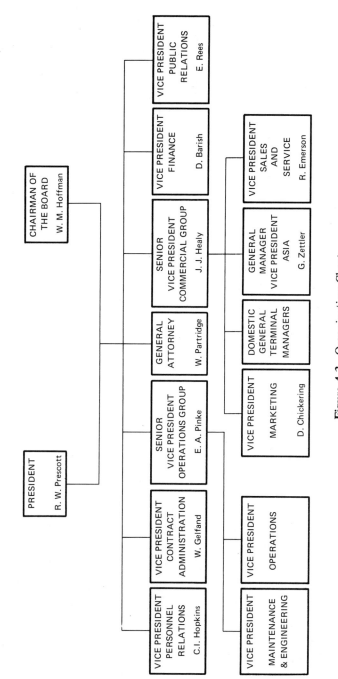

Figure 4-3. Organization Chart

office equipment, and so on. The effect of these two acquisitions may be judged from Tables 4-2 and 4-3.

In the air-cargo operations, the importance of war-related operations continued to decline from 51 percent of airline revenues in 1969 to 20 percent in 1972. The Pacific operation contributed 13.5 percent in 1969 and 46.8 percent in 1972. It had become Tiger's main source of profit, contributing $12.9 million to pretax profits in 1970 and 1971. In the same years, domestic operations incurred losses of $1.7 million and $1.1 million, respectively. A turnaround came in 1972, when domestic operations showed a pretax profit of $2.6 million, the first profit since 1966. It made Tiger the only profitable domestic operator in air freight in 1972.

Table 4-2
Consolidation Statement of Income, 1971-1972
(thousands)

	1971	1972
Revenues		
Common carrier		
Domestic	$ 39,228	$ 48,802
International	66,467	77,610
Military	34,091	32,862
Equipment leasing	60,093	86,482
Other	9,671	11,455
	209,550	257,211
Costs and expenses		
Airline operations	94,357	103,191
Leasing operations	10,615	13,645
Selling, General and Administrative	21,660	31,052
Depreciation and amortization	24,984	30,729
Interest and preferred dividends of subsidiary	23,688	27,636
	175,304	206,253
Income before taxes	34,246	50,958
Income tax provision	13,868	21,148
Net income	20,378	29,810
Primary earnings per share	1.91	2.54
Fully diluted per share	1.65	2.28

Terminal Profit-center System

In early 1968, Tiger began to implement a profit-center program for the airline's twenty-three major cargo terminals under the guidance of Joseph J. Healy (then Senior Vice President-Terminals, but later given responsibility for all commercial activities). The basis of the system was that one man, the general terminal manager (GTM) was in charge of each major terminal and had the responsibility to run the operation and make a profit.

As part of his duties, the GTM had to formulate an annual profit-center plan containing estimated costs, traffic, revenue, and other projections of his terminal's activity for management review. An essential ingredient in the system was personal negotiation and agreement between GTMs. Cargo revenue for each flight—as well as all line-haul costs—was divided between the managers of two points in a shipment, so the managers made "deals" to develop cargo movements between their terminals. Healy observed that these deals, in practice, were not restricted to two-way negotiations. If an imbalance in the direction of demand existed, groups of three or four managers would often get together to work out a complete routing for an aircraft. Once a "deal" was made, the interested GTMs would notify the H.Q. scheduling group, whose task was to integrate the requested flight or flights into a new schedule. The total projected impact on the system was then assessed and the new schedule submitted to the Scheduling Committee (Healy, Pinke, Barish, Gelfand, and Chickering). Changes in the schedule occured as often as once every three weeks.

Company Goals and Development Policies

In discussing Tiger's long-term goals, Healy stated:

We want to serve the top fifty major centers of commerce in the world by 1985. (The top sixty freight airports in 1971 are listed in Table 4-4). We believe we can achieve this goal by a combination of route applications to the CAB and acquisitions. We are constantly talking to foreign governments ourselves to explore the opportunities for obtaining authority. We also want to carry 18 to 20 percent of the world's commerce by 1985. Up to 1980, we expect a 25 percent growth in revenues each year, and expect to achieve an operating ratio of 78 percent (down from our current 82 percent). In terms of rate of return, we are aiming for 17.6 percent pretax, which will just bring us in under the CAB limit of 12 percent after tax. This compares with our present 14.5 percent (pretax).

We do not set market share goals as such in individual markets but we are well aware of what we have. For example, we have 61 percent of the Boston-Los Angeles market, and American, TWA, and United share the remaining 39 percent. For Detroit-L.A. we have 72 percent and N.Y.-Seattle 78 percent.

Table 4-3
Consolidated Balance Sheets, 31 December 1971 and 1972

Assets	1971	1972
Current assets		
Cash	$ 45,757	$ 35,550
Short-term investments	6,942	45,080
Receivables	35,922	11,354
Materials and supplies	9,900	
Prepaid expenses and others	3,673	7,768
Total current assets	102,284	99,752
Lease receivables	57,378	107,347
Less unearned income	22,888	46,711
	34,490	60,636
Plant, property and equipment		
Equipment for/or under lease	576,439	605,072
Equipment used in airline operations	117,643	132,267
Buildings and leasehold improvements	13,378	16,148
Shop and terminal facilities	18,602	18,760
Less accumulated depreciation and amortization	230,409	243,295
	495,653	528,952

Liabilities	1971	1972
Current liabilities		
Current portion of LTD	$ 20,407	$ 27,447
A/P and accrued liab.	27,974	36,408
Accrued income taxes	389	2,429
Total current liabs.	48,770	66,284
LTD		
Equipment obligations	290,149	308,894
Notes and lease contracts	76,773	52,460
Subordinated debt	32,594	31,739
Total LTD	399,516	93,083
Deferred credits	65,523	81,335
Stockholders' equity	17,356	20,372
Additional paid-in capital	90,404	103,431
Retained earnings	36,531	51,401
	144,291	175,204
Total liabilities and stockholders' equity	658,100	715,904

Other assets		
Cost in excess of fair value of net assets of acquired business	16,189	16,167
Long-term receivables	6,682	5,782
Unamortized debt expense and other assets	2,802	4,615
	25,673	26,564
	658,100	715,904

Table 4-4
Top Sixty Freight Airports of the World in 1971

Rank	Airport	Country	Freight[a] (tons)
1	John F. Kennedy	United States	681,443
2	O'Hare International	United States	475,745
3	Los Angeles International	United States	435,588
4	Heathrow	United Kingdom	327,902
5	Frankfurt-Main	West Germany	306,775
6	San Francisco International	United States	277,143
7	Miami International	United States	262,666
8	Tokyo International	Japan	227,789
9	Orly	France	185,303
10	Schiphol	Netherlands	175,422
11	Honolulu International	United States	121,835
12	Ciampino/Fiumicino	Italy	111,904
13	Kastrup	Denmark	110,710
14	National	Belgium	109,225
15	Montreal International	Canada	102,737
16	Zurich	Switzerland	97,867
17	Toronto International	Canada	92,433
18	Osaka International	Japan	83,854
19	Linate/Halpensa	Italy	78,984
20	Tan-Son-Nhut	Vietnam	76,454
21	Eldorado	Colombia	76,202
22	Seattle-Tacoma International	United States	75,700
23	Hong Kong International	United Kingdom	75,557
24	Barajas	Spain	73,689
25	Sydney International	Australia	70,555
26	Beirut International	Lebanon	64,803
27	LeBourget	France	55,570
28	Wellington	New Zealand	54,296
29	Maiquetia	Venezuela	54,237
30	Melbourne International	Australia	52,487
31	Mexico City International	Mexico	42,268
32	Soledad	Colombia	40,786
33	Vancouver International	Canada	39,291
34	Dublin	Ireland	38,254
35	Jan Smuts	South Africa	37,204
36	Manchester	United Kingdom	36,854
37	Barcelona	Spain	36,072
38	Tocumen	Panama	30,151

Table 4-4 (cont.)

Rank	Airport	Country	Freight[a] (tons)
39	Dusseldorf	West Germany	29,712
40	Arlanda	Sweden	29,216
41	Hamburg	West Germany	27,952
42	Athens	Greece	27,897
43	Galeao	Brazil	27,003
44	Cointrin	Switzerland	26,521
45	Stuttgart	West Germany	26,512
46	Ezeiza	Argentina	26,292
47	Pudahel	Chile	26,040
48	Templehof	West Germany	25,979
49	Singapore International	Singapore	25,806
50	Bangkok	Thailand	25,277
51	Fort Lamy	Chad	24,739
52	Munich	West Germany	24,252
53	Congonhas	Brazil	23,024
54	Lisbon	Portugal	22,173
55	Kennedy International	Bolivia	21,124
56	Karachi International	Pakistan	20,512
57	Douala	Cameroons	18,303
58	Nairobi	Kenya	18,108
59	Schwechat	Austria	18,108
60	Fornebu	Norway	17,924

Source: ICAO Airport Traffic, 1971.

[a]Total loaded and unloaded freight in commercial air transport.

We are a marketing-oriented airline. Our marketing approach is defined by the process of perceiving the *needs*, not necessarily the expressed *wants* of the customer. It is then our task to design a product to fit those needs, and to examine carefully the profitability of the product. Other major airlines too often listen and react to the customers wants, and take too much of a production view of their cargo operation, just offering the services of their aircraft. Part of our strategy is providing the frequency of departures that the customer needs.

Forwarders? Given the high capital intensity of this industry, the airlines *must* retain the point of contact with their ultimate customer. We don't want to put ourselves in the hands of the wholesalers.

It may be seen from Figure 4-3 that Healy had both a marketing vice president and a sales vice president reporting to him. This distinction was institutionalized in 1968 with the formation of a "marketing development group" to stimulate Tiger's commercial revenues to compensate for declining military business. The first task of the newly formed group was to recover all Tiger air waybills back to 1963, have them keypunched, and utilize a computer to analyze who Tiger's customers were and where they were shipping. It was discovered at that time that 20 percent of the accounts produced 85 percent of Tiger's commercial revenues, and these major accounts, referred to as the "core," were singled out for special attention. The first step in Tiger's profit planning was a forecast by salesmen of the likely demands of the core group. As a result of the efforts of the market development group, Tiger's customer base had been expanded such that, in 1973, 85 percent of commercial revenues were accounted for by 40 percent of the customers.

Tiger's largest customer was UPS, which in 1971 had begun to offer what was, in effect, an air-forwarding service in addition to its small-package trucking operation. In 1973, UPS accounted for 21 percent of domestic revenues, and Tiger estimated that it received approximately one-fourth of UPS's total air traffic. In domestic operations, other forwarders accounted for an additional 29 percent of revenues, and in international operations, where forwarders were the norm for the whole industry, 86 percent of revenues came from this source.

Traffic Distribution

Tables 4-5 and 4-6 give the breakdown of total Pacific and Domestic cargo traffic and revenues for 1970-1972. Tables 4-7 and 4-8 give airport activity statistics for domestic and Pacific service, respectively, and Table 4-9 shows the city-pairs most densely served by Tiger. Imbalance in the direction of freight existed to the extent that, for all scheduled operations, approximately 70 percent of revenues in 1971 and 1972 came from eastbound flights. However, in the Pacific operation, a sharp reversal of directionality was experienced. In 1970, 40 percent of revenues was eastbound; in 1972 this proportion rose to 60 percent.

Seasonality of traffic also existed to some extent. For domestic operations, the four quarters of the year yielded 21 percent, 23 percent, and 29 percent of total annual revenues; for Pacific operations the figures were 20 percent, 23 percent, 27 percent, and 30 percent. As far as was possible, Tiger accommodated the seasonality by switching aircraft from commercial to military operations and other charter work. Average annual load factors in 1972 were 55 percent for domestic operations and 66 percent for international, whereas the average stage lengths were 1200 miles and 1350 miles, respectively.

On the Pacific route, where the most commonly transported articles were wearing apparel, telecommunication equipment, electrical machinery, textiles, and tape recorders, Tiger faced major competition from Japan Air Lines (JAL),

Table 4-5
Distribution of Operating Revenues, 1970-1972

	1970	1971	1972
Domestic Service			
Transport			
U.S. mail (priority)	$ 477,758	$ 973,040	$ 1,056,697
U.S. mail (nonpriority)	903,638	1,298,946	832,003
Foreign mail	–	–	–
Express	303,432	393,655	460,890
Freight	28,932,910	36,605,257	46,270,123
Miscellaneous	52,373	79,498	211,865
Total	30,670,111	39,350,396	48,831,578
Incidental revenues (net)	(172,796)	(121,930)	(29,803)
Total operating revenues	30,497,315	39,228,466	48,801,775
Pacific Service			
Transport			
U.S. mail (priority)	8,635,245	7,806,078	8,790,301
U.S. mail (nonpriority)	21,292,014	13,571,522	11,501,170
Foreign mail	–	–	–
Express	–	–	–
Freight	20,276,527	35,187,188	52,319,338
Miscellaneous	8,314	3,403	13,256
Total	50,212,100	56,568,191	72,624,065
Incidental revenues (net)	(28,896)	(4,195)	79,217
Total operating revenues	50,183,204	56,563,996	72,703,282

Source: CAB Form 42.

Pan American, and Northwest Orient. The number of freighter flights per week between the United States and Tokyo offered by each of these airlines in 1973 is shown in Table 4-10.

Competition on domestic routes came mainly from TWA, American Airlines and United (the main traffic being automotive parts, perishables, wearing apparel, and electrical and nonelectrical machinery). Tiger found that there was a strong interaction between their domestic and Pacific markets, with 65 percent of the U.S.-to-Orient traffic originating east of the Mississippi and 60 percent of the Orient-to-U.S. traffic terminating there.

Operating Aircraft

During the early 1950s, the company's main aircraft were the C-46, the DC-4, and the DC-6A. In 1955 a commitment was made for ten Super Constellations,

Table 4-6
Aircraft Statistics, Scheduled Services, 1970-1972

	1970	*1971*	*1972*
Domestic Service			
Revenue tons enplaned			
U.S. mail (priority)	1,252.71	2,571.66	2,597.49
U.S. mail (nonpriority)	4,422.22	4,957.36	4,313.70
Foreign mail	–	–	–
Express	1,101.87	1,341.27	1,536.47
Freight	103,609.03	129,599.13	159,708.62
Total	110,385.83	138,469.42	168,156.28
Revenue ton-miles			
U.S. mail (priority)	1,663,892	3,675,105	3,710,991
U.S. mail (nonpriority)	6,517,202	6,929,620	5,722,032
Foreign mail	–	–	–
Express	1,420,734	1,801,703	1,976,684
Freight	203,460,202	234,780,044	277,933,158
Total	213,062,030	247,186,472	289,342,865
Revenue aircraft departures	6,446	7,822	N/A
Pacific Service			
Revenue tons enplaned			
U.S. mail (priority)	5,384.96	5,311.88	5,665.04
U.S. mail (nonpriority)	27,124.03	21,515.30	16,270.94
Foreign mail	–	–	–
Express	–	–	–
Freight	20,337.68	43,949.68	62,107.21
Total	52,846.67	70,776.86	84,043.19
Revenue ton-miles			
U.S. mail (priority)	30,264,965	27,783,634	31,490,952
U.S. mail (nonpriority)	159,825,824	105,435,650	85,345,266
Foreign mail	–	–	–
Express	–	–	–
Freight	100,034,823	190,306,193	295,022,161
Total	290,125,612	323,525,477	411,858,379
Revenue aircraft departures	5,757	6,881	

with delivery to commence in 1957. Except for one C-46, the operating fleet at the end of 1958 consisted solely of Super Constellations. In 1961, the turboprop Canadair CL-44D (which has a swing tail for easier loading of freight) was introduced into the fleet, and until 1965, only this aircraft and the Super Constellation were employed (Table 4-11).

Table 4-7

Domestic Service Airport Activity Statistics (Scheduled Service), Quarter Ended 30 June 1973

Airport	Departures Performed	Enplaned Cargo (tons)[a]	Enplaned Freight (tons)
Logan (Boston)	152	3,810	3,548
Cleveland	64	1,914	1,755
Detroit	156	4,278	4,193
Newark	341	8,012	6,488
JFK (NY)	180	4,669	4,221
Los Angeles	357	12,728	12,222
Chicago	715	12,644	11,682
Portland	8	–	–
Seattle	143	3,620	3,605
San Francisco	288	7,166	6,685
Hancock (Syracuse)	63	1,366	1,158
Total	2467	60,207	55,557

[a]Includes freight, express, and mail.

Table 4-8

Pacific Service Airport Activity Statistics (Scheduled Service), Quarter Ended 30 June 1973

Airport	Scheduled Departures	Enplaned Cargo (tons)	Enplaned Freight (tons)
Bangkok	75	960	287
Hong Kong	143	2,346	2,100
Manila	26	306	163
Okinawa	103	546	36
Osaka	57	301	301
Seoul	66	1,355	1,131
Saigon	66	98	17
Taipei	145	1,810	1,629
Tokyo	464	4,970	3,687
Subtotal	1145	12,692	9,351
Los Angeles	78	1,485	1,401
Chicago	77	2,173	2,148
San Francisco	149	2,738	1,373
Seattle	235	1,771	1,015
Subtotal	539	8,167	5,937
Total	1684	20,859	15,288

Table 4-9
Most Densely Served City-pairs,[a] August 1973

Direct (Nonstop) Flights Only			Direct and Indirect Flights		
From	To	Flights/Week	From	To	Flights/Week
Los Angeles	Newark	18	Los Angeles	Newark	19
San Francisco	Los Angeles	14	Newark	Chicago	18
Chicago	Los Angeles	14	Newark	Los Angeles	16
Tokyo	San Francisco	13	Chicago	Los Angeles	15
San Francisco	Chicago	13	Tokyo	San Francisco	13
Chicago	San Francisco	11	Chicago	San Francisco	11
Newark	Chicago	11	Detroit	Los Angeles	11
Newark	Detroit	10	Newark	San Francisco	11
Chicago	Seattle	10	San Francisco	Tokyo	10
			San Francisco	Chicago	10
			Newark	Detroit	10

[a]If Newark and John F. Kennedy airports are taken as serving the single market of New York, then the following numbers of flights result:

	Direct	Total
New York to Chicago	18	27
New York to Los Angeles	9	18
Los Angeles to New York	19	20
Chicago to New York	14	15
New York to San Francisco	4	11
San Francisco to New York	3	10
New York to Detroit	10	10

The company's first jet aircraft, two Boeing B-707-300Cs, were leased in 1965, but by 1966, plans had begun for a complete conversion of the fleet. The low operating cost of jet aircraft had led competing carriers to introduce low air-freight rates, and Tiger's fleet became increasingly uneconomical. During 1966 a contract for ten DC-8-63F was signed (with an option for the purchase of four more) at an aggregate cost of approximately $100 million. (Negotiations and analysis for the purchase had begun in 1964, even though the aircraft was not expected to make its first flight until 1968.) During 1967 the option was exercised and an additional three aircraft ordered. The purchase of the first ten was financed with a $51 million public offering of equipment trust certificates and a $38 million private placement, and the remaining seven were financed through leases. Delivery of the aircraft was scheduled to commence in June 1968, and all seventeen were expected to be in service by the end of 1969.

Table 4-10
Number of Flights per Week Between United States and Tokyo, 1973

	Eastbound	*Westbound*
Flying Tiger	19	20
JAL	15	15
Pan American	13	8
Northwest	6	6

The DC-8-63F (known as the "stretch" DC-8) had a lift capacity of 108,500 lbs., 40 percent more than the 707-320C and 85 percent more than the CL-44. It could accommodate eighteen pallets or containers, compared to the 707's thirteen and the CL-44's ten. This extra capacity was expected to raise direct operating costs per mile by only 13 percent.

Advance planning for the introduction of the new aircraft into the fleet was extensive. Training of maintenance personnel was completed in 1967, and construction began in the same year of a $2.25 million flight training center for pilots, incorporating a 63F simulator. Also started was a $25 million program of modernization for eight domestic stations, incorporating automatic systems that could load or unload the new aircraft in forty-five minutes.

Changes in pricing and marketing strategies to secure increased volumes at

Table 4-11
Fleet Mix, 1960-1972

Year	1049H Super Constellation	CL-44D	707-300C	DC-8F	DC-8-63F
1960	14				
1961	12	6			
1962	8	10			
1963	11	10			
1964	11	10			
1965	9	15	2		
1966	8	15	4		
1967	8	15	4		
1968				2	9
1969				2	15
1970					17
1971					19
1972					20

profitable levels were also necessary. Tiger began to press the CAB for a simplified rate structure, with less distinction between "levels of service" but added containerization incentives.

Also crucial to the new equipment strategy was the addition of new route authority over the Pacific, granted in 1969, to exploit the long-haul capabilities of the new aircraft. Prior to the new Pacific operations, Tiger's DC-8-63Fs were averaging 6.8 to 7 hours per weekday over the domestic routes and there were no weekend operations. In 1971, the fleet averaged 10.3 hours per day, seven days per week.

Aircraft Evaluation

Tiger engaged in continual communication with manufacturers of both airframes and engines. An analysis of wide-body jets, such as the Boeing 747, commenced during 1971, and the impact of increased power, carrying capacity, and takeoff and landing distances was investigated. Tiger executives were concerned about reducing the empty weight of the aircraft, maximizing volume usage, developing ground-service equipment, and achieving the optimum cargo-loading systems, door sizes, heights, and so on.

Tiger did not anticipate that an aircraft specifically designed for cargo operations (rather than a modification of an existing passenger design) would come from manufacturers in the foreseeable future. Such an investment on the part of the manufacturers could run to as much as $1 billion and would clearly not be justified by the potential market for such an aircraft unless support was forthcoming from the government directly or through the military. This possibility was less desirable than the modification of passenger designs. In the words of one Tiger pilot "The primary operating characteristic of military cargo aircraft is that they can land in ten feet of mud."

The potential advantages of a cargo-designed aircraft would include a high wing to allow truck-bed-height loading and an airframe design that allowed a high degree of volume utilization.

The two aircraft that Tiger was prepared to consider were cargo versions of the wide-body Boeing B-747 (the B-747F) and the McDonnell-Douglas DC-10 (the DC-10-30AF). Comparative specifications of the B-747F, the DC-10-30AF and the DC-8-63F are given in Table 4-12. No cargo version of the other wide-body jet, the Lockheed L-1011, had been proposed by the manufacturer, and development work was only beginning on a long-range version of this basically medium-range aircraft.

Both Boeing and McDonnell-Douglas submitted analyses of the performance of their respective aircraft on several Tiger routes. These are summarized in Tables 4-13 and 4-14. These reports also included estimates of the direct operating costs (DOC) and are shown in Figure 4-4. Estimates of total line-haul

Table 4-12
Comparative Aircraft Specifications

1 Ton	DC-8-63F	B-747F	DC-10-30AF
Max. takeoff wt.	355,000 lbs.	800,000 lbs.	555,000 lbs.
Max. landing wt.	275,000 lbs.	630,000 lbs.	436,000 lbs.
Max. zero fuel wt	261,000 lbs.	590,000 lbs.	412,000 lbs.
Length	187'5"	231'4"	181'4.75"
Height	42'5"	63'5"	58'0"
Wing span	148'5"	195'8"	161'4"
Fuel capacity	24,275 gals.	51,000 gals.	35,800 gals.
Engine thrust (per engine)	19,000 lbs.	52,000 lbs.	49,000 lbs.
Cubic capacity	10,788 cu.ft.	26,420 cu.ft.	19,788 cu.ft
Payload @ 8 lbs. /cu.ft.	86,304 lbs.	220,378 lbs.	158,304 lbs.
Structural limit payload	110,068 lbs.	220,378 lbs.	192,075 lbs.
Price ($M)	10.056	33.411	24.6
Cost/engine ($M)	0.300	1.211	1.211
Cruising speed	0.82Mach (550-570 mph)	0.82Mach (550-570 mph)	0.82Mach (550-570 mph)

Assumed common characteristics of DC-8-63F, B-747F, and DC-10-30AF

Airframe spares ratio, ATA formula	10%
Airframe spares ratio, modified formula	5%
Engine spares ratio, ATA formula	40%
Utilization	4380 hours/year
Crew	3 men
Fuel price (cents/gallon)	
International	12.5
Domestic	13
Depreciation	14 years–15%
Insurance (% per year of study price)	2

costs, as Tiger defined them, traffic-servicing costs, and other indirect costs were not included. However, in 1972 Tiger's experience had been that indirect costs equaled 100 percent of DOC on domestic flights and 61 percent on international flights. Thus, it would be necessary to make an investment in additional ground-service equipment.

Tiger executives welcomed the opportunity to discuss the B-747F and the DC-10-30AF, but they did not want to rush into a purchase of either of these aircraft. Management agreed that the DC-8-63F continued to be the most

Table 4-13
Payload Comparisons[a]

	Weight Limited Payload (tons)			70% L.F. Payload (tons)		
	DC-8-63F	747F	DC-10-30AF	DC-8-63F	747F	DC-10-30AF
TYO-ANC[b]	45.11	110.19	78.66	37.81	77.34	58.62
ANC-TYO	40.92	106.19	72.95	37.81	77.34	58.62
(3459)						
ANC-JFK	44.84	110.19	78.39	37.81	77.34	58.62
JFK-ANC	41.79	108.27	74.15	37.81	77.34	58.62
(3377)						
JFK-LAX	54.01	110.19	83.74	37.81	77.34	58.62
LAX-JFK	52.87	110.19	83.74	37.81	77.34	58.62
(2469)						
JFK-SFO	52.98	110.19	83.74	37.81	77.34	58.62
SFO-JFK	52.87	110.19	83.74	37.81	77.34	58.62
(2579)						
ORD-LAX	54.01	110.19	83.74	37.81	77.34	58.62
LAX-ORD	54.01	110.19	83.74	37.81	77.34	58.62
(1741)						

[a]These payloads are based on "75 percent annual winds," that is, a 75 percent probability that winds will be less than the standard forces over the given routes.

[b]ANC denotes Anchorage, Alaska, which served as a refueling point for transpacific flights.

Table 4-14
Direct-Operating-Cost Comparison
(cents/ton-mile)

	Weight Limited Payload (100% Load Factor)		
	DC-8-63F	747F	DC-10-30AF
TYP-ANC	3.94	3.21	3.47
ANC-TYO	4.76	3.67	4.07
ANC-JFK	3.96	3.22	3.47
JFK-ANC	4.73	3.60	4.07
JFK-LAX	3.81	3.71	3.78
LAX-JFK	3.32	3.21	3.23
JFK-SFO	3.93	3.67	3.69
SFO-JFK	3.30	3.20	3.22
ORD-LAX	3.88	3.82	3.88
LAX-ORD	3.42	3.40	3.38

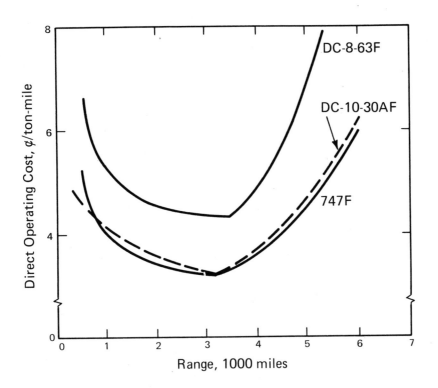

^aBased on density of 8 lbs./cu. ft. and 100% load factor.

Figure 4-4. Direct-operating-cost Comparison[a]

efficient cargo aircraft in existence, in both performance and size. Healy believed that even the DC-8-63F was too big for all but the nine largest markets that Tiger served and that only a 40 to 50 percent share of the top market (NY-LA) would justify operating a 747F, for example. In discussing alternatives open to Tiger, Pinke commented, "We now have the best cargo aircraft flying today. Staying with the 63F is our best alternative. The B-747F? Disastrous! The DC-10? Even worse!"

Management was also reluctant to lose the advantages of operating a single-aircraft fleet. Hoffman had been quoted as saying that it would take a 40 percent reduction DOC to overcome the loss of these advantages, but industry observers considered this to be an overstatement and a more likely range to be 20 to 25 percent.

Because the B-747F was already in existence, whereas the DC-10-30AF had yet to fly, Pinke, senior vice president of operations, considered that the B-747F was "out front technically." However, the smaller size of the DC-10-30AF meant that Tiger could "grow into it sooner." Jack Elliot, a subordinate of Pinke who had worked at McDonnell-Douglas on the development of the DC-8-63F, pointed out that although relations with that company were cordial, the benefits of greater familiarity with their personnel would only influence the selection decision "if everything else were exactly equal."

Although Tiger did not have a "minimum purchase quantity," it considered the purchase of just one wide-body jet highly unlikely. Apart from the economics, a prime consideration would be frequency of service. Any wide-body jet purchased would probably be placed in service in the NY-TYO market, with a stopover at Chicago, Seattle, San Francisco, or Los Angeles. Because such a round trip might take the best part of two days, a daily service could not be offered with just one aircraft, and thus a purchase order of three or four would be the minimum that Tiger might consider.

The real question for Tiger's management, however, was how soon the market could support such a service. They expected to have to purchase used DC-8-63Fs to support their growth in traffic for a number of years to come.

Used DC-8-63F Market

Flying Tiger management knew of the whereabouts of every one of the DC-8-63Fs in existence (a few of the sixty originally made by McDonnell-Douglas had been destroyed in crashes, including one of Tiger's). Unfortunately for Tiger, all current DC-8-63F owners were aware of Tiger's continuing interest in purchasing used DC-8-63Fs. Apart from this factor, the favorable operating characteristics of the aircraft made its current owners reluctant to part with the aircraft. Among American carriers, only the other all-cargo carriers owned DC-8-63Fs; Seaboard World owned five and Airlift International, four. Seaboard expected delivery of the first of its three on-order B-747Fs in early 1975.

In 1972, a European charter airline had gone bankrupt and placed three DC-8-63Fs on the market. Tiger had not purchased any of these aircraft because the company anticipated that its short-term needs would be served by the return of two of its own fleet that were out on lease until late 1973. It also considered the asking price for the aircraft to be too high. Pinke assessed that the 1973 price for a used DC-8-63F would be in the region of $11 million. He also recognized that a significant investment might be necessary to convert navigational and other cockpit equipment to the Tiger requirements. The size of this investment would depend on the existing cockpit configuration, but could be expected to be $500,000 on average.

The crew-training supervisor, Russ Kissinger, observed that the standard cockpit layout and equipment in all of Tiger's aircraft was much appreciated by the company's pilots, who could move from one aircraft to another without having to adjust to different equipment type or location in the cockpit.[a] Conversion of one of the aircraft returned to Tiger from its lease was to be carried out during ongoing maintenance and was not expected to be completed until three months after the return of the aircraft.

A final consideration in the purchase of used DC-8-63Fs was that many of them were not constructed as pure freighters, but in a convertible configuration. The reduction in payload of these aircraft from the freighter configuration was on the order of 5000 lbs.

Underlying consideration of continued purchases of the DC-8-63F was the fact that the future of the DC-8-63F was threatened by recent FAA legislation requiring that aircraft noise be reduced. The DC-8-63F, one of the noisier aircraft, created more "noise pollution" than the 747F or the much quieter DC-10. To conform with the new standards would require an investment of approximately $1 million per aircraft and take each aircraft out of service for two weeks while changes were being made. Also, the "retrofitting" process that would be employed would cause a 2.5 to 3 percent degradation of engine performance.

Pinke was aware of the development of an increased fan size for the JT3D-7 turbofan engines used on the DC-8-63F that would allow noise standards to be met and would *increase* engine performance by 2.5 to 3 percent. Development work had not been completed on the new fan size by Pratt and Whitney, the engine's manufacturers, but Pinke estimated that, when and if it became available, conversion costs would be $2.5 million per aircraft.

In weighing the alternatives before them, Tiger's management had many factors to consider besides operating characteristics of the aircraft. "Of particular importance were the subjects of terminal operations and airport restrictions."

Terminal Operations

Flying Tiger was known to have a conservative approach to terminal automation. The standard operating procedure for loading and unloading aircraft at the terminal involved three types of equipment. A "loader," which cost $30,000 and was operated by one man, was wheeled to the side of the aircraft. It lowered (or raised) containers and pallets from the aircraft onto ground transporters. These transporters, of which up to three might be used per operation, cost $15,000 each and were used to carry the containers from the aircraft to the terminal's traveling elevator storage system. This system, also operated by one man, had cost $40,000 when installed in 1968 at Detroit, Newark, Los Angeles, Chicago,

---

[a]Mr. Kissinger estimated that initial training of crews for any new aircraft would be approximately $35,000 per three-man crew and that ten crews per aircraft would be needed for any new type of plane.

and San Francisco. (All had three levels, except the San Francisco system, which had one.) However, the system being installed at Tiger's new JFK terminal had cost $95,000. A similar expenditure was anticipated at Tiger's other new terminals (to be opened in 1974) at Seattle, San Francisco, and Tokyo.

The main impact of the introduction of wide-body jets on terminal operations would be in the new container sizes and weights that would be necessary. New loaders and transporters would be required at all terminals that the wide-body jet served. Traveling elevator systems that Tiger was installing during 1973-1974 could be modified relatively easily to accommodate new container sizes, but the older systems would require extensive adjustments and perhaps complete replacement.

At one airport, Los Angeles, it would be impossible to employ the wide-body jets, because the terminal and the runways were separated by an overpass crossing a highway. The overpass could not support the weight of a loaded B-747F, and despite requests from all major airlines, the authorities refused to strengthen it because of pressure from environmental-protection groups who wanted to discourage the growth of air traffic at L.A.

Airport Restrictions

Among other environmental factors that could affect Tiger's equipment strategy were the problems of restricted takeoffs and curfews. At Tokyo Airport, Tiger had to negotiate each year with the Tokyo government about the total number of flights per week it could operate into and out of the airport. In the past, Tiger had always been able to obtain the flights it wanted and had already negotiated increases for 1974 and 1975 over its 1973 level of 76 operations (i.e., 38 takeoffs and 38 landings), but it recognized that it was becoming increasingly difficult to increase its allocation and that the time might come when the number of operations could no longer be increased. At Tokyo itself, a possible easing of this problem lay in the opening of the new airport at Narida, but the Japanese government had been unable to open the completed airport due to an inability to lay a fuel pipeline to the airport. The government had no compulsory purchase powers and had been unable to persuade landowners and house owners to allow a pipeline to be laid. No one in the airline industry knew when Narida airport would open, if ever.

The problem of restricted operations was not confined to Tokyo. During certain hours, Tiger was restricted also at JFK, and there existed the constant possibility that at some time in the future many American airports would seek to ease their congestion problems by allocating landing frequencies among the airlines.

Another, more profound threat to Tiger lay in the possibility of the spread of another Asian airport practice to the United States: at all Asian airports that

Tiger served, with the exception of Taipei, the airport closed down between 11:30 p.m. and 6:00 a.m. This practice complicated the scheduling task, but the long flying times meant that little real compromise was forced on Tiger's operation. However, should environmentalist pressure groups succeed in their efforts to enforce curfews at American airports, then the basic night-freighter nature of Tiger's operation would be seriously threatened.

5

Eastern Airlines December Schedule

Introduction

On Sunday, 3 December 1972, Captain Mike Fenello, vice president of operational coordination for Eastern Airlines, was still thinking about the meeting that had taken place the previous evening. He and several members of Eastern's Operations Group had been up until 2:30 a.m. working on an air-crew scheduling problem that might have a major impact on the company's flight schedule for that month. Events during the past weeks indicated that flight crew utilization for December would be extremely tight, and Captain Fenello was not sure that Eastern had enough total available pilot hours to operate the December flight schedule as it stood. If there would be a shortage, it would possibly be to Eastern's advantage to cancel some less-profitable flights during the early part of the month to avoid cancellation of flights toward the end of December when passenger traffic and load factors were always high. On the other hand, flight cancellations of any kind were always dreaded and meant giving up revenues as well as passenger good will to Eastern's competitors.

If flights were to be canceled, Captain Fenello was unsure of how many total pilot hours he should attempt to save. Also, he wondered what criteria should be used to decide which flights to cancel. As vice president of operational coordination, Captain Fenello was responsible for this decision. However, he knew that he would be expected to justify his actions before Eastern's Capability Committee, which met regularly on Wednesday afternoons. This committee consisted of the following members (see Figure 5-1):

Colonel Frank Borman—senior vice president of operations group (chairman);

David Kunstler—vice president of schedules and airline planning;

Captain Walter Krepling—vice president and chief pilot;

Captain Mike Fenello—vice president of operational coordination.

Other members of these departments were also present. To prepare for the meeting, Captain Fenello decided to review once again the events affecting the situation.

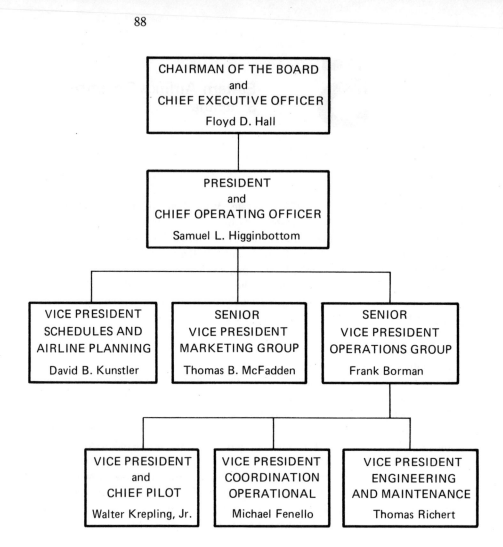

Figure 5-1. Partial Organizational Chart

Company Background

Eastern Airlines began operation on 1 May 1928, having won a government contract to carry mail by air between New York and Atlanta. From this base (passenger service was initiated in 1930), the company's routes quickly expanded to include Daytona Beach, Orlando, Tampa, and Miami, Florida; Newark, New Jersey; Philadelphia; Baltimore; and Washington, D.C. In 1938, Captain Eddie Rickenbacker, World War I flying ace, and a group of associates acquired control of the company. Captain Rickenbacker served as chief executive officer until 1963. After Eastern encountered a period of economic difficulty at the start of the jet age, Floyd D. Hall (now chairman and chief executive officer) joined the company in 1963 as president and chief executive officer. He led a new management team which guided Eastern back to profitability and growth.

By 1972, Eastern had become one of the "big four" domestic airlines in the United States—the others being United Airlines, Trans World Airlines, and American Airlines. Total operating revenues for the calendar year 1971 were $1.054 billion, over 90 percent of which came from the 22.8 million passengers the airline carried that year. A more complete picture of Eastern's financial history is presented in Table 5-1.

Eastern's system network comprised 33,080 route miles, linking 101 CAB-designated cities in 29 states plus the District of Columbia (see Figure 5-2). In addition, Eastern provided air service to Canada, Mexico, Puerto Rico, the Virgin Islands, Bermuda, the Bahamas, and Jamaica. Including the company's Air Shuttle operation between Boston-New York/Newark-Washington, scheduled departures averaged 1526 per day.

In December 1972, Eastern's jet fleet (summarized in Table 5-2) consisted of the Lockheed 1011, the company's newest aircraft; the Boeing 727; and the McDonnell-Douglas DC-8 and DC-9. The average airspeed for these jets (block to block) was 575 miles per hour. In addition, Eastern owned and operated sixteen Electras, which were primarily used as backups for the airline's shuttle operations.

The company was built on a substantial volume of business travel. However, it was very aware of the role of the importance of customers who were traveling for pleasure or personal reasons. As part of an effort to develop these markets, Eastern developed a joint advertising program to promote Disney World in Florida and a series of television commercials describing vacation-planning services available from the airline. These activities were all part of a program headed "Eastern—the wings of man."

Eastern suffered financial difficulties between 1969 and 1972, but reported profits through November 1972 had increased some $20 million over the same period in the previous year. With a good showing in December, Eastern hoped to earn $25 million on total revenues of approximately $1.3 billion (see Table 5-3). Crucial to this improvement was an upsurge in revenue passenger-miles (RPMs) during the latter part of 1971 and continuing into 1972. This increase in traffic was expected in light of the improved condition of the national economy during this period.

Eastern's improved performance during the period of 1969 through 1971 resulted from cost cutting and overall "belt tightening" by the company. The management allowed attrition to reduce the level of the work force in nearly every classification. Because flight crew salaries represented a significant cost item, Eastern was particularly conscious of the aggregate number of pilots it

Table 5-1

Comparative Income Account, 31 December 1965-1971

($000)

Income Accounts	1965	1966	1967	1968	1969	1970	1971
Operating revenue							
Passenger (first class)	$118,661	$ 99,880	$124,888	$136,624	$154,941	$158,544	$ 143,962
Passenger (coach)	352,329	355,430	480,694	543,485	633,915	738,165	803,519
Passenger (economy) }							
Mail	8,472	7,748	9,876	10,644	12,527	12,206	13,894
Freight	16,293	15,185	21,427	28,219	36,222	44,606	44,895
Other	11,768	18,039	20,919	25,805	31,958	17,528	47,487
Total	507,523	496,282	657,804	744,777	869,563	971,049	1,053,757
Operating expenses							
Flying operations	131,503	134,464	177,368	208,018	253,384	270,765	324,848
Maintenance	86,591	87,277	108,926	128,796	133,482	149,564	158,459
Passenger service	42,749	44,239	59,247	72,639	82,166	91,641	97,563
Aircraft and traffic servicing	75,009	77,839	103,827	123,049	142,830	163,507	181,828
Promotion and sales	62,554	67,947	88,691	103,210	116,558	123,737	126,657
General and administrative	19,648	21,055	27,386	36,081	39,804	44,610	49,197
Depreciation and amortization	48,932	39,209	48,147	65,238	77,494	83,336	79,372
Total	466,986	472,030	613,592	737,031	845,718	927,160	1,017,924
Operating profit	40,537	24,252	44,212	7,746	23,845	43,889	35,833
Nonoper. income and expenses							
Gain on dispos. of property	342	277	29	1,062	2,834	1,893	2,431
Interest expense	13,005	13,089	15,239	28,109	33,331	37,793	33,769
Other	cr 1,799	cr 3,583	cr 2,856	cr 3,556	cr 3,419	cr 3,138	cr 2,986
Pretax net income	29,673	15,023	31,858	(15,745)	(3,233)	7,341	7,481

Income taxes							
Provision for deferred taxes			7,741	cr 3,809	cr 911	1,877	1,787
Total			7,741	cr 3,809	cr 911	1,877	1,787
Net income	29,673	15,023	24,117	(11,936)	(2,322)	5,464	5,694
Revenue passenger-miles flown (000,000)	8,053	7,945	11,225	12,513	14,003	15,493	15,502
Average yield per RPM (cents)	6.0	5.9	5.5	5.6	5.8	6.0	6.3

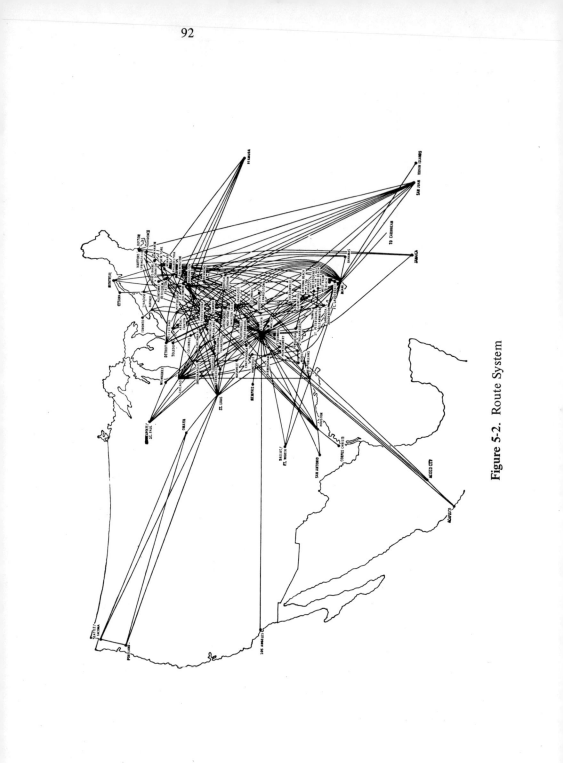

Figure 5-2. Route System

Table 5-2
Fleet Composition, December 1972

	Number of Seats per Aircraft (basic configuration)
Jets	
12 Lockheed 1011 Whisperliners	226
16 McDonnell-Douglas DC-8-61	203
10 McDonnell-Douglas DC-8-21	139
80 McDonnell-Douglas DC-9 Whisperjet II	90
75 Boeing B-727 Whisperjet	94
34 Boeing B-727-200 Whisperjet	163
16 Lockheed Electra (for use strictly as the second sections of the shuttle)	87
On order	
27 Lockheed L-1011 Whisperliners	
7 Boeing B-727-200 Whisperjets	
On option	
13 Lockheed 1011 Whisperliners	
Reserved delivery positions	
6 British/French Supersonic Concordes	
Available for sale or lease	
10 DC-8-21	
16 Electras	

Table 5-3
Net Income (Loss) After Taxes, 1968-1972
($000)

	1968	*1969*	*1970*	*1971*	*1972*
January	$1,201	$(1,937)	$2,781	$ (253)	$4,296
February	1,035	(2,720)	2,514	(1,969)	1,517
March	2,688	5,681	6,656	(522)	6,917
April	2,246	1,791	3,205	3,835	7,162
May	(843)	491	991	(844)	(178)
June	1,051	(916)	791	212	1,463
July	274	(470)	1,080	2,655	3,437
August	2,154	2,387	1,771	3,684	4,105
September	(7,234)	(6,579)	(7,586)	(7,445)	(5,547)
October	(6,981)	(2,754)	(8,559)	(4,478)	(1,853)
November	(7,424)	(1,106)	(2,903)	2,697	687
December	(106)	3,809	4,720	8,118	
Total	(11,939)	(2,323)	(5,461)	$5,690	

employed at any one time. The company tried to hire and train additional pilots only after careful analysis of the flight schedule indicated that an increase was necessary. Normally, it took about six weeks to hire, train, and fit an experienced pilot into Eastern's schedule. Variations depended on the type of aircraft the pilot was being trained to fly, as well as the availability of flight simulators, instructors, and training aircraft. Prior to July 1972, Eastern had not hired any new pilots for almost two years. As a result, the total number of "line pilots" had decreased to approximately 3700. During July and August, the airline had hired 150 pilots in preparation for the increased activity forecast through 1973. Most of these had recently begun flying as second officers aboard the company's B-727s.

Eastern's Relations with Its Pilots

Like most of the larger domestic and international airlines, Eastern's pilots were represented in all wage and contract negotiations by the Air Line Pilots' Association (ALPA). In the previous twenty years ALPA had been quite successful in improving the hours, pay, and working conditions of its pilots. In 1950 an average commercial pilot might have earned an annual salary of $15,000 for working 192 days in the year. By 1970, this figure had increased to around $30,000 and senior captains could earn as much as $65,000 for working approximately 144 days in the year.

Under the terms of the contract in 1972, Eastern's pilots could fly a maximum of eighty "pay hours" per month. Pay hours not only referred to a pilot's actual flying time (block to block), but also included the time spent briefing and preparing for a flight and traveling to or from a flight. For example, the pay hours of a pilot based in Miami who was scheduled to take a flight from Miami to Chicago to Atlanta and terminate in New York would include all his flight time as well as a portion of the time required to fly him home from New York to Miami. Similarly, if the flight originated in Atlanta, part of the pilot's time traveling as a passenger from Miami to Atlanta would count towards his eighty hours. For any month, this scheduled "dead head" or credit time averaged approximately 25 percent of a pilot's actual block time.

Eastern's Bid System

Eastern's pilots were usually qualified to operate only one type of aircraft, so substitutions of aircraft on a flight (say a DC-8 series aircraft for a B-727 series aircraft) necessitated a change in flight crew. This was part of the company's bid system covered by the ALPA contract. Under this system, pilots could bid twice a year for domicile (or base point) location and type of aircraft within Eastern's fleet they would fly. Results of this bidding depended on a pilot's seniority within his classification. Eastern's pilots were classified captains, first officers, or second officers. One of each was required in each of the aircraft operated by Eastern, except for the DC-9, which required a crew of only two. The most senior captain necessarily received his first choice of base location and type of aircraft, as did the most senior first officer and the most senior second officer. However, when a pilot advanced his classification, for bidding purposes his seniority was reduced.

A pilot who was assigned to a new type of aircraft was required by both the Federal Aviation Agency (FAA) and Eastern to undertake simulated and actual flight training in that aircraft prior to his first flight carrying passengers. Thus, after every bid, a certain number of Eastern's pilots were taken off the line and trained on the company's time. Normally, training took six to seven weeks, but it was usually spread out among the pilots so as not to interrupt the current flight schedule. Because of the seasonality of Eastern's operations, bids were conducted so that all training would be completed prior to 1 June and 1 December of each year. This arrangement permitted maximum utilization of pilots during the peak periods in Eastern's schedule. Once the date for a bid had passed and a pilot had been trained for a different type of aircraft, under the terms of the contract he could not fly any other aircraft, even though he may have been qualified to do so.

Flight Scheduling

Because Eastern was the second largest passenger carrier, flight scheduling was an immensely complicated task. According to David Kunstler, vice president of schedules and airline planning, the airline had to look at the feasibility of serving any particular city-pair within the context of the entire system. It was not enough to know that development of a certain market share on a route would yield a lucrative return. Alternative uses of aircraft and flight crews had to be considered along with the possible reactions of Eastern's competitors. Consequently, new ways were constantly being sought to improve Eastern's level of service in a way that would complement existing operations. The scheduling process was further described as follows:

A perfect schedule is rarely, if ever, attainable. The many varied requirements, many of which are inherently in conflict with one another, simply cannot be simultaneously satisfied. For example, the schedule planner must endeavor to provide adequate ground time for servicing and maintenance, and at the same time keep aircraft in the air for economic utilization. He must provide departure times that are compatible with known customer preference, or build complexes of connecting flights at major gateways, and at the same time avoid excessive peaking of station activity. He must strive for schedule stability for the convenience of both passengers and employees, and at the same time display the flexibility to rapidly adjust to new competitive threats or other developments. He must recognize that public service obligations will sometimes work in the opposite direction from strictly economic considerations, and at the same time remember that his airline could not provide any service at all without a sound financial position. And the conflicts go on and on.

In short, by attempting to optimize the allocation of the airline's principal assets—its aircraft, facilities, personnel and selling resources—considering its route opportunities as well as its route obligations, the resulting patterns must be satisfactory to essentially meet the combined goals of public service, competitive effectiveness, operational performance and profitability. During much of the process, there is very little black or white—but a great deal of gray.

At Eastern, we try hard to insure that the scheduling process is not an "Ivory Tower" approach that disregards the comments, suggestions and recommendations of those responsible for revenue production, operational performance and cost. To the contrary, there is considerable coordination, and in fact, required inputs from each of the involved departments. It is the schedule planner's job to somehow accomplish as many of the justifiable requests as possible.

Normally, Eastern's schedule of flights was written for a year in advance and updated quarterly as passenger forecasts and competitors' schedules changed. This schedule was used by Eastern's operations and maintenance departments to plan for the delivery and utilization of different types of aircraft and the hiring, training, and scheduling of air crews and flight attendants. In the short run, however, the realities of the airline industry often dictated that this order be reversed. At any one point in time, there was very little flexibility in aircraft and crew availability, and any unexpected change in the condition of one of these factors usually required some alteration of Eastern's flight schedule. For example, if a B-727 that was scheduled to fly from New York to Miami experienced maintenance problems, the company might have another B-727 assigned as a backup in New York. If so, the substitution was made, and the original aircraft would become a reserve when the repair work was completed. However, if a reserve aircraft was not available in New York, Eastern could either cancel the flight entirely or delay operations until another reserve aircraft could be flown in from another city. The latter alternative necessitated breaking out another crew of pilots to fly the reserve aircraft into New York and then either fly that aircraft to Miami or turn it over to the original crew and "dead head" to their next assignment.

Once the schedule for a quarter had been approved, it was turned over to the operational coordination department, which was charged with operating the schedule as smoothly and efficiently as possible. Any alteration of the schedule or cancellation of flights past this point due to maintenance difficulties, flight-crew problems, or whatever reason was the responsibility of operations coordination, and this department was held accountable for the results.

Because of the high demand for travel during the Christmas holidays,

Eastern typically scheduled additional capacity during the latter half of December. The impact can be seen in the daily available seat-miles offered in 1972, shown in Table 5-4. It was planned that such a schedule would take effect again in December 1973, as the manpower plan shown in Table 5-5 reflects.

Events Preceding the December Situation

There was always some increase in activity in December and Eastern expected it, but it was preferable to fall short of available pilot hours at this peak point of the annual operations rather than to carry an excess number of pilots during slack periods. However, this year the situation was worse than normal. ALPA had invoked a clause of the contract that required Eastern to place more pilots into training than had been predicted. This action prevented these pilots from being used in December. Compounding this difficulty was the fact that delivery of Eastern's new L-1011 aircraft was running significantly behind schedule. It had been hoped that the company would be able to use these aircraft in December and the allocation of crews had been based on this expectation. Consequently, Eastern was unable to use these large-capacity aircraft (300 seats each), nor could it reassign pilots covered by the ALPA contract.

The operational coordination department had difficulty meeting the November schedule. Because of these factors and extremely inclement weather, Eastern had exhausted all available monthly pilot hours in the B-727 and DC-9 aircraft categories. Consequently, it had been forced to cancel forty flight segments between 28 and 30 November. Of the 1828 passengers scheduled on those flights Eastern had been able to satisfactorily reschedule 275 passengers on another Eastern flight; 974 were rescheduled on other carriers and 579 were left "unprotected." Unprotected in this context meant that Eastern was unable to reschedule a passenger from a canceled flight on another flight that would arrive at his original destination within two hours of his original arrival time. Because the November cancellations had all come during the last three days of the month, the percentage of passengers rescheduled on another Eastern flight was extremely low. Captain Fenello thought that had he been able to selectively cancel the same amount of flights, he could have rescheduled approximately 50 percent of the inconvenienced passengers.

In actuality, the situation was worse than indicated. To complete a number of flights during the last two weeks of November, the operations group had scheduled some supervisory and instructor pilots on regular Eastern flights. Although these crews were fully qualified to operate Eastern's aircraft, they were not considered "line pilots" under the terms of the ALPA contract. Thus, they could be scheduled for flights, but they could not take flight time or pay hours from the regularly scheduled line pilots. Whatever flight time they accumulated in a line capacity had to be credited to a line pilot's record for

Table 5-4
Forecast ASMS and Load Factor, December 1972

Date	Day	ASMs (000)	Load Factor (percent)
1	Fri.	130,575	61.4
2	Sat.	131,169	54.3
3	Sun.	132,240	62.7
4	Mon.	128,035	56.1
5	Tues.	125,428	50.7
6	Wed.	126,962	50.6
7	Thurs.	127,537	57.0
8	Fri.	129,084	64.4
9	Sat.	131,127	47.3
10	Sun.	131,948	59.5
11	Mon.	127,984	55.8
12	Tues.	124,979	49.2
13	Wed.	153,215	45.5
14	Thurs.	159,137	51.1
15	Fri.	160,833	59.6
16	Sat.	158,815	57.6
17	Sun.	164,365	48.6
18	Mon.	161,104	48.8
19	Tues.	161,932	53.4
20	Wed.	165,538	68.2
21	Thurs.	165,889	76.2
22	Fri.	165,935	79.1
23	Sat.	166,932	65.4
24	Sun.	160,107	58.3
25	Mon.	150,725	66.9
26	Tues.	159,575	76.0
27	Wed.	158,463	66.7
28	Thurs.	156,414	69.6
29	Fri.	157,941	57.8
30	Sat.	160,682	69.5
31	Sun.	162,918	68.6
		4,597,588	60.3

scheduling and pay purposes. Most pilots had used up their allowed eighty hours for November, so this time was credited on their records for December. The result was that Eastern had started the month of December with some pilot pay hours already expended.

Table 5-5
Flight Operations Manpower Planning Report for December 1972, Summary

	Maximum Capability of Crew Pay Hours[a]	Allocated Crew Pay Hours	Margin Above Allocated Pay Hours
Prepared 11/21/72			
L-1011	3,823	3,675	+148
DC-8-60	3,500	3,557	−57
DC-8	2,633	2,565	+68
B-727	43,296	43,780	−484
DC-9	29,795	30,127	−332
L-188	3,718	3,588	+130
Total	86,765	87,292	−527
Prepared 11/28/72			
L-1011	3,823	3,675	+148
DC-8-60	3,500	3,564	−64
DC-8	2,633	2,558	+75
B-727	43,296	43,780	−484
DC-9	29,795	30,156	−361
L-188	3,718	3,550	+168
Total	86,763	87,283	−518

[a]These figures reflected the entire flying operations crew and were not "man-hours." For example, the L-1011 required a flight operations crew of 3. The total allocated man-hours for December were 11,025 (i.e., 3675 × 3).

Flight Operations Reports

Eastern made weekly projections of the total pilot hours (block hours and pay hours) required to operate the flight schedule for a particular month. Current records were also kept of the maximum available pilot capacity for the month. These figures were compared to give an indication of the leeway or cushion existing in this area. So long as the aggregate number of available pay hours for a particular type of aircraft exceeded the allocated number of hours, the schedule was considered manageable. As the two figures approached one another, Captain Fenello knew that things got tight. Once allocated pay hours had exceeded the maximum capability, aircraft and/or flights had to be rescheduled to bring the two into balance. One common approach to the problem was to try to substitute one type of aircraft for which excess pilot hours existed on a flight series for another type of aircraft where pilot hours were scarce. For example, it might be possible to substitute a DC-8 for a B-727 run provided that the DC-8 was not already committed that an alternate adjustment could be made.

The figures for the previous four weeks caused Captain Fenello to become increasingly concerned. The latest Flight Operations and Manpower Planning

Report for December indicated a shortage in pilot hours for the B-727 of 484 hours and of 361 hours for the DC-9 (see Table 5-5). Even if the aggregate number of pilot hours equaled the hours required, there might be schedule problems. Captain Fenello felt that it was necessary to have a few extra hours (perhaps 1 or 2 percent) to accommodate mislocations of pilots or other problems that tended to arise when specific schedules had to be filled.

The figures shown in Table 5-5 assumed "poor" December weather conditions. The company felt reasonably confident about the forecasts stated in the Flight Operations Manpower Planning Report, but the individuals responsible for scheduling were concerned by recent long-term weather forecasts. If good weather were to occur, the demand for pilot hours would be substantially lower and Eastern would just meet the required hours.

Weather

General flying conditions up and down the East Coast were the worst in years during November and caused considerable delays and stranded crews at all major airports. Eastern's meteorologists were forecasting continued fog along the Middle Atlantic States and considerable sleet and icing around the northeastern airports. The monthly forecasts were accurate approximately 70 percent of the time and were taken into account in Eastern's Manpower Planning Reports. In other words, Eastern felt that there was a 70 percent probability that the 28 November manpower requirements projected in Table 5-5 would prove accurate, whereas there was approximately a 30 percent probability that there would be sufficient bad weather to allow the company enough pilot hours to avoid schedule failure. The use of supervisors as pilots in a pinch in December would do little more than accommodate Captain Fenello's desire for a 1 to 2 percent margin of safety in good weather.

Competition

Captain Fenello was concerned about the effect that the actions of Eastern's competitors would have on the situation. Delta Airlines, the nation's fifth largest carrier and Eastern's chief rival along the East Coast, did not normally add as many flights to the winter schedule as Eastern because Delta's route system was more diversified than Eastern's and subject to less seasonality regarding the overall demand on the system. Moreover, Delta had recently completed a merger with Northeast Airlines, and under the terms of the merger agreement, Delta had assimilated all of Northeast's pilots as well as most of its routes. Because of extensive rescheduling following the merger, Delta found that they had inherited a larger cushion of pilots than anticipated. Attrition would eventually reduce this cushion, but there would be increased flexibility regarding pilot scheduling for the next few months.

On the other hand, American Airlines, which was experiencing relatively poor pilot relations at this time, had announced that pilot hours for the month were already known to be particularly tight. Nevertheless, American was expected not to cancel any flights during the early part of December and to try to operate its entire schedule as published.

Southern Airways, Inc.

Introduction

In July 1972 Frank Hulse, president and founder of Southern Airways, Inc. (SO), was meeting with his Board of Directors to decide whether to purchase thirteen used DC-9 jets from Delta Airlines. The decision involved weighing the importance of fulfilling the continuing need to upgrade service through frequency, competitive equipment, and nonstop flights against the precarious financial position, cash-generating ability, and rules of thumb on prudent rates of growth.

For the previous five years (1967-1971), SO had been in a loss position despite markedly increased revenues. Rapid capacity expansion, more sophisticated equipment, alterations in regulatory policies, obligations to serve new routes, and a decline in the rate of growth in demand had contributed to losses for SO and for the rest of the local service industry. The year 1972 appeared to be a turning point. SO began to plan for investment, which had been severely curtailed during the loss years. Building on its operating and management strengths, SO was determining niches of profitable market opportunities to exploit even as the smallest local service carrier. In addition, a creative finance group and persuasive president were placating banks and other creditors and promising future growth to those who would help them through the rough years (see Table 6-1).

Company History

Frank Hulse founded Southern Airways (SO) in 1944 when he applied to the CAB for extensive route authority throughout the Southeast. His involvement in aviation began long before that however:

As a boy I was fascinated with airplanes. Fortunately we lived two miles from the airport in Augusta. During high school I went to the airport everyday and became a handyman. Someone gave me my first flight in 1927 and I was hooked. I worked for flying lessons and received my private license in 1929 at the age of 17.

I left planes to go to college. Since there was no future in aviation I went to work for Coca-Cola when I graduated. Then the Depression hit so I went back to what I knew, the airport. We operated charter flights, student instruction, and

Table 6-1
Financial and Operating Data, 1957-1971
($000 unless stated otherwise)

	1957	1958	1959	1960	1961	1962	1963	1964	1965	1966	1967	1968	1969	1970	1971
Operating revenues															
Passenger	2,393	2,799	3,248	3,622	5,718	7,778	8,622	10,214	12,723	15,184	17,155	20,503	28,050	37,187	45,302
Mail, express, freight	2,253c	2,601c	2,816c	306	495	654	706	852	1,160	1,397	1,637	1,950	2,163	2,866	3,090
Public service revenue				3,068	4,395	5,352	5,893	5,107	5,199	4,541	4,255	4,038	3,580	4,823	6,974
Charter		37	47	10	80	204	277	403	508	519	564	1,934	3,358	3,835	4,067
Other		24	28	26	31	45	83	231	297	413	643	857	684	736	901
Total	4,646	5,461	6,138	7,032	10,718	14,033	15,582	16,835	19,888	22,054	24,256	29,300	37,836	49,447	60,334
Operating expenses															
Flying operations	1,375	1,504	1,851	2,198	2,913	3,772	4,418	4,633	5,385	6,117	7,050	9,118	12,659	18,072	20,950
Maintenance	861	967	1,197	1,498	2,067	2,961	3,333	3,315	4,037	4,493	5,217	5,121	6,111	9,045	10,808
Aircraft and traffic servicing	1,261	1,442	1,706	2,115	2,859	3,478	4,152	4,344	4,799	5,507	6,518	7,502	9,079	11,851	13,523
Passenger service	208	224	304	373	580	716	750	766	822	926	1,102	1,283	1,875	2,661	3,314
Promotion and sales	406	441	490	623	730	899	1,063	1,188	1,395	1,518	1,852	2,306	3,003	4,273	4,774
General and administrative	274	302	350	452	534	695	698	852	880	1,006	1,130	1,608	2,286	3,192	3,921
Depreciation and amortization	179	210	188	316	424	557	538	573	694	862	1,454	1,770	2,396	2,632	2,617
Total	4,547	5,090	6,085	7,576	10,108	13,078	14,953	15,671	18,012	20,428	24,324	28,707	37,409	51,227	59,927
Operating income	99	371	53	(544)	611	955	629	1,164	1,875	1,626	(68)	593	426	(1,780)	407
Other deductions (income)															
Interest on long-term debt	8	13	22	34	127	185	205	169	214	250	585	1,136	1,720	1,789	1,078
(Gain) on disposal of property	—	17	—	—	—	—	(37)	(100)	(27)	(37)	(11)	(90)	—	—	—
Tax effect[a] less applicable income taxes	60	192	10	(239)	304	482	138	425	803	595	(369)	(212)	(487)	—	(235)
Other[b]	2	2	1	(7)	(20)	(23)	57	105	(53)	(43)	(35)	(30)	16	(235)	22
Net income	33	147	22	(332)	200	310	266	566	938	860	(238)	(211)	(822)	(3,333)	(1,059)
Per share ($)	.12	.53	.08	(1.18)	.70	.96	.71	1.17	1.40	1.03	(.23)	(.21)	(.50)	(3.25)	(1.02)
Assets															
Current assets	970	1,336	1,530	1,965	3,612	3,601	3,359	5,184	7,089	7,535	7,048	15,754	12,308	12,380	14,336
Plant and equipment, gross	1,766	2,076	2,595	3,144	4,966	6,837	7,152	8,156	9,957	12,545	26,402	26,606	28,818	30,485	30,027
Plant and equipment, net (includes prepayments, deposits)	624	715	1,030	1,239	2,565	3,836	3,724	4,624	5,791	7,956	21,178	20,333	21,086	20,336	18,739
Other assets (including deferred charges)	53	75	95	164	324	268	223	70	88	5,360	1,028	1,824	2,171	1,968	1,490
Total	1,648	2,127	2,655	3,367	6,498	7,705	7,305	9,877	12,968	20,851	29,254	37,911	35,775	35,252	34,854
Liabilities															
Current liabilities	1,013	1,213	1,486	2,469	2,825	3,150	2,958	3,578	4,408	5,130	6,255	7,696	8,847	10,665	10,944

Long-term debt	18	–	195	21	1,450	1,988	1,493	2,833	4,280	5,743	13,468	12,228	9,903	9,408	8,535
Convertible subordinated debentures	–	–	–	189	1,300	1,000	1,000	–	–	5,000	4,682	12,682	12,682	12,682	12,682
Equity															
Common stock	757	793[d]	831[d]	859[d]	864	948	1,240	2,005	2,010	2,010	2,050	2,050	2,050	2,050	2,124
Preferred stock	–	–	–	–	–	–	–	–	–	–	–	–	–	–	421
Other paid-in capital	3	3	3	23	26	58	148	521	525	525	798	1,230	1,230	1,230	3,373
Retained earnings	(28)	118	140	(192)	6	316	402	941	1,745	2,444	2,001	1,790	969	(2,365)	(3,423)
Total Equity	732	914	974	689	896	1,323	1,790	3,466	4,280	4,979	4,849	5,070	4,248	915	2,493
Total liabilities	1,648	2,127	2,655	3,367	6,498	7,705	7,305	9,877	12,968	20,851	29,254	37,911	35,775	35,252	34,654
Common shares outstanding (000)	252	252	252	285	288	346	413	668	670	1,005	1,025	1,025	1,025	1,025	1,062
Authorized shares (000)	400	400	400	550	1,000	1,000	1,000	1,000	1,000	2,000	2,000	2,000	5,000	5,000	7,500
Traffic data (scheduled services)															
ASM ($000)	101,400	105,100	124,600	147,400	215,600	263,900	301,000	314,640	363,000	403,666	483,644	554,516	763,748	1,111,287	1,222,289
RPM ($000)	38,300	41,800	45,600	46,700	71,300	95,400	110,000	137,228	156,421	196,366	222,142	254,028	323,472	430,736	527,552
Load factor (%)	37.8	39.8	36.6	31.7	33.0	36.2	37.2	43.5	43.2	48.6	45.9	45.8	42.4	38.8	43.2
Passengers enplaned (000)	217	226	258	261	402	518	599	721	848	1,052	1,180	1,271	1,377	1,589	1,875
Average revenue per passenger ($)	11.03	12.38	12.59	13.88	14.22	15.02	14.39	13.90	14.69	14.39	14.49	16.08	20.33	23.36	24.11
Yield (cents)	6.2	6.7	7.1	7.8	8.0	8.2	7.8	7.4	8.1	7.7	7.7	8.1	8.7	8.6	8.6
Aircraft in fleet															
DC-3	13	15	19	23	26	25	22	16	14	9	0	0	0	0	0
Martin 404	0	0	0	0	5	8	14	20	24	25	23	16	14	13	13
DC-9	0	0	0	0	0	0	0	0	0	0	3	6	14	15	15
Number of employees at year's end	518	550	830	932	991		1,100	1,157	1,248	1,365	1,499	1,538	1,747	1,757	1,994
Plane miles flown (000)	3,901	4,076	4,809	5,669	8,213	9,172	9,581	9,865	10,661	11,287	11,803	12,260	14,679	18,580	20,003
Average length of hop (miles)	176.5	184.9	176.7	178.9	177.3	184.2	183.6	190.3	184.4	186.7	188.2	199.8	234.8	143.2	143.8
Average length of haul (miles)	176.5	184.9	176.7	178.9	177.3	184.2	183.6	190.3	184.4	186.7	188.2	199.8	234.8	271.0	281.3
Total cost per ASM (all services) (cents)	4.5	4.8	4.9	5.1	4.7	4.9	4.95	4.8	5.0	4.9	5.0	4.9	4.5	4.3	4.6
Average passenger load (number)	9.8	10.3	9.5	8.2	8.7	10.4	11.7	14.3	15.3	18.0	19.4	22.3	24.3	25.2	28.3
Route miles operated	2,023	2,620	3,108	5,248	5,544	6,045	5,537	6,190	6,202	6,741	6,745	6,741	8,061	8,061	6,741
Airports served	30	33	35	45	52	55	48	50	50	50	50	56	56	56	50

[a] Includes income tax, tax loss carry forward, and investment tax credit.

[b] Includes after-the-fact reduction of public service revenues based upon maximum ROIs as defined by the CAB.

[c] For these three years, mail, express, freight, and public service revenue are combined.

[d] Includes installment payments by employees for purchase of stock.

aircraft sales and service including airplane and engine overhaul. In 1936 the manager left, then the owner decided to get out of the business. I managed to borrow $6000 to buy him out and became president of Southern Airways, forerunner to Southern Airways, Inc.

In this business one had to be a jack-of-all-trades. For example, in Augusta I was the Delta contractor. An hour before the Delta flight would come in I would take off my coveralls, put on my Delta hat, meet the Delta passenger and put on the sack of mail.

The operation expanded to other airports and businesses. SO soon had fixed-base operations in Greenville, South Carolina, Birmingham, and Atlanta plus an air school offering civilian pilot training programs (CPTPs) in coordination with affiliated colleges.

I happened to be in the right place at the right time because the war clouds were gathering. The government needed pilots. In 1939 I became a contractor with the Army Air Corps to run CPTPs. By 1944 we had trained over 25,000 pilots and developed significant knowledge from operating some 400 planes, managing 500 employees, and becoming familiar with towns throughout the Southeast.

When the CAB announced it would conduct area cases for local commercial carriers, I was eager to apply for the Southeast. On January 7, 1944 the application was filed and we officially began Southern Airways, Inc., separate from the fixed base operations.

The first route authorization came three years later. The only thing lacking was money to put the first flight in the air. All the major banks turned their backs, but SO found a Birmingham brokerage firm that would float a stock issue.

We traded stock for engine parts, work, cheap office space, a variety of things. The offering circular stated we were to receive $255,000, but after noncash items and repaying some debt we struggled into operation with our first flight on June 1, 1949 with less than $100,000 in the bank.

Within ninety days service was instituted to the thirteen cities in which SO was certified. By the end of the first year of operation SO had carried 21,763 passengers over 3,665,215 passenger-miles. Financial concerns were far from over, however. It took ingenuity to pay the bills and keep the airline operating. One frequently cited example is about financing fuel. Hulse recalls:

We had about run out of money. Then someone hit on an idea. Why not give the pilots gasoline courtesy cards? Our pilots began fueling their DC-3s on automobile gas credit cards. We soon owed Standard Oil $50,000. A representative from aviation sales came to visit us and we worked out a deal where we agreed to pay him $1000 per week. I didn't tell him we were going to double our schedule the next day because he didn't ask.

DC-3 Era

The period 1949-1960 was a time of expansion for SO as well as for the rest of the industry. After initial start-up costs SO began to profitably expand its operations under the subsidy system in effect. Numerous new route awards from the CAB and improved consumer acceptance of air transport helped annual volume grow to 260,000 passengers flown over 45 million passenger-miles by 1959. To serve this demand SO's fleet of reconditioned government surplus DC-3s expanded to twenty-six by 1959. Growth occurred in spite of the uncertainty in subsidy rates and the amount of retroactive adjusted compensation the carrier would receive.

Capital was scarce. Nevertheless, Hulse was fastidious with maintenance and quality of the aircraft. SO maintained a perfect safety record. Aircraft improvements were in line with the uncertain levels of revenue and limited funds.

We redesigned our airplane paint scheme to provide for a white top, which makes the airplane cabin as much as 10 percent cooler in the summertime. We have also initiated a program of naming our airplanes for famous Confederate personalities. The company has received a most favorable public reaction to these programs.

In 1958, as part of Phase II, the CAB announced its intention to develop a new more predictable subsidy formula to go into effect on or as soon after 1 July 1959 as possible. Hulse saw in the program relief from the long periods of uncertain financial results experienced under the current system. The new method, named the Class Rate, went into effect on 1 June 1961. For the first time he felt the local service industry would be in a position to plan on a long-range basis and to exercise greater responsibility and managerial judgment.

In addition, through route realignment, SO was authorized to serve fifty-nine communities over 4830 route miles by the end of 1959, whereas less than one year before service was being provided to thirty-seven cities. In eight of these cities and 1249 route miles SO was replacing trunk service.

Hulse felt upgraded equipment and additional capacity would be needed both to cover new routes and to provide more schedules on the existing system. He estimated the fleet requirements at twenty-three DC-3s and five pressurized aircraft. It was estimated that $4 million in capital would be required to expand operations. Development of a financial program to meet that requirement wihtout selling additional common stock, was announced. Hulse bought five Martin 404s from Eastern to be delivered in 1961. In retrospect, Hulse commented:

We had to upgrade. It was a question of capacity. We had moved through DC-3s carrying 21, 24, and 26 passengers with baggage respectively. But in our part of the world an un-air-conditioned aircraft is a pretty uncomfortable critter in the summertime. The Martins were a must. More seats, more speed, more comfort. And they were more competitive.

Martin 404 Era

The year SO began changing over to the Martin 404s (1961) was the most successful in SO's history. Profits after tax were $204,349, or 70 cents a share. Seven new stations were opened, bringing the total to fifty-two serving sixty-one cities. By year's end, five Martins were operating. Hulse felt this investment had moved SO a quantum jump ahead in the industry. According to the 1961 annual report:

The acquisition of these fast, 40-passenger, pressurized, air-conditioned planes enabled Southern to upgrade its corporate image throughout the industry. The planes were christened "Southern aristocrats" and have been widely acclaimed by travelers.

Moreover, with the initiation in 1961 of the new rate policy, Hulse foresaw a continued favorable environment:

Under the new, long-awaited rate formula, the industry can enjoy record profits while, at the same time, providing better service for the traveling public. Advance planning, more efficient scheduling and utilization of equipment, and concentration of service where most needed are improvements which, among others, should result.

More expensive equipment and higher passenger volume made concentration on operating efficiency in flight operations and passenger processing mandatory. The profitability SO enjoyed by achieving these goals made it possible to add a few frills and to promote the new service.

Flight dispatch was expanded to twenty-four hours a day. All incoming Martins were equipped with the latest weather radar. Shop and hangar facilities were expanded. Twenty-five thousand hours of in-house training in Martin operations was provided. The high level of dedication continued so that by the end of 1963 SO ranked as one of the most efficient operators in the industry.

Once the fleet was flying smoothly, safely, and on time, attention turned to efforts that could fill the expanded capacity. The reservations system was modernized. Services were consolidated first regionally and then at a central reservations office in Atlanta. Low-cost improvements in aircraft appearance were made. The Martins' exteriors were painted "to dramatize the trim lines of the airplane." Interior design colors were chosen "to be comparable to those found in jet equipment—pastel."

Promotion was primarily a multimedia advertising program based on the slogan "We've got good connections." Consistent with the practice of the rest of the industry, SO offered discount fares to youth, military standbys, groups, weekend travelers, and families.

Transition

By late 1965 success was at hand. Record sales of $14.7 million and profits of $938,000 came from serving 866,648 passengers, 20 percent more than the previous year. The fleet stood at twenty-five Martins and fourteen DC-3s. The directors unanimously voted a three-for-two stock split and recommended a 20 percent increase in the common stock dividend, which had been paid for the first time the year before. In 1966 load factors were at an all-time high.

When the CAB announced it would embark on a program of route strengthening, SO began preparing route applications and contemplating required additional resources. Attention focused on the need for additional capacity. It had been evident for several years that the DC-3s were no longer competitive from either an operating or a marketing point of view. Moreover, the technology embodied in the Martins had been eclipsed by propjets almost immediately after the Martins had been purchased. All projections indicated continued market growth and thus further capacity constraints. Proposals were prepared and circulated with recommendations ranging from converting the Martins to propjets to replacing them with newer turbojet equipment. No answer came from the executive suite. Then, at a press conference on 24 August 1965 Hulse announced "Southern will enter the jet age with the purchase of three new DC-9s."

An order was placed with Douglas for three jets to be delivered in January, February, and March 1967. Options were taken on three additional planes. Total costs for three DC-9s and related spare parts were estimated at $11 million. Long-term bank loans of $8 million were arranged. Cash flow and cash on hand were expected to fund the difference.

Preparation for the jets began. A program for inventory management was instituted. Evaluations were made of needed parts, components, tooling, test equipment, and systemwide ground-handling equipment. Extensive employee training programs were begun for those who would be involved in day-to-day maintenance of the new aircraft. Data and accompanying instructions concerning DC-9 operations over the route system were prepared in house, an effort that smaller carriers usually purchased from the trunks. Facilities were modified, new tools and test equipment manufactured, and provision was made for administration of manufacturers' warranties. Flight personnel were trained for DC-9 qualifications.

Sales reported a record number of passengers boarded and longer lengths of haul. Promotional fares were expanded to fill otherwise empty seats. Modernization of the central reservations office was begun to provide for computerized connections with other airlines by mid-1967. A new corporate logotype, "ACCENT S," which would appear in all advertising and on each aircraft was announced.

Finance raised $5 million through the sale of 5.75 percent convertible subordinated debentures in 1966 "to provide a stronger financial base for future expansion," for which 312,500 shares were reserved. Other financing was arranged with banks and the equipment manufacturer for the purchase of the first three DC-9s and the exercise of the options. Plans were in the offing to sell the remaining DC-3s.

Route applications were filed requesting authority to provide service to markets suited for jet aircraft where SO felt it would have a competitive advantage. These included routes where SO would have exclusive authority and could develop a strong feed from other points currently on the system or offer direct service between cities superior to existing connecting service. Expansion routes included New York, Washington, Dallas-Ft. Worth, Chicago, Detroit, St. Louis, Louisville, Cincinnati, Greensboro-High Point-Winston-Salem, and Raleigh-Durham. In addition, requests to link Jacksonville with New Orleans operations and to provide a comprehensive pattern of local service for the state of Florida were filed.

Hulse's confidence in the future resounded throughout the industry. In the 1965 annual report, Hulse said:

Looking toward 1966 and beyond, we see continued opportunities for healthy growth and correspondingly good earnings. The impact of the jet airplane on the airline industry is evident in the strong position of most of the carriers, and it is certainly your management's intention to use this new tool to its fullest advantage. During the past five years your Company has doubled its size in terms of customers served and increased its earnings over four times. Your management will strive to better this record during the years ahead.

DC-9 Era

SO celebrated taking delivery of its first DC-9 on 10 June 1967 by setting a world speed and distance record from the Douglas plant in Long Beach, California, to Charleston, South Carolina, of four hours, thirteen minutes, and twelve seconds. The 75-seat DC-9-10 went into scheduled service on 15 June. By 1 August, three jets were in operation over eighteen cities and by year's end they were generating approximately one-third of total revenue. The remaining DC-3s were sold at a small profit. The fourth, fifth, and sixth jets arrived in 1968, financed by a twelve-year term lease. In spring of 1969 SO took delivery of three 95-seat DC-9-30s, two financed by twelve-year term leases and the third purchased from part of the proceeds of a 1968 debenture issue. During the remainder of the year the company entered into short-term lease agreements for six additional DC-9-10s all of which were to be in operation by 1 April 1970. It was expected that these would be replaced with larger DC-9-30s within a few years as traffic warranted and financing could be arranged.

With the introduction of jets and anticipated awards under route strengthening, SO felt it could implement a "by-pass Atlanta" strategy. By offering comparable service between cities on a direct-flight basis as an alternative to connecting to a trunk carrier in a congested airport such as Atlanta, SO reasoned it could capture a significant share of the market. This appeared to be a viable niche in the southeast market served by several trunk carriers.

SO was one of the last carriers to hear the results of the majority of its route filings. The first award came in mid-1968 and on 3 September service was inaugurated on the 1011-mile segment from Elgin AFB, Florida, to New York via Columbus, Georgia, and Washington's Dulles Airport. Compared to existing routes, this haul was so long that in December three daily round trips were generating nearly 25 percent of SO's revenue passenger-miles. Additional cities were authorized as summarized in Table 6-2. As an indication of the rate of expansion, during spring 1970 SO increased its available seat-miles over 75 percent within a 45-day period! Figures 6-1 and 6-2 show SO's network before and after expansion.

Hulse's pride in and outlook for SO's progress were expressed in his 26 March 1970 letter to the shareholders:

The year 1969 was perhaps the most significant year of progress in the history of our Company, in spite of disappointing financial results. During the period SO received major route awards which substantially expanded the area we serve, and which will enable us to participate in vastly stronger markets.

The CAB granted the Company authority to provide nonstop service in many long-haul markets. Some of these are Chicago-Memphis, Miami-Memphis,

Table 6-2

New Route Authority Granted by the CAB to Southern Airways Since 1967

Date Service Began	Newly Awarded Off-line Points	Service Provided from On-line Points
Sept. 1968	Washington, New York	Columbus, Ga.; Dothan, Ala.; and Eglin AFB, Fla.
July 1969	St. Louis	Memphis and points south and east on original system
Feb. 1970	Tallahassee, Orlando, and Miami	Memphis, Birmingham, and other points in Alabama, Florida, and Georgia
April 1970	Chicago	Memphis, and points south and east on original system

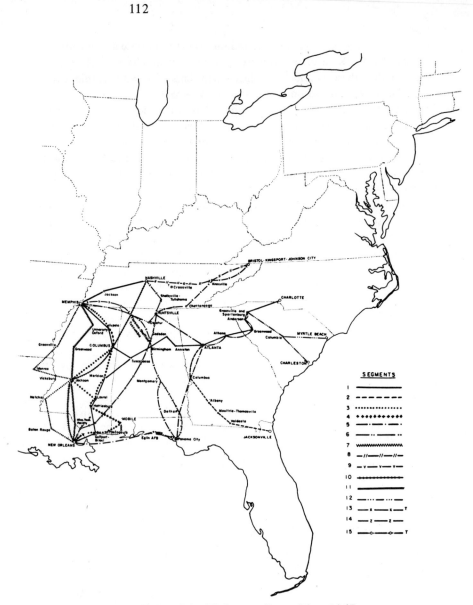

Figure 6-1. SO System Route Map, 1967

and Miami-Birmingham. Our present system now consists of 8061 unduplicated route miles, more than twice the route mileage at the beginning of 1968.

Aside from relatively minor start-up costs in connection with the inauguration of Chicago service on April 1st (1970), the major costs of expanding our system, training personnel, and obtaining new equipment were incurred in 1969 and the first quarter of 1970. Likewise, much of the developmental costs of new markets is behind us.

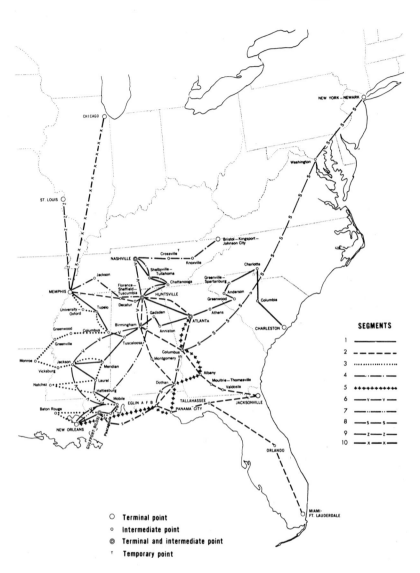

Figure 6-2. SO System Route Map, 1972

Then in May the bottom fell out of the market and SO lost $3.3 million, or $3.25 a share, by the end of the year. In the words of an SO spokesman, "the nation, and particularly the Southeast, entered into a long and severe recession." In addition, decreasing military activity, a vital component of traffic from some of SO's smaller cities, did not generate the volume of long-haul traffic expected.

Revenues increased 10, 21, and 29 percent in 1967, 1968, and 1969 respectively; however, this increase was insufficient to offset associated increases in operating costs of 19, 18, and 30 percent. In spite of successful efforts to reduce direct operating costs per seat-mile, in 1969 alone, expenditures for employee wages and benefits were up 21 percent, fuel was up 39 percent, depreciation and lease rentals were up 67 percent, and other operating expenses were up 32 percent over the previous year. Moreover, over the three-year period, expenses associated with the magnitude of investment were staggering by historic comparison. From 1966 till 1969 depreciation increased 18 percent and interest payments went up sevenfold (see Table 6-3). As a result, SO incurred losses from 1967 through 1971. Capital that had been intended for the acquisition of additional equipment to exploit the new authority and achieve full market potential was consumed.

During this period SO actively pursued programs to decrease costs and increase passenger revenues on available capacity. Sophisticated methods were implemented to support the jet fleet. Schedule reliability was increased by an automatic flight-control system and a low-visibility approach capability that were among the most advanced in the industry. A significant contribution to reduce costs came in 1968 when a system of continuous maintenance for the DC-9 was introduced. With computer support it became possible to schedule the jet fleet for overhaul and maintenance at night after the aircraft had returned from their last flights. This procedure minimized nonproductive ground time. Revolving the rotations of each jet made it possible to schedule a different one each night for the central maintenance facility. These and similar efforts made SO one of the industry leaders in maintenance cost and operating performance.

Concurrent with the introduction of new aircraft, management decided to introduce a new stewardess look in 1967. After considering prestige for the stewardesses and publicity benefit to the company, SO selected a world-renowned Paris designer, Pierre Balmain, to create a new look. A new theme, "Southern Style," emphasizing that "courteous, friendly, and efficient service is our product" was introduced in 1968 in the most extensive advertising program ever undertaken by SO.

SO faced a new promotion problem. They had to gain wide exposure in a short period of time in large metropolitan markets at a minimum overall

Table 6-3
Depreciation and Interest, 1966-1969

Year	Depreciation	Interest
1966	$ 861,826	$ 250,038
1967	1,454,350	584,621
1968	1,769,762	1,135,812
1969	2,395,905	1,719,541

expense. A saturation program of spot commercials in prime time on major networks was launched. Simultaneously, ads were to run in the *New York Times* featuring the themes "Skip the battle of Atlanta" and "Sherman went through Atlanta, but you don't have to" to emphasize the advantages of not having to connect in Atlanta. Soon resources would be channeled exclusively to TV, a departure from SO's former multimedia philosophy.

SO management found that over 70 percent of the passengers emplaned in Atlanta had initiated their trip at another airport and were in Atlanta only to change planes. Also, approximately 88 percent of the emplanements were on Eastern Airlines and Delta Airlines.

Reservations training programs were conducted to increase productivity related to length of time per call handled. Telephone lines linking New York and Washington, D.C., markets were answered with "a pleasant Southern accent." In-flight meal service received new attention. Longer flights, better serving facilities on jets, and competition required development of full meal service. A marketing analysis department was created "to survey present and potential markets to determine the best revenue opportunities for the company."

Studies were made to refine market identifications leading to more accurate passenger traffic forecasting and new tactics to capture that traffic. Factors limiting traffic growth were identified. New scheduling methodologies were considered. Looking forward to a time when profitability would be resumed and taking advantage of rigorous cost estimates and controls that produced results extremely close to budget, profitable rotations for additional aircraft were developed.

The effects of capital expansion, market growth, regulatory policy (both route awards and subsidy), and organizational response were expressed most clearly in financial actions and programs. Leasing arrangements were made for the last eleven of the twelve jets even though debt financing was available for at least two of them. In November 1968, $8 million, 6.5 percent convertible subordinated debentures were privately placed. Proceeds were used to purchase one DC-9-30, cover losses, add to working capital, and repay previous obligations. Additional shares were authorized both in 1968—3 million common—and in 1971—2.5 million common and 2 million preferred—on a base of 2 million shares.

In late 1969, arrangements were begun for a financing program "to provide for slackening in the economic climate served." The program involved raising equity and deferring certain payments due during 1971 and 1972. By 31 January 1971, SO had not made certain payments to lessors of aircraft and other creditors in anticipation of deferment. (The failure to pay constituted default under the long-term debt and lease agreements.) Ernst & Ernst's opinion in the 1970 annual report included the following note:

The Company's continuation as a going concern is dependent upon (1) its ability to develop future profitable operations, which contemplates receiving public service revenue based upon the new formula, (2) obtaining amendments to its agreements with creditor banks, lessors of aircraft, and suppliers providing for the deferral of approximately $3,200,000 of payments due in 1971 and 1972, and (3) obtaining proceeds of $2,500,000 from the sale of its equity securities.

Because of the materiality of the matters discussed in the preceding paragraphs and the uncertainty of their resolution, we are unable to and do not express an opinion for the years ended December 31, 1970 and December 31, 1969.

A clean opinion was granted in 1971.

Management maintained its belief in a profitable future for the company. Hulse commented in the 1970 annual report:

The growth enjoyed by Southern in 1970 was by no means universal in the industry. Indeed, I believe this growth—soundly based upon valuable long-haul route additions—points the way to a better future for your Company if the economy improves.

And again in 1971:

Expansion during the recent period of depressed airline traffic was expensive, but it has enabled Southern to build a strong base for future earnings.

Delta Offer

In May 1972, Delta Air Lines contacted Hulse with an offer to sell its entire fleet of thirteen 75-passenger DC-9-14 aircraft at $1.9 million each. A quick decision was necessary. Delta would grant SO sixty days to respond before opening the offer to others in the industry. The price was attractive because it offered Delta the opportunity to negotiate terms with and convert the aircraft to the needs of a single buyer. For SO this offer provided the opportunity to fulfill its marketing objectives, to catch up with its recent route awards, to become competitive in the marketplace, and to keep pace with market growth. These jets represented a quantum leap in both quality and quantity of service provided—a leap, some believed, upon which the viability of the airline depended.

No equipment additions had been made to SO's fleet since early 1970. Since then, due to improved equipment utilization, passenger-miles had increased 38 percent although available seat-miles had increased 15 percent. Table 6-4 lists the top 20 markets in which SO operated. By early 1972, economic recovery, higher load factors, and a revised subsidy formula had enabled SO to break even. SO forecast a 1972 profit of $1,327,000. Although it was a healthy comeback, recovery from five years of losses totaling $5.66 million and repayment of several refinancing agreements still had to be accomplished. Fleet additions were

Table 6-4
Top Twenty Markets in RPMs, 1972

Market[a]	SO Passengers 6 Months 1972	Total Market 6 Months 1972	SO Share	Competition	Nonstop Mileage
CHI-MEM	24,323	140,907	17.3%	Delta	486
ATL-HSV	65,538	65,538	100.0	None	151
ATL-VPS	36,566	36,566	100.0	None	250
ATL-GPT	19,918	19,919	100.0	None	352
ATL-PEN	28,050	28,050	100.0	None	247
MIA-TLH	17,917	33,853	52.9	Eastern	403
ATL-DHN	37,037	37,037	100.0	None	171
IAD-VPS	8,127	8,127	100.0	None	783
MEM-STL	24,679	78,333	31.5	Delta	256
ABY-ATL	41,734	41,734	100.0	None	146
CSG-LGA	6.777	15,787	42.9	DL, EA, Connex[b]	831
MCO-MIA	27,095	94,853	28.6	DL, EA, NA	196
CSG-IAD	7,833	10,267	76.3	DL, EA, Connex[b]	619
GPT-MEM	10,488	10,488	100.0	None	325
MEM-MOB	11,467	11,467	100.0	None	317
ATL-MOB	10,587	50,280	21.9	Eastern	302
HSV-MEM	19,871	19,871	100.0	None	185
BHM-MEM	16,947	20,127	84.2	Delta	211
MCO-TLH	15,005	15,005	100.0	None	225
ATL-MEI	12,652	18,883	67.7	Delta	267

[a]Airports are designated by three-letter codes. Appendix 6A identifies the airport codes in SO's system.
[b]Connex indicates competition offers connecting service over ATL.

under consideration; however, thirteen aircraft represented close to a 90 percent increase in the size of the jet fleet, a large chunk of capital to swallow under any circumstances.

Marketing favored the purchase. Marketing people argued that the only way SO could profitably serve its network was to expand its fleet to provide greater frequency, fewer stops, higher market visibility, and scheduling flexibility to enable collection of feeder traffic. Moreover, additional aircraft would allow them to institute superior service to existing routes served by competition. A proposal was prepared justifying at least thirteen additional jets; two for added frequency in current markets, two for normal growth and constraint relief, four to replace five Martin 404s, four to provide first available direct service between points as an alternative to connecting flights through hubs, and one as a maintenance spare. Excerpts from the study advocating purchase are presented below:

Efforts fall short of providing adequate jet service to all our potentially good markets. For example, in Orlando-Miami, our current five round trips daily are not adequate to meet the demand created by the enormous success of Walt Disney World. In other markets, we are forced to offer only multi-stop service.

There is no question remaining that there is a decided customer preference for fan-jet aircraft over *any* propeller-driven aircraft. In fact, propeller aircraft cannot compete successfully with the Interstate Highway System.

Additional opportunities are present in markets for which we have current operating authority but do not have the aircraft to provide the service.

Historically, traffic in our region has been controlled by a large trunk carrier whose strategy has been to consolidate all regional traffic in Atlanta and provide connections to other national cities. This has caused Atlanta to become one of the very busiest of U.S. airports even though approximately 70 percent of the traffic represents transient passengers. Atlanta is also now known for its "holding delays on arrivals and departures." This creates a ripe opportunity to offer "by-pass Atlanta" service throughout the region.

In particular, to fly from Florida cities Jacksonville (JAX), Miami (MIA), and Orlando (MCO) to Birmingham (BHM), Memphis (MEM), or Nashville (BNA) and from Jacksonville (JAX) to St. Louis (STL), a passenger had to change planes in Atlanta (ATL).[a] The size of these markets is shown in Table 6-5. SO participated in the ATL-MEM, BHM, and BNA legs only in a minor way, as shown in Table 6-6, usually when the passenger had booked through SO.

The market share SO could hope to capture was a function of the relative number of flights offered and their convenience. The CAB had developed a measure called the Quality of Service Index (QSI), which reflected these factors.

Table 6-5
Existing SO Markets,[a] 1972

	Round-trip Passengers/Year			
	Birmingham (BHM)	Memphis (MEM)	Nashville (BNA)	St. Louis (STL)
Jacksonville (JAX)	18,000	19,000	15,000	20,000
Orlando (MCO)	26,000	30,000	12,000	25,000
Miami (MIA)	35,000	55,000	32,000	N/A

[a]All current service connects over Atlanta with six nonstop flights between each city and Atlanta.

[a]Airports were designated by three-letter codes. Appendix 6A lists the codes for airports served by SO.

Table 6-6
SO Share of Existing Carriage, 1972

Routing	Segment Offered by SO	SO Share of Segment (%)	Annual SO Round-Trip Revenue from Segment
JAX-BHM via ATL	ATL-BHM	8	$34,775
JAX-BNA via ATL	ATL-BNA	12	55,440
JAX-MEM via ATL	ATL-MEM	5	38,000
MCO-BHM via ATL	ATL-BHM	8	50,230
MCO-BNA via ATL	ATL-BNA	12	44,350
MCO-MEM via ATL	ATL-MEM	4	48,000
MIA-BHM via ATL	ATL-BHM	5	42,260
MIA-BNA via ATL	ATL-BNA	8	78,850
MIA-MEM via ATL	ATL-MEM	3	66,000

A simplified version of this technique is calculated by assigning points to each flight based on the type of service: 1.0 for nonstop to destination; .5 for one-stop; .3 for two-stop or nonstop connecting with nonstop; .1 for three-stop. The sum of these points over a city-pair was the QSI. A carrier's service share was computed as the ratio of its QSI to the total QSI in the market. For example, 6 flights/day were offered from MCO-MEM connecting over ATL with nonstop service on each leg. If SO offered 1 flight/day nonstop MCO-MEM, its anticipated service share would be 36 percent (competition: 6 flights/day $\times$ .3 pt./flight = QSI of 1.8; SO - 1 flight/day $\times$ 1 pt. = QSI of 1. Service share = 1/2.8 = .36.) This method was usually reliable within a 10 to 15 percent tolerance. In addition, experience had shown that due to the creation of new gateways and more convenient travel patterns, the first direct nonstop service in a market had a stimulative effect of 10 percent, whereas the first direct one-stop service had a 5 percent stimulative effect.

Given the constraints imposed by its operating authority, SO identified seven possible bypass-Atlanta aircraft itineraries. Table 6-7 characterizes these itineraries and gives net per-passenger revenues for the associated segments. Competitors were offering six daily round trips connecting over ATL in the nine markets connecting JAX, MIA, and MCO with BHM, MEM, and BNA and in JAX-STL. Other than those nine markets associated with the proposed rotations, such as MIA-MCO, MEM-STL, and BHM-STL, were generally so large that a certain amount of traffic would accrue just because of a carrier's presence. SO expected to board an average of ten passengers per departure in these markets. However, two- and three-stop service from MIA and MCO to STL was deemed uncarriable due to superior available service.

Table 6-8 illustrates the QSI calculation for proposed Itinerary 1 in Table 6-7. The first step of the analysis is to break down the itinerary into component

Table 6-7
Proposed SO Itineraries

Proposed Itineraries	One-way Flight Time
1. MIA-MCO-BHM-BNA	2 hrs. 30 min.
2. MIA-MCO-MEM	2 hrs. 20 min.
3. MIA-BHM-MEM-STL	3 hrs. 12 min.
4. JAX-MEM-STL	2 hrs. 18 min.
5. JAX-BHM-MEM-STL	2 hrs. 32 min.
6. MIA-MEM	2 hrs.
7. MIA-MCO-BHM-MEM-STL	3 hrs. 27 min.

Net One-way Revenue[a]

	JAX	MIA	MCO	BHM	MEM	BNA	STL
JAX		N/A	N/A	42.50	57.50	N/A	67.50
MIA			29.15	62.50	74.15	70.80	86.65
MCO				50.80	63.30	60.00	75.00
BHM					30.80	27.50	45.80
MEM						N/A	34.15
BNA							N/A
STL							

Note: N/A: No fare filed. Nonviable segment under current authority.

[a]10 percent dilution fares (net tax) due to·discount fares, joint fares, and travel agent commissions.

origin-destination combinations. Next, the QSI for the existing service is calculated for each segment. The QSI for the proposed additional SO service is calculated and the resulting SO share of the total QSI is multiplied by the existing market and any adjustments from stimulation due to new service. The expected SO revenue is then calculated for the proposed itinerary. The diversion from existing SO flights serving segments of these trips (shown in Table 6-6) must be deducted. This operation gives a net increase in revenue expected from the new itinerary. Table 6-9 shows the results of a series of calculations of the type illustrated in Table 6-8.

Direct operating cost per hour was $800 based on nine and a half hours daily utilization. This amount included approximately 85 percent operating expenses except fixed overhead such as promotion, sales, and general and administrative expense, plus an allocation for ownership, which included depreciation and interest.

Table 6-8
Sample OSI and Revenue Calculation for Aircraft Itinerary 1

Market	QSI Current Service Level	QSI Proposed Service	SO Share of Market	Market Size Round Trip PAX/Year	SO Base PAX	Stimulation Factor	Total Round Trip PAX/Year	Revenue per PAX($)	Gross Revenue ($)
MIA-MCO	I[a]						7,300	$29.15	$212,795
MIC-BHM	1.8	.5	22%	35,000	7,700	5%	8,085	62.50	505,312
MIC-BNA	1.8	.3	14	32,000	4,571	0	4,571	70.80	323,627
MCO-BHM	1.8	1	36	26,000	9,286	10	10,214	50.80	518,871
BHM-BNA	1.8	.5	22	12,000	2,640	5	2,772	60.00	166,320
BHM-BNA	I[a]						7,300	27.50	200,750
Total									$1,927,675

Diversion from Current Segments

Market	SO Segment	SO Revenue
MIA-BHM	ATL-BHM	$42,260
MIA-BNA	ATL-BNA	78,850
MCO-BHM	ATL-BHM	50,230
MCO-BNA	ATL-BNA	44,350
Net Revenue		215,690
		$1,711,985

[a]I = incidental market producing 7300 PAX/year round trip.

Table 6-9
Estimated Results of Adding Proposed Itineraries

Proposed Itinerary	Net Revenue/Year	Direct Operating Cost/Year	Contribution/Year
1	$1,711,985	$1,460,000	$251,985
2	1,793,874	1,362,666	431,208
3	2,509,540	1,868,800	640,740
4	1,136,675	1,343,200	(206,525)
5	1,783,757	1,479,466	304,291
6	1,548,987	1,168,000	380,987
7	2,853,753	2,014,800	838,953

The finance department of SO estimated the total new capital required to acquire the Delta aircraft would be:

13 DC-9-10 aircraft modified to SO's configuration at $1.9 million each	$24,700,000
Spares and support equipment	4,429,000
Preoperating costs and working capital	5,871,000
Total requirement	$35,000,000

In addition, $7 million would be needed to repay outstanding bank loans.

There was indication that financing could be obtained. The purchase question before the board hinged on the financial and operational implications of an enormous capacity increase and the position expressed by marketing that SO's survival was dependent upon fleet expansion and that new equipment could be profitably used. As Hulse considered the past five years he wondered about the influence of managment on performance, the prudence of expansion, and how it might change the way SO was managed.

Appendix 6A
Airport Codes of Cities
Served by Southern

Code	City
ABY	Albany, Ga.
AHN	Athens, Ga.
ANB	Anniston, Ala.
ATL	Atlanta, Ga.
BHM	Birmingham, Ala.
BNA	Nashville, Tenn.
BTR	Baton Rouge, La.
CAE	Columbia, S.C.
CHA	Chattanooga, Tenn.
CHS	Charleston, S.C.
CLT	Charlotte, N.C.
CSG	Columbus, Ga.
DHN	Dothan, Ala.
GAD	Gadsden, Ala.
BLH	Greenville, Miss.
GWO	Greenwood, Miss.
GPT	Gulfport/Biloxi, Miss.
GSP	Greenville/Spartanburg, S.C.
GTR	Columbus/Starkville/ West Point, Miss.
HSV	Huntsville/Decatur, Ala.
IAD	Washington, D.C. (Dulles Intl. Airport)
JAN	Jackson/Vicksburg, Miss.
JAX	Jacksonville, Fla.
LGA	New York, N.Y. (LaGuardia Airport)
MCO	Orlando, Fla.

Code	City
MDW	Chicago, Ill. (Midway Airport)
MEI	Meridian, Miss.
MEM	Memphis, Tenn.
MGM	Montgomery, Ala.
MGR	Moultrie/Thomasville, Ga.
MIA	Miami, Fla.
MKL	Jackson, Tenn.
MLU	Monroe, La.
MOB	Mobile, Ala.
MSL	Muscle Shoals/Florence/ Sheffield/Tuscumbia, Ala.
MSY	New Orleans, La.
ORD	Chicago, Ill. (O'Hare Airport)
PFN	Panama City, Fla.
PIB	Laurel/Hattiesburg, Miss.
STL	St. Louis, Mo.
TCL	Tuscaloosa, Ala.
TLH	Tallahassee, Fla.
TRI	Bristol/Kingsport/ Johnson City, Tenn.
TUP	Tupelo, Miss.
TYS	Knoxville/Oak Ridge, Tenn.
UOX	University/Oxford, Miss.
BLD	Valdosta, Ga.
VPS	Eglin A.F.B./Ft. Walton Beach, Fla.

7

Federal Express Corporation (1)

Introduction

In November 1973, Federal Express Corporation (FEC) was attempting to raise over $50 million in long-term financing in order to continue operation of the small-package jet delivery service it had commenced seven months previously. Under the direction of its founder, Frederick W. Smith, Jr., a 29-year-old ex-Marine pilot, the company had engaged New Court Securities, a New York City merchant bank, to raise $26 million of privately placed equity financing. In addition, $26 million of long-term debt financing was sought.

Company History

Fred Smith traced the origin of Federal Express back to an academic assignment completed while he was a student of political science and economics at Yale. He had examined the air-freight industry and had concluded that many needs of the air shipper were not being served. Smith worked his way through college by flying aircraft and came from a family with close ties to the transportation industry. His father had founded Dixie Greyhound, a bus company later sold to the Greyhound Corp.; his grandfather had been a riverboat captain.

Fred Smith joined the Marines as an aviator. After flying more than 200 combat missions, he earned the Silver Star, Bronze Star, Navy Commendation Medal, Vietnamese Cross of Gallantry, Purple Heart, and Combat Action Medal. After his tour of duty with the Marines, he bought controlling interest of Arkansas Aviation Sales. He changed the nature of its business from a "fixed-base operator" servicing general aviation aircraft into buying and selling used jet aircraft. Under his direction, sales increased in two years from $1 million to $9 million and earnings increased from a loss of $40,000 to a profit of $250,000.

By 1971 Smith had formulated his plans for a small-package air service and incorporated Federal Express in Delaware. He commissioned two studies at a total cost of $150,000 to examine the market potential for his idea. The consultants selected were A.T. Kearney, a well-known and respected consulting group, and Advanced Aerospace Planning Group (AAPG), a company with which he had personal connections. Both studies were optimistic about the concept. Several members of the consulting teams jointed FEC as officers.

125

Upon receiving confirmation that his plans were feasible, Smith and his officers began searching for a small jet aircraft that could be adapted for use as a cargo aircraft. A prime consideration in selecting aircraft was the maximum loaded weight. In September 1972, the Civil Aeronautics Board had ruled that operators flying aircraft with a payload of 7500 lbs. could be classified as "air-taxi" operators. This designation allowed the operator to fly to any city in the United States without having to file for a certificate of public convenience and necessity. Larger transportation companies had to obtain such a certificate for each city-pair (i.e., route between two cities) they wanted to serve. To obtain the certificate, the applicant had to prove, over the objections of existing carriers, that there was a need for a new carrier. No new scheduled cargo carrier had received a certificate in over twenty years. Because FEC desired to provide a nationwide service, the exemption from this certificate eliminated the prohibitive cost, legal contests, and time that such a process involves.

The aircraft finally selected was the Dassault Fanjet Falcon, which was marketed in the United States by Pan American Airways as an executive jet.[1] Federal Express assisted in the funding and design of a prototype cargo version of this aircraft. The main alteration, the installation of a large cargo door, necessitated many other minor but intricate structural changes. Modification costs ran to $400,000 per aircraft. The Falcon had a speed of 520 mph and a range of 1400 to 2000 miles. Its payload, after the installation of a 74-inch door and a roller-bed floor, was 6000 lbs. and its capacity was 500 cu. ft. Addition of "single point refueling" meant that the aircraft could be refueled and loaded simultaneously. Due to the sizable order of thirty-three planes that Federal had placed, the price per aircraft was set at $1,297,345, some $350,000 less than the market price for a single plane.

Little Rock Airmotive, a company engaged in modification of aircraft, was purchased in January 1973 and, as a subsidiary of FEC, performed all the conversions of the Fanjet Falcons received from Dassault. FAA approval of the modification was received in 1972, as was the CAB certificate as an air-taxi operator.

Federal Express Concept

The central principle under which FEC operated was the use of a single "hub" facility, located in Memphis, Tennessee. Aircraft stationed throughout the United States left their base cities at night, loaded with parcels, and all flew into Memphis, with one or two stops along the way for some aircraft. At the Memphis facility packages were unloaded, sorted, and reloaded, whereupon the aircraft returned to their destinations. The service was offered five days per week. Friday afternoon shipments were delivered Monday morning.

The "single-hub" concept had many advantages. First, it allowed the maximum number of cities to be served with the minimum number of aircraft. Second, the fact that all sorting was done at one location allowed tight control and efficiency of ground handling and provided the basis for an effective tracing service. However, the fact that no aircraft could depart Memphis until the last inbound flight had arrived and its load sorted narrowed the margin for error.

The hub concept was used by many motor carriers and by United Parcel Service. The area served by the hub usually had a radius of approximately four hours of driving time. FEC applied the same principle, except its radius was four hours of flight time at an average speed in excess of 500 miles per hour. In this way, the whole of the contiguous forty-eight states of the United States was within the Memphis hub area.

Memphis was carefully chosen to be the hub facility. First, it was considered relatively close to the "center of gravity" of the United States with respect to package movements. Second, its record of only twenty-four hours per year of closure due to weather conditions made it a reliable base point. Finally, the Memphis airport authority was prepared to lease considerable space to Federal Express on favorable terms. A $2.9 million bond was issued by the authority for restoration of three large hangars and construction of a sort facility. The twenty-year lease issued to Federal required payment of 1.25 times the annual principal and interest on the bond. The sort facility, which was completed in March 1973, had facilities for docking thirty aircraft simultaneously.

The second principle of the Federal Express concept was that, from shipper's dock to consignee's door, the package was handled entirely by Federal Express. At each of the cities served, Federal leased vans, painted in Federal's purple, orange, and white colors, to perform pickup and delivery (Figure 7-1). This system enable Federal to offer a premium package service and to guarantee next-day delivery. In other words, Federal would undertake to deliver a package to· any of the cities it served by noon of the day following pickup. A reduced rate, second-day service was also offered. A third service offered was a "Courier Pak," by which the company would transport anything that could fit into a manila foolscap envelope for a flat fee of five dollars.

The third principle of the Federal Express concept was the limitation of parcels to 50 lbs. and under, with an additional dimensional limit of no more than 108" total for the three dimensions. By standardizing the product, FEC hoped to gain the same efficiency of operating procedures as United Parcel Service had gained from instituting a similar set of restrictions. Included in the A.T. Kearney feasibility study was a cost of operation estimate, shown in Table 7-1.

Competition

The domestic air-freight market had grown between 1961 and 1971 at a compound growth rate of 17 percent to reach a total of 3 billion ton-miles.

FEDERAL EXPRESS

The World's Only Small Package Airline

Figure 7-1. Example of Advertising

AAPG estimated that 300,000 tons fell into the category of priority air freight (shipments less than 100 lbs., picked up by 5:00 p.m. and delivered by 9:00 a.m. the following day). A.T. Kearney further estimated that in 1970 there had been 20.4 million air shipments of 50 lbs. or less and that an average shipment weighed 11.25 lbs. The latter report went on to establish that 37,000 manufacturing plants in the United States accounted for 86.4 percent of all air shipments.

Both of the consulting studies had independently discovered from field interviews and mail questionnaires that there was considerable dissatisfaction with existing services, and there was evidence of a strong degree of support for the type of system Federal was operating. Many organizations served the existing

Table 7-1
Operating Expenses for Package Service

Flying operations			
Aircraft			
Fixed[a]			8,367,000
Variable[b]			7,222,000
			15,589,000
Maintenance			247,000
Operations			2,249,000
			18,085,000
Cargo operation			
23 Terminal cities	@	36,720	844,560
87 on-route cities	@	17,930	1,559,910
1 Hub city	@	1,009,000	1,005,000
			3,409,470
General and administration			
Salaries			828,000
Systems			291,000
Advertising			300,000
Legal Fees			300,000
All Other			284,000
			2,003,000
Total			23,497,470

[a]Based on twenty-six aircraft.
[b]Based on 36,000 flying hours/yr.

small-package air market. First, the scheduled airlines carried all forms of freight, although their rate structures discouraged small shipments. Many of the trunk airlines did offer a small-package service, such as Delta's "Dash" system, but they provided no pickup and delivery service and were generally high priced ($20-$60 per shipment).

The air-freight forwarders, the single-fastest-growing segment in the air-cargo market, aimed particularly at small shipments that they consolidated and tendered to the airlines for line haul. The forwarders did perform pickup and delivery, but they tended to delay shipments in order to achieve consolidation economies. The forwarders also had to hand the shipment to the airlines and thus could not provide a full tracing service. For this reason, Federal felt that it had a competitive edge. However, one forwarder, Emery, had an excellent reputation for reliability and speed and in 1972 earned $8.3 million on $142 million of revenues. Federal also recognized that the airlines favored and encouraged the growth of the forwarders, who accounted for 40 percent of the air freight market, because, by providing pickup and delivery services, they complemented the service of the airlines. The forwarders had a large number of salesmen in the top markets.

A third group of competitors were the air taxis and commuter airlines flying small aircraft. In 1970 these lines had accounted for 21,000 tons of cargo, and the forwarders were increasingly relying on them. Unique among the air taxis was Priority Air Dispatch, which had put together a network of ninety operators to provide a service for high value and critical freight. However, Priority's rates ($700 for a 20 lb. shipment between New York and Chicago) were such that it addressed a very different market than that of Federal.

REA Air Express was the forerunner of air-cargo operations, having handled *all* air-cargo shipments prior to 1944. However, with the development of the airlines and freight forwarders, REA lost its dominant role, although it remained unique in that its shipments had prior claim on available aircraft space, second only to the U.S. mails. REA had a reputation for unreliability and suffered a continuous decline in market share, although it attracted some shippers simply because it did not delay shipments for consolidation and it would deliver to any point in the United States.

American Courier Corporation, a division of Purolator, which concentrated on very high-value priority shipments requiring guard service, experienced a dramatic growth of revenues (surface and air) in 1970 and 1971 of $48 million and $72 million, respectively. The company maintained sixteen aircraft, of which five were used to serve thirteen cities in the northeast on a regular basis.

A major competitor was United Parcel Service (UPS), which, apart from its ground operations, offered a "Blue Label" air package service. Of the more than 500 million shipments handled by UPS in 1970, some 8 million were air shipments. Thus, UPS was one of the dominant air-freight forwarders. It had a good reputation for reliability and promoted two-to-three-day service to the forty-one states that it served. Although this service was extremely competitive with respect to cost, some customers complained about a lack of tracing services. In addition, unless the customer subscribed to the ground UPS services, no pickup service was available, and the customer had to deliver the package to the UPS terminal.

One of Federal's largest rivals (in terms of volume) was the U.S. Postal Service, which derived approximately 16 percent of its revenues from parcels, although only a small portion of this was "air parcel post." The postal service reported 158 million ton-miles of air parcel post in 1970, with an average haul of 894 miles. The main users of this service were the mail-order houses, because the reputation of the Postal Service for speed was exceedingly low.

A comparison of Federal's rates and those of its competitors at the start of the small-package service is provided in Table 7-3. Market shares in the small-package industry are given in Table 7-4.

Table 7-2
Cities Served

ABQ	Albuquerque	MKC	Kansas City
ATL	Atlanta	LEX	Lexington
BAL	Baltimore/Washington, D.C.	LIT	Little Rock
BED	Boston	LAX	Los Angeles
BUF	Buffalo	SDF	Louisville
CAK	Canion/Akron	MEM	Memphis
ORD	Chicago	MIA	Miami
CVG	Cincinnati	MKE	Milwaukee
CLE	Cleveland	MSP	Minneapolis/St. Paul
CWH	Columbus	MLI	Moline
DAL	Dallas	BNA	Nashville
DAY	Dayton	MSY	New Orleans
DEN	Denver	LGA	New York City
DSM	Des Moines	EWR	Newark
YIP	Detroit	OAK	Oakland/San Francisco
GRR	Grand Rapids	OKC	Oklahoma City
GSO	Greensboro	PHL	Philadelphia
BDL	Hartford	PIT	Pittsburgh
HOU	Houston	ROC	Rochester
IND	Indianapolis	STL	St. Louis
JAX	Jacksonville	ICT	Wichita

City Selection

As seen above, most of FEC's competitors used the scheduled airlines for the line haul between cities. It was here that FEC felt it held the competitive advantage. Art Bass, senior vice president for planning, explained, "There is a wide gap between the needs of the shipper and the service offered by the airlines. Packages are slaves to when and where the carriers want to move people, which just happens not to be when and where most parcels have to be sent."

Fred Smith pointed out that with the introduction of wide-body aircraft such as the Boeing 747 and the McDonnell-Douglas DC-10, the airlines now had a great deal of "belly" capacity available for cargo on their passenger flights and thus the relative importance of cargo aircraft to the airlines would diminish. He stated:

Our consulting reports showed that over three-fourths of all the cargo moved in the U.S. has an origin or destination outside of the twenty-five top markets. Yet airlines schedule 25 percent of all their flights into four cities. Over 25 percent of the cities served by the airlines have only one or two flights per day. We

Table 7-3
Comparison of Representative Air-Transportation Rates for Small Packages,[a] 1 April 1973 Rates

Weight (pounds)	700 Miles					1800 Miles				
	1	5	10	25	50	1	5	10	25	50
Federal Express										
Overnight	$ 8.10	$10.50	$13.50	$22.50	$37.50	$ 8.50	$12.50	$17.50	$32.50	$57.50
Two-day	6.40	8.00	10.00	16.00	26.00	6.60	9.00	12.00	21.00	36.00
Courier Pak	5.00	–	–	–	–	5.00	–	–	–	–
Emery Air Freight	14.61	14.61	18.55	23.71	30.41	11.97	11.97	17.58	24.21	32.00
Airlines	17.75	17.75	17.75	17.75	17.75	20.85	20.85	20.85	20.85	20.85
REA Air Express	9.50	9.50	9.50	11.00	15.15	9.50	9.50	11.25	15.65	22.26
UPS (Blue Label)	1.54	2.44	3.64	7.30	13.30	1.69	3.25	5.20	11.05	20.80
American Courier (Sky Courier)	27.00	27.00	27.00	27.00	27.00	27.00	27.00	27.00	27.00	27.00
Express Mail (USPS)	25.00	25.00	25.00	28.00	32.00	25.00	25.00	25.00	28.00	32.00
Air Mail-Special Delivery	1.60	3.77	6.72	15.12	29.12	1.60	4.83	8.98	20.98	40.98
Air Parcel Post	1.00	3.02	5.82	14.22	28.22	1.00	4.08	8.08	20.08	40.98

Note: Not all competitive services are available between all city-pairs and certain services take up to seven days to effect delivery. The Federal Express overnight and two-day rates include $1.00 for the daily pick-up call based on a $5.00 per week subscription fee. Federal adjusted its rate schedule in May 1973. The overnight service rates for heavier packages closely approximated those of Emery Air Freight, the two-day service rates were patterned after UPS's Blue Label Service.

[a]Includes pickup and delivery charges where applicable.

therefore intend to aim our service at the neglected markets. We anticipate that we could get only 5 percent of the total small-shipment air freight through Chicago, but 30 percent in cities like Rochester, and maybe 50 percent in Des Moines.

A list of cities currently served by FEC is shown in Table 7-2.

Operations

Prior to commencement of the small-package business, Federal Express used nine aircraft that it had already converted in order to service seven air mail contracts and to perform charter work for customers such as Ford, NASA, GM, Emery, and IBM. It was planned, however, that both air mail and charter service would be phased out relatively quickly as small-package business increased. Other forms of revenue to the company came from the aircraft modification performed for outside customers by Little Rock Airmotive and from pilot training for the Dassault Fanjet Falcon in the VA-approved school set up in November 1972. For the fiscal year ending 3 June 1973 the following revenues were generated: charter operations, $1,361,000; air mail contracts, $2,981,000; aircraft services, $796,000; training, $1,519,000; and small parcels, $113,000. These revenues totaled $6,770,000, but unfortunately, operating expenses totaled $9,841,000 so operating losses were over $3 million.

In its first six to seven months the small-package service proved itself in the marketplace. As a new operation in April, with two aircraft serving twenty-three

Table 7-4
FEC Estimates of Market Shares of Competitors

	Projected 1974 Volume (millions of packages)	*Percent*
Priority (next-day) shipments under 50 lbs.		
REA Air Express	22.0	47
Forwarders	16.9	37
Airlines	7.2	16
Second-day shipments under 50 lbs.		
U.P.S.	750.0	80.8
Parcel Post	160.2	17.2
U.P.S. Blue Label	16.9	2.0

cities, FEC had a first-night volume of four packages. However, by October the average nightly volume rose to over 2500 packages, and nineteen aircraft served forty-two cities (see Tables 7-5 and 7-6).

Mike Fitzgerald, senior vice president for sales and customer service, reported that the company initially met some market resistance: "There was a 'show me' attitude prevalent. Traffic managers have had their fill of extravagant promises from carriers. But we stressed the totality of our system, which seemed to work, and in addition the traffic managers really seemed to be impressed with our Fanjet Falcon."

Some customer confusion had arisen over the use of Memphis as a hub city. Commented one customer, "A customer shipping from Boston to Albany is going to be very mad if a package gets fogged in at Memphis."

In general, however, customer reaction to Federal Express' service was very encouraging. The expected customer resistance to separating parcels of 50 lbs. and under from their other shipments had not proven to be too much of a problem.

The company did have to change its pricing policy. In the first month of operation, it was discovered that the rate structure was excessively biased to favor packages under 15 lbs. Although this structure, in part, was intended to discourage the harder-to-handle larger packages, the effect had been to deter them entirely. Overnight rates for heavier packages were made competitive with those of air freight forwarders; second-day rates were made competitive with UPS's Blue Label Service for all weight classes. FEC aimed to obtain a core of regular shippers by offering to call on the customer every day for a flat fee of five dollars per week. Nonsubscribers were required to pay one dollar per package for pickup.

Table 7-5
Monthly Package Volumes

	No. of Cities	No. of Days	Volume ($)	Package Volume/Month	Average No. of Subscribers[a]
May	28	20	N/A	9,453	N/A
June	28	24	166,000	16,517	N/A
July	33	19	194,000	17,304	214
August	34	20	299,000	28,388	284
September	34	24	640,000	48,316	367
October (est.)	42	20	693,000	50,330	429

[a]For $5 fee, Federal would call on subscribers every weekday. Nonsubscribers were required to pay $1 per package for pickup.

Table 7-6
Flight Schedule, October 1973

Scheduled Arrivals at Memphis		Scheduled Departures from Memphis	
6 p.m.-7 p.m.	1	3:00 a.m.-3:30 a.m.	5
7 p.m.-8 p.m.	0	3:30 a.m.-4:00 a.m.	7
8- 9	2	4:00 a.m.-4:30 a.m.	2
9-10	2	4:30 a.m.-5:00 a.m.	1
10-11	4	5:00 a.m.-5:30 a.m.	1
11-12	2	5:30 a.m.-6:00 a.m.	1
12-1 a.m.	3	6:00 a.m.-6:30 a.m.	2
1 a.m.-2 a.m.	9	6:30 a.m.-7:00 a.m.	0
Total	23	7:00 a.m.-7:30 a.m.	1
		7:30 a.m.-8:00 a.m.	1
		Total	21[a]

[a]Total not equal to 23 because two departures take place early in the night only to arrive back at Memphis after a short journey. In October, FEC had nineteen Fanjets dedicated to the small-package service.

Hub Operations

The ability of the company to sort packages at a single location was considered a key element by FEC in optimizing the capital and manpower resources employed in the small-packages system. As of November 1973, FEC had installed a $36,000 three-belt conveyor system in its 12,000 sq. ft. sort facility in Memphis. This unit had a capacity of five to seven thousand packages per hour. Approximately thirty-five men were employed in the facility as unloaders, sorters, and checkers, of whom twelve were full-time employees and the rest part-time, hired at $3 per hour for a minimum of four hours.

It had been arranged that early in 1974 two more conveyor belts would be added at a cost of $40,000. The capacity of the new system would be between 8000 and 12,000 packages per hour. Replacement of the belts with an automatic tilt-tray sorting system would take place when volume was sufficient to support such a system. The proposed $1.3 million system, which had a capacity of 11,000 to 22,000 packages per hour, would cut manpower requirements by 60 percent.

Because there was a little more than an hour between the arrival of the last plane and the departure of the first, efficient operations at the facility were essential. Fortunately, some aircraft arrived much earlier, allowing the bulk of the sorting to fall outside the critical one-hour period. The proposed schedule for the full 82-city system implied that thirty-three aircraft would be on the ground at Memphis at midnight each day (Figure 7-2). Note that this schedule would require many planes to make two round trips a day, compared to the October schedule of just over one trip per day per plane.

Staffing

Among the executives of the company were Roger J. Frock (age 37), general manager. Frock had been a principal of A.T. Kearney, one of the groups that had performed the feasibility study for FEC. Art Bass, former president of AAPG, the other consulting group, joined FEC as a senior vice president. Mike Basch (35) and Mike Fitzgerald (37), both of whom had executive experience at UPS, were also recruited to the management team. The organizational structure of the company was based around the particular talents and experience of each of these men. As may be seen in Figure 7-3, there were two major operational

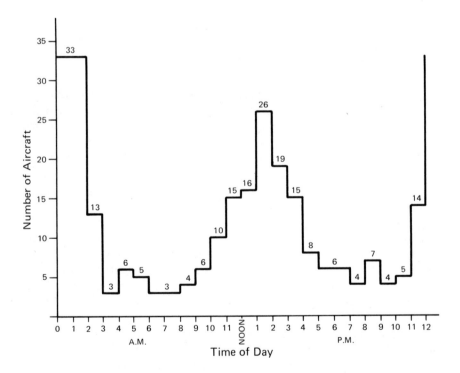

Figure 7-2. Proposed Eighty-Two-City Schedule: Net Aircraft at Memphis

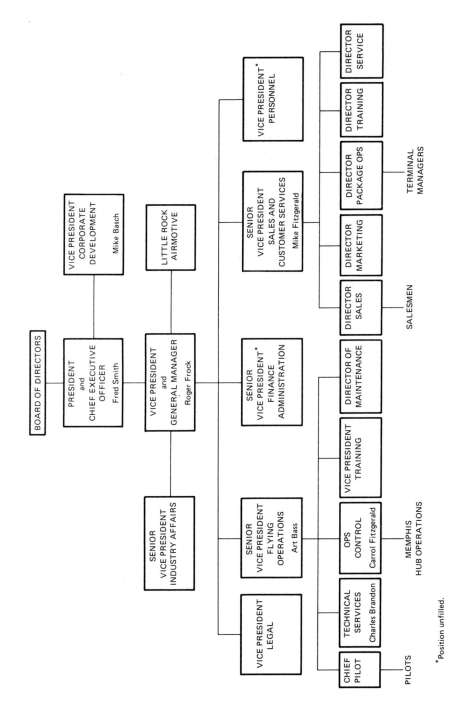

Figure 7-3. Organization, October 1973

*Position unfilled.

groups in the structure: Flying Operations (reporting to Art Bass) and Sales and Customer Service (reporting to Mike Fitzgerald).

Financing

In March of 1973, FEC attempted to raise $20 million in long-term financing by means of a private placement of $16 million in equity and $4 million in second-mortgage notes. The attempt at private placement was unsuccessful. A mass mailing of the prospectus to venture capitalists and many institutional lenders yielded some interested inquiries, but no financing. Among the best prospects that arose from the financing attempt was General Dynamics (GD), which, although hesitant to commit funds immediately, began an exhaustive analysis of Federal's business. Meanwhile, the FEC package service began in April. Federal's option on eighteen undelivered aircraft was due to expire in mid-May 1973. General Dynamics agreed to guarantee a bank loan that enabled Federal to purchase the aircraft. In return, GD negotiated an option to purchase an 80 percent share in Federal Express Corporation (FEC) for $16 million.

After fifteen GD analysts had completed their study of FEC, they recommended to GD's board that the option be exercised. Four times the recommendation was presented, and four times the board rejected it. By now, FEC was in effect bankrupt (Table 7-7). However, bankruptcy was *not* declared.

On 19 July the company approached a New York venture capitalist, New Court Securities, in a second attempt at financing. New Court Securities, a division of Rothschild's, was a merchant banking operation that handled intermediary functions and also managed massive amounts of capital. An arrangement was made for New Court to handle the placing of equity, while General Dynamics looked for placement of bank debt.

Of the $52 million to be raised in the placement, over $37 million was required to service and refinance existing debt committments, $7 million was to be used to complete the purchase and modification of aircraft, and $5 million was needed to increase working capital. The remainder was to be used to purchase engines, a training "simulator," and sundry other items. The pro forma change in capitalization that resulted from placement is shown in Table 7-8. Traffic forecasts are given in Table 7-9, together with a pro forma income statement in Table 7-10.

Notes

1. The average density of all air cargo shipped during 1972 was 8.5 lbs./cu. ft.

Table 7-7
Consolidated Balance Sheet, 3 June 1973

Current Assets		Current Liabilities	
Cash	$ 11,678	Notes payable to banks	$35,933,543
Receivables	1,405,800	Notes payable to stockholders	175,000
Other	2,084,155	Notes payable to vendors	1,015,193
		Current maturities of long-term debt	406,525
		Overdraft at bank	406,525
		Accounts payable	4,579,154
		Accrued interest	434,551
		Accrued income taxes	245,000
		Taxes (other)	464,275
		Other current	288,538
Total current assets	$ 3,501,633	Total current liabilities	$44,948,653
Net property and equip.	$51,085,208	Long-term debt	$11,532,810
Deferred charges and other	2,183,726	Common stock	4,750,000
		Acc. deficit	(4,460,896)
Total assets	$56,770,567	Total liabilities	$56,770,567

Table 7-8
FEC Capitalization, 1973

	Outstanding 9/30/73	To Be Outstanding After Securities Are Issued
Notes payable to banks	$36,033,543	$ 0
Notes payable to stockholder, vendor and others	1,847,386	0
Current maturities of long-term debt	1,986,360	1,574,880
Long-term debt		
Three-year note, secured by LRA[a] stock		2,286,395
Note, secured by aircraft	10,863,750	11,238,750
Monthly Installment Note	82,855	80,615
Subordinated notes due Oct. 1981		12,250,000
Subordinated note, payable in 24 quarters beginning Aug. 1975		2,250,000
Revolving loan agreements with banks		19,149,000
Total long-term debt	10,946,605	47,504,760
Capital stock		
Class A preferred		8,750,000
Class B preferred		3,500,000
Common	4,750	6,620
Additional paid-in capital	4,750,000	4,745,250
Total capital stock	4,754,750	17,001,870

[a]Little Rock Airmotive, a subsidiary of FEC.

Table 7-9
Small-package Revenue Projection Assumptions, 1974 Fiscal Year

	No. Calendar Weeks	Flight Hours			No. of Aircraft In Service	Airports Served	Small Packages (1000 lbs.)			
		Small Package	Other	Total			Quantity[a]	Estimated Weight[b]	Total Lift (Weight) Available[c]	Load Factor
June 1973	5	1,083	1,043	2,126	13	29	14,521	203.3	1,440.0	14.1%
July	4	862	783	1,645	14	34	17,336	242.7	1,254.7	19.3
Aug.	4	968	970	1,938	14	34	28,590	502.6	1,320.0	38.1
Sept.	5	1,198	955	2,153	14	35	47,645	667.0	1,584.0	42.1
Oct.	4	1,922	615	2,537	19	41	63,000	882.0	2,100.0	42.0
Nov.	4	2,816	630	3,446	19	41	110,545	1547.6	3,150.0	49.1
Dec.	5	4,134	870	5,004	20	41	200,273	2803.8	5,820.0	48.1
Jan. 1974	4	3,840	590	4,430	22	48	177,025	2478.4	4,992.6	49.6
Feb.	4	4,700	680	5,380	24	55	269,273	3755.8	6,180.7	60.8
Mar.	5	7,439	805	8,244	29	70	388,091	5433.3	10,060.6	54.0
April	4	6,593	787	7,380	32	79	328,700	4601.8	8,849.6	52.0
May	4	7,286	679	7,965	33	82	340,550	4767.7	9,730.0	49.0

[a]Assumed average revenue per package is $11.00.
[b]Assumed average weight per package is fourteen pounds.
[c]Assumed weight available per cycle is 6000 pounds.

Table 7-10

Actual and Projected Statement of Operations, 1974 Fiscal Year

($000)

	Actual						Projected						Total Year
	June	July	Aug.	Sept.	Oct.	Nov.	Dec.	Jan.	Feb.	Mar.	Apr.	May	
No. calendar weeks	5	4	4	5	4	4	5	4	4		5	4	
Revenues													
Sm. package	$166	$194	$299	$640	$693	$1216	$2,203	$2,142	$2,962	.6	$4,269	$3,746	$22,146
Postal	354	262	268	305	260	260	320	260	260	320	260	260	3,389
Charter	31	66	105	68	41	41	51	41	41	51	41	41	618
Training	209	155	196	180	210	210	110	150	180	200	215	225	2,240
Service center	3	34	99	9	115	125	75	100	100	125	125	125	1,035
Subscription charges					12	14	24	23	28	43	41	50	235
Insurance	2	4	6	10	5	9	13	16	27	38	34	37	201
Total	765	715	973	1,212	1,336	1,875	2,796	2,732	3,598	5,046	4,332	4,484	29,864
Operating Expenses													
Flt. operations	551	545	502	560	716	821	1,075	1,056	1,181	1,588	1,473	1,502	11,670
Training	84	77	63	59	78	86	57	70	79	80	82	80	905
Line maint. and eng.	196	266	321	324	295	370	390	383	401	429	462	481	4,318
Sales and cust. serv.	332	388	397	495	477	515	585	605	751	835	920	970	7,270
Marketing and traffic	26	15	21	20	77	105	95	85	75	65	55	55	694
Corp. development	11	11	11	9	17	16	19	22	22	22	22	22	204
Finance	23	27	31	29	37	41	46	48	57	68	64	67	538
Administrative	55	52	40	48	70	62	68	75	79	76	77	76	778
Data processing	22	23	39	38	47	54	57	60	64	65	66	68	603
Executive	25	22	12	12	25	24	24	25	25	27	25	23	269
Total oper. expenses	1,325	1,426	1,437	1,694	1,839	2,094	2,426	2,429	2,734	3,255	3,246	3,344	27,249
Oper. income (loss)	(560)	(711)	(464)	(482)	(503)	(219)	370	303	864	1,791	1,086	1,140	2,615
Other expenses (income)													
Interest	195	257	242	296	287	333	363	411	458	501	532	532	4,407
Other	(15)	172	28	(140)	64	63	62	121	60	59	59	58	591
Net income before taxes	(740)	(1,140)	(734)	(638)	(854)	(615)	(55)	(229)	346	1,231	495	550	(2,383)

Manning the Boeing B-737

Introduction

On 12 December 1967, the Federal Aviation Administration's western region announced that the Boeing B-737 short-range jet would be certified for a minimum flight crew of two. Despite this finding, the Air Line Pilots Association (ALPA) and the management of United Air Lines continued to negotiate the question of whether a third pilot was necessary in the new plane. It appeared quite possible that the pilots would strike the airline unless a satisfactory manning agreement were reached. It seemed that another "evaluation" program would be required, but there was no agreement between the parties as to how the tests should be conducted.

In addition, Boeing announced that there would be a delay in the delivery of the aircraft. Operations over United's routes could not begin until the second quarter of 1968 at the earliest.

United Air Lines was the nation's largest air carrier. In 1966, despite a 43-day strike against United, Trans World, Northwest, Eastern, and National by the International Association of Machinists, United netted $38.3 million on a gross of $857 million.

The carrier had been the last of the major trunks to order the short-range twin jets. In 1967, American Airlines was flying the British Aircraft BAC 1-11. Trans World Airlines and Eastern were operating Douglas DC-9s. Both the BAC 1-11s and DC-9s carried two-man crews. Table 8-1 shows operating and financial data for the BAC 1-11 and DC-9.

Boeing B-737

The B-737 was designed originally to carry fifty-five to sixty passengers, significantly fewer than the BAC 1-11 or DC-9. But in response to the requests of potential customers, Boeing substantially increased the plane's weight, size, and capacity between planning and production stages. As of late 1967, 189 737s had been ordered at an average cost of $3.5 million per plane. There were two basic models. The B-737-100 carried 101 passengers. The "stretched" 737-200 had a capacity of 117 persons. Table 8-2 contains descriptive information concerning the 737, two models of the DC-9, and the BAC 1-11.

143

Table 8-1

Selected Operating and Financial Data, (twelve months ending 30 June 1967)

	BAC 1-11		DC-9	
	AA	Braniff	Delta	TWA
Crew salaries (\$/block hrs.)	\$ 95.68	\$ 78.88	\$ 99.21	\$140.77
Total flying operations (\$/block hrs.)	\$187.26	\$158.70	\$199.03	\$236.46
Total maintenance (\$/block hrs.)	\$110.12	\$120.42	\$ 99.74	\$115.38
Depreciation and rentals (\$/block hrs.)	\$100.35	\$ 69.99	\$ 92.93	\$125.45
Total aircraft operating expenses[a] (\$/block hrs.)	\$397.73	\$346.11	\$391.70	\$477.29
Cost/revenue-mile	158.7 cents	120.7 cents	134.0 cents	170.8 cents
Cost/seat-mile	2.45 cents	1.92 cents	1.99 cents	2.44 cents
Utilization, block hours/day	7:17	9:38	9:55	8:08
Average speed, block hours (mph)	272	289	314	285
Revenue passenger-miles (millions)	960	533	651	368
Available seat-miles (millions)	1268	837	912	538
Average seats/mile	64.8	62.9	67.3	70.0
Average flight length (miles)	272	250	267	248
Passenger load factor	75.72%	63.59%	71.46%	68.43%

Source: *Air Transport World*, November 1967, pp. 48, 50. Reprinted with permission.

[a]Total aircraft operating expenses—also known as direct operating costs—include: flying operations (crew salaries; fuel, oil, and taxes; insurance; other), direct maintenance, burden, and depreciation and rentals.

United Orders the B-737

On 5 April 1965, United placed the first domestic order for the B-737. It chose the B-737-200 over the DC-9 primarily because of its compatibility with United's fleet of Boeing trijet B-727s. It was anticipated that the first three planes of the forty plane order would be delivered by December 1967, with the remainder placed into service during 1968. Additional B-737s (ten in November 1966 and twenty-five in July 1967) were ordered for 1968-1969 delivery.

At the time of the initial order, a trade journal reported that the expected B-737 direct operating cost per mile would be a dollar or less for ranges greater

Table 8-2
Descriptive Data, Selected Domestic Short-range Jet Aircraft, 1967

Aircraft	Passengers	Normal Gross Weight (lbs.)	Maximum Landing Weight (lbs.)	Maximum Speed (mph)
DC 9-10	90	77,700	74,000	559[a]
DC 9-30	115	98,000	93,000	565[a]
BAC 1-11-200	79	78,500	67,500	550
B-737-100	101	107,000	95,000	580+
B-737-200	117	107,000	97,000	580+

Source: Reprinted by permission of *Aviation Week & Space Technology.*

[a]Best cruising speed.

than 400 miles. But by February 1966 a Boeing official estimated that the stretched versions of the B-727 and B-737 would operate at approximately the same seat-mile costs. In 1967, the seat-mile costs of the B-727 varied from 1.3 cents to 2.1 cents depending on the individual airline. United's B-727s operated at a seat-mile cost of 1.7 cents.

Events in 1965 and 1966

In the fall of 1965, representatives from United's ALPA pilots and the FAA were briefed and shown a mockup of the B-737 cockpit design. The cockpit was not animated and had no lights, dials, or means of simulating emergencies. The FAA advised Boeing that it could not make a preliminary determination about certification, and the United pilots stated that they disapproved of the two-man-crew concept.

A year later, Boeing completed a simulated cockpit that could be used to test crew workloads. The United pilot group evaluated the new cockpit and concluded that the B-737 would have to carry a three-man crew.

In November 1966, at ALPA's Nineteenth Biennial Board of Directors meeting, a resolution was adopted requiring three pilots on the B-737 in all services. It was pointed out, however, the union's bylaws provided that exceptions to the three-man-crew rule could be made by a two-thirds vote of the directors.

Meanwhile, during October 1966, two events of major importance took place. Contract negotiations between ALPA and United began and the B-737 manning question became a major issue. Also, the FAA notified Boeing by letter that the B-737 cockpit was tentatively acceptable for two-man operation, barring changes that might occur as a result of the flight-test program.

Events in 1967

By April 1967, negotiations between ALPA and United had failed to reach an agreement on the crew consist question. United insisted that two men could safely operate the B-737. A mediation board was appointed, but it recessed 25 July without resolving the issue. A strike vote taken at United revealed that 92 percent of the pilots favored striking if the B-737 were not operated with three-man crews.

During the summer, ALPA made a proposal to the FAA's western region and the FAA administrator that three-man crews operate the B-737, the BAC 1-11, and the DC-9. The union's proposal stated: "The FAA by establishing a requirement for a three-man crew for airline jet transport operations could insure that no carrier would have economic incentive to provide service with less than the highest possible degree of safety in the public interest." Later, following instructions from its membership, the union informed the FAA that it was seeking three crew members only on the B-737, although it appeared likely that if the B-737 were operated with three men, ALPA would reopen the questions of BAC 1-11 and DC-9 manning. A key FAA official commented, "We'll have to go back and take a hard look at both the nine and the one-eleven if it is determined that the B-737 needs a three-man crew."

In September, the Air Transport Association of America and the Aerospace Industries Association filed a report with the FAA that supported the two-man crew position. The union then responded with a letter to the FAA Administrator rebutting each of the AIA-ATA arguments point by point. Some of the issues in dispute included:

1. What happens if a pilot is incapacitated? Will there be overburdening responsibilities on the other pilot?
2. If there is an unruly person in the cabin, would an extra crewman be necessary?
3. Should there be a "third set of eyes" to decrease the possibility of midair collisions?
4. In view of the increased FAA and company radio traffic, one crewman is essentially a radio operator most of the time. Should there, therefore, be an additional pilot on board?

During the Thanksgiving holiday week in 1967, the FAA conducted flight tests of the B-737 in the Boston-Washington corridor using a two-man crew (one FAA and one Boeing). Two daily round trips were made on each of six days. The forty hours of flight time included day and night flights, IFR and VFR weather, below minimum conditions requiring diversion to an alternate airport, and simulations of instrument failures and crew incapacitation.

Excerpts from the Report

The FAA's statement, issued 12 December 1967, contained the following:

The far reaching evaluation of the Boeing B-737 was started in September, 1965, with an evaluation of the cockpit mockup. Continuous evaluations over the past two years included regular operations of the aircraft in a high-density air traffic environment to determine workload, complexity, and safety of operations on a fail-safe concept.... These flights were a part of the very extensive flight testing program accomplished by the FAA and Boeing personnel.... The technical findings coming out of these evaluations are that the aircraft can be safely flown with a minimum of two pilots.

ALPA's Reaction

ALPA officials challenged both the methodology and conclusions of the FAA tests. The union charged that the FAA had "failed to utilize up-to-date, state-of-the-art methods and techniques for accomplishing a valid study of crew workloads." It criticized the Agency for failing to consult the FAA's own aeromedical experts "for advice in setting up a study upon which the decision was based." The union said that it had "sought advice and assistance from independent authorities who are eminently qualified on this subject. These authorities concluded that a valid safety question would be raised by operating the B-737 with a crew of two." The authorities included two members of the University of Southern California's Institute of Aerospace Safety and Management.

The union called for an "objective evaluation" including a "realistic sampling of day-to-day operation in an airline environment." Until the evaluation was completed, "the only safe course of action to protect the public interest is to require a crew of three."

Problems at Other Airlines

Western

Negotiations on a new pilot contract became stalled on other issues. The carrier hoped to receive its first B-737 in mid-1968. It stated that it was relying on the FAA's decision and saw no need for another evaluation program.

Piedmont

The company was to receive its first B-737 in May and was negotiating with its pilots. It was determined to fly with two-man crews. A company official stated,

"If it was not for the B-737 issue, there is no question the contract would have been settled by now. . . . I don't see what (an evaluation program) would accomplish." It was willing to increase crew compensation in exchange for two-man crews if another carrier set a pattern.

Frontier

The president of Frontier felt that a three-man crew was a safety hazard. He criticized any evaluation program because "I don't see why we should introduce an unsafe operation for the sake of compromising a labor problem." He was particularly concerned over the negotiations at United: "If United caves in—and it would be disturbing to me if it does—it will be due to the iron might of the union. It could spread to other carriers, but I'm hopeful our boys will see the light."

Pacific Southwest

The California intrastate carrier planned to fly its 737s with two-man crews. Its pilots were not ALPA members.

Australia's Domestic Carriers

During this same period, two of Australia's domestic carriers, Ansett-A.N.A. and Trans-Australia Airline, were in the midst of a dispute with the pilots on the manning of the DC-9-30. An evaluation program using two- and three-man crews had been conducted, but the results were in dispute. (The third man was a flight engineer, not a pilot.) The FAA had sent a representative to Australia and claimed that the evaluation program was still in progress as of the end of 1967. ALPA sources countered that the Australian tests had been completed with the majority of the evaluation group favoring three-man crews.

Negotiating the Evaluation Program

On 16 January 1968, negotiations resumed between United and ALPA with the help of the National Mediation Board. The primary objective was to reach agreement on the ground rules for another evaluation of the 737, one that ultimately might lead to a settlement. The questions raised included the following:

1. *Scope*: ALPA said that any meaningful evaluation of the crew-complement issue must be interdisciplinary, including medicine, aviation psychology, and human factors.
2. *Arbitration*: United favored arbitration if the parties could not agree on the results of the evaluation program. The union resisted arbitration, but proposed that if all other tie breaking machinery failed, a single neutral party would determine "what procedure shall be utilized for the purpose of finally resolving and settling the dispute. . . . This neutral could make a decision to require arbitration."
3. *Duration of the evaluation*: United wanted a ninety-day in-service trial period. The union wanted a much longer period.
4. *Manning during the evaluation*: The union insisted that three-man crews be used, although the third man could be inactive at the discretion of the captain during the evaluation.
5. *Duties of the third man*: Inasmuch as his position would be in a jump seat behind the captain in a cockpit designed for two men, the functions of the third crew member were unclear.

On 18 January 1968, the company withdrew its evaluation proposal and ended negotiations. If the parties rejected arbitration (the next step under the Railway Labor Act), the union would be free to strike in early March. The union did not take any immediate action to set a strike date. But a union spokesman remarked:

It would now appear that the company did not expect the pilots to meet their demands for a final, legal, and binding resolution at the end of the evaluation program. It appears the thirty-eight total days of conferences spent discussing an evaluation program since October were a waste of time, money and considerable effort. The only conclusion that can be reached is that the company was looking for the first opportunity to ditch the evaluation program.

A United official told a member of the press, "We fully anticipate a resumption of discussions."

CP Air Passenger Reservations

Introduction

During the late 1960s CP Air, one of Canada's two transcontinental air carriers, (the other being the government-owned Air Canada), was considering the introduction of an electronic processing system to replace its manual passenger reservations system. In 1970, CP Air (CPA) had commissioned a consulting firm to appraise the type of system to be adopted and to recommend the timing of the introduction of a computer-based system. The consultant had recommended that, based on CPA's passenger traffic projections, a "stand-alone" system could not be justified before 1976. However, in 1972, CPA's director of customer service development believed that such a system might be needed before that date, but had been unable to present a sufficiently convincing case to top management to cause them to act contrary to the consultant's recommendations.

Company History

CPA (formerly Canadian Pacific Airlines) was officially formed in 1942 when ten small independent air services were amalgamated. By 1944 the airline operated routes in the British Columbia/Yukon Region, across the Prairies and Northern Ontario and along the St. Lawrence Valley. However, CP Air (CPA) was not content to be a feeder to the government-owned Trans-Canada Airlines (which became Air Canada) and in 1944 applied for a new route in Southern Ontario which would have created a connected, if not direct, transcontinental service. The Canadian Government denied this application to protect the public airline, TCA.[1]

By 1949 CPA was entering the international market with the addition of the Orient/South Pacific route which Trans-Canada Airlines rejected. Then in 1955 the Amsterdam and Mexico/South America routes were added. The Mexico route was obtained from Trans-Canada in exchange for the St. Lawrence Valley routes.

In 1958 CPA requested, and finally received, the right to operate a single, daily transcontinental flight between Vancouver, Winnipeg, Toronto, and Montreal. Nine years later, CPA was allowed to further expand this transcontinental service with the restriction that CPA capacity on this route was less than 25 percent of Air Canada's capacity on the route.

In recent years the Trans-pacific routes had been the most profitable while the European and South American routes returned only marginal profits. Domestically, the transcontinental routes provided modest profits while the Western Canadian regional routes provided satisfactory rates of return but only small absolute dollar returns. (The average two-way revenues per passenger were $180 on trans-continental service, $100 on B. C. regional service, $135 on trans-border service and $280 on international service. All these figures are approximations.)

The satisfactory return from the Pacific trade was due mainly to a higher per-mile fare than on other routes. CPA had benefited from the general increase in Pacific Rim trade, and hence, air travel. The Vancouver-Hawaii route had attracted large increases in traffic in recent years.

By 1972 CPA's route pattern radiated from Vancouver, Canada in the form of a giant X, linking five continents and all major cities in Canada. Within this route pattern lay 7,700 domestic miles (including 3,976 route miles on the trans-continental service). The international routes linked North, Central, and South America with Europe, Japan, and Australia. An abbreviated route map is given in Figure 9-1.

Within the domestic market CPA's growth rate had been limited in several markets. First, on the transcontinental routes (which accounted for 35 percent of company revenues) CPA was limited to 25 percent of Air Canada's capacity. Also, the Canadian Transport Commission had required that CPA originate and terminate all transcontinental flights from Vancouver in Montreal. Second, the regional service in Western Canada (which accounted for 10 percent of revenues) was limited by the fairly small populations of many of the communities served by that service. CPA's competition on this service came mainly from a regional carrier (Pacific Western Airlines).

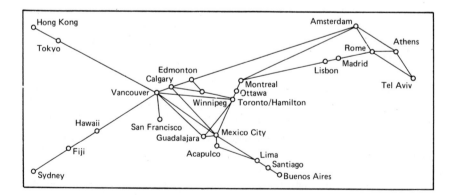

Figure 9-1. CPAIR Route Map

The airlines growth on the Canadian/United States trans-border service (5 percent of revenues) was limited by several factors including the designation of Air Canada as the Canadian flag carrier, the size of the market, and the amount of competition from competing air lines (mostly American).

Finally, in its international services, (50 percent of revenues) CPA was constrained by a large number of competing air carriers. CPA faced competition both directly from air carriers which served the same route and indirectly from carriers which served locations within close proximity of CPA destinations.

The 5,400 employees of CPA were part of the larger Canadian Pacific Limited which was a widely diversified transportation and natural resource development company. In 1972 Canadian Pacific Limited operated 16,600 miles of railway line in Canada and controlled another 4,621 in the United States. It operated modern containerships on the North Atlantic and an expanding fleet of tankers and bulk cargo vessels on the oceans of the world. Canadian Pacific Limited also operated a trucking company, a telecommunications firm, and a consulting firm. Through Canadian Pacific Investments, the company was involved in resource-oriented industries such as oil and gas, coal, and other mining operations, the recycling and disposal of waste products, real estate, forest products, and steel manufacturing. Balance sheet information for CPA is given in Table 9-1, operating statement data in Table 9-2, and selected operating statistics in Table 9-3.

Airline Reservations Systems

During the 1960s the air transportation industry had given considerable attention to the development of passenger reservation systems. The use of computers to maintain space availability records and passenger name records was becoming common among trunk carriers in the United States.

Reservations systems were tailored to the anticipated volume of traffic of the particular carrier (or carriers) involved. A carrier handling 10,000 passengers per month usually found it more efficient and economical to manually process reservations. Carriers with 500,000 passengers per year found a relatively nonsophisticated seat inventory reporting system adequate. However, for carriers with 1.5 million passengers a year, a computerized reservation processing system provided benefits (speedily accessible passenger records indexed by name, accurate and easily confirmed flight availability records) that could not be overlooked. Smaller carriers often found it advantageous to participate with other carriers having computerized reservations systems through time-sharing or similar arrangements.

Many airlines have off-line computer installations which handle functions such as general accounting, cost and budget problems, and flight and market data. However, computer reservations systems are designed to be on-line for 24

Table 9-1

CP AIR Balance Sheet, December 31, 1969-1971

(In 1,000 Canadian Dollars)

	1969	1970	1971
Assets			
Cash	$ 2,029	$ 1,767	$ 4,490
Deposits	–	13,887	19,718
Accounts Receivable	11,804	14,025	13,387
Material & Supplies	4,574	6,450	6,087
Prepaid Expenses	592	629	695
Total Current Assets	18,999	36,759	44,377
Dep. Aircraft Assets	4,110	–	–
Sundry Investment	1,032	788	–
Property Net of Depreciation[a]	132,207	139,091	141,602
Deferred Charges[b]	–	–	720
Total Assets	156,348	176,638	186,699
Liabilities			
Accounts Payable	25,767	22,342	23,987
Accounts Payable to Affiliates	3,630	878	100
Demand Loan	6,500	18,000	18,000
Unearned Transportation Revenue	7,007	6,941	8,719
Long Term Debt Due	8,593	9,488	12,412
Total Current Liab.	51,497	57,649	62,948
Long Term Debt	69,988	76,209	78,614
Defer. Inc. Taxes	8,513	9,610	11,710
Preferred Shares ($5)[c]	9,750	10,000	10,000
Ordinary Shares[c]	13,000	20,000	20,000
Retain Income	3,600	3,170	3,877
Total Liabilities	156,348	176,638	186,699
Depreciation[a]	43,912	58,844	73,498

[a]Depreciation
[b]Severence Pay
[c]2,000,000 Preferred Shares;
4,000,000 Ordinary Shares

hours a day, 7 days a week. Future computer systems of this kind are projected to handle fare quotations, personnel records, cargo computerization and auto-mated check-in.

Prior to automated reservation systems, processing of a reservation trans-action, with its complex behind-the-scene filing procedures, could require as much as 45 minutes. Computerizing this operation reduced the average time to perform the same task to approximately three seconds.

Computerized reservation systems for air carriers had been developed to a sophisticated level, utilizing specially designed computer processing equipment,

Table 9-2
CP AIR Operating Statement, 1967-1971

(In Canadian $1,000)

	1967	1968[a] (1)	1969	1970	1971
Operating Revenues	$	$	$	$	$
Passenger	79,649	89,055	107,314	121,560	129,418
Cargo	7,097	9,302	10,804	10,490	11,789
Mail	6,418	6,514	7,360	7,720	8,196
Charter	555	267	6,102	6,596	5,792
Other	1,505	1,560	2,137	2,767	3,020
Total Operating Revenue	95,224	106,698	133,717	149,583	157,945
Operating Expenses					
Flying Operations	32,586	26,551	31,170	34,919	36,709
Maintenance	12,357	12,629	14,398	18,954	16,684
Passenger Service	9,428	11,006	15,143	17,802	17,923
Fleet, etc. Service	10,582	12,787	15,639	18,669	20,726
Sale Promotion	19,755	21,961	26,153	28,517	30,328
General & Administrative	4,140	5,038	7,249	8,885	9,578
Depreciation	1,940	8,799	12,288	15,286	16,649
Development	55	–	–	–	–
Total Operating Expense	91,113	98,771	122,040	143,032	148,597
Net Operating Income	4,111	7,927	11,677	6,551	9,348
Investment Income	1,428	782	483	1,911	1,607
Interest on Debt	–	dr 3,829	dr 5,413	dr 6,398	dr 6,715
Gain from Assets Sold	–	24	438	–	–
Total	5,539	4,904	7,185	2,064	4,240
Income Tax Prov.	2,330	2,529	3,690	1,061	2,100
Net Income	3,209	2,375	3,495	1,003	2,140
Retained Income Balance, Jan. 1	1,430	747	1,538	3,600	3,170
Gain from Assets Sold	185	–	–	–	–
Total	4,825	3,122	5,033	4,603	5,310
Preferred Dividends	4,078	1,584	487	500	500
Ordinary Dividends	–	–	946	933	933
Retained Income Balance, December 31	747	1,538	3,600	3,170	3,877

[a]Restated to conform with presentation adopted for 1969.

cathode ray tube agent terminals, high-speed communications links, and software programs to provide fast and accurate service to the passenger. Computerized systems fall into two broad classifications: the seat inventory availability systems; and the passenger name record (PNR) seat inventory availability system.

Table 9-3
Selected Operating Statistics (Scheduled Services Only), 1967-1971

		1967	1968	1969	1970	1971
Revenue Passengers Carried	(000)	886	1,036	1,277	1,437	1,520
Revenue Passenger Miles	(million)	1,492	1,652	1,985	2,369	2,410
Available Seat Miles	(million)	2,636	3,279	3,952	4,520	4,414
Passenger Load Factor		56.6	50.4	50.2	52.4	54.6
Yield Per RPM		n/a	n/a	5.41	5.13	5.36
Revenue Ton Miles	(million)	183	210	274	313	323
Available Ton Miles		383	472	581	659	635
Personnel		n/a	n/a	5,012	5,510	5,364

Seat Inventory Availability Systems

Developed in the late 1950s, seat inventory availability systems operated in real-time, usually with hard-copy typewriters and special input/output devices to maintain and update file data. All necessary information other than passenger name data was transmitted to the central computer where accuracy of input was checked, seat inventory files adjusted, and reservations confirmed. Typically, information was not indexed by the passenger's name.

During the 1960s, an inventory space-availability system had successfully handled reservations operations for United Air Lines and Trans World Airlines. For air carriers not requiring passenger name information on a real-time basis, this type of system would continue to be adequate. Because fewer items of information were transmitted to the central processor, computers of lower capacity than required for a PNR system could be used.

Passenger Name Record Systems

A logical progression from space availability system to PNR systems began when American Airlines first introduced this concept in its SABRE system (1962). A PNR system included all of the capabilities of a seat reservation availability system plus the ability to add passenger information to the reservation file. The advantages of a PNR system were directly related to improved passenger services (for example, faster schedule information and faster reservation confirmations). Most important, a positive check of a passenger's itinerary by name was possible. Errors and omissions were more easily detected, and preparation of flight manifests and no-show lists was facilitated. Functions such as limited-fare quotation, seat selection/assignments, and automated ticketing could also be included in some software packages.

The most popular systems in the late 1960s were IBM's Programmed Airline Reservation System (PARS) and a revised version for international airlines called IPARS. The PARS program package was developed as a real-time reservation system which would provide instant access to all passenger records for an entire airline. The application programs were concerned primarily with passenger reservation operations. The principal reservation functions performed were:

1. Maintenance and display of flight schedules and availability—Sales agents could obtain quick access to the current availability and status of any flight on their airline plus selected flights of other airlines.
2. Recording of passenger and itinerary.
3. Maintenance of Passenger Name Record—this information included the passenger name, telephone number, ticketing information and other information as directed by the airline.
4. Reconfirmation, changing or cancellation of passenger records—system provided quick access to all passenger records.
5. Teletype message handling—required for access to/from those locations on an airlines system where no direct computer links were provided.
6. Auxiliary functions such as meal and beverage orders—the system provided passenger counts by class of service, which was used to notify the caterer of the number of beverages or meals to be loaded on the flight.

CP Air Manual Reservation System

Two principal groups were responsible for the CPA manual system in effect in 1971. These groups were the Sales and Service Section and the Payload Control Section. However, many other groups were involved, including Communications, Dispatch (Operations), Administration, the City and Airport Ticket Offices, interline carriers and travel agents.

Sales and Service

The Vancouver Reservations Center is representative of the other CPA centers in Winnipeg, Toronto, and Montreal. The Vancouver Sales and Service Section was divided into two basic subsections, which were, in fact, physically divided. These two subsections were known as Sales and Records. The Vancouver office served eight major cities: Los Angeles, San Francisco, Seattle, Portland, Calgary, Victoria, Nanaimo, and Vancouver. Direct Customer requests and inquiries from any one of the eight cities entered the Sales subsection via telephone. Each call entered an automatic switching system that attempted to evenly distribute agent load. (In Vancouver, CPA received 2.5 calls for every passenger boarded.) Each sales agent had three basic tools: a telephone, an airline Ready Reference Book and a stack of (T-124) booking cards.

The sales agent's procedure was fairly basic. Upon receipt of a prerecorded city identifier message which told the agent the origin of his next call, the agent opened his airline Reference Book to the appropriate section. The Reference Book contained information for schedules, arrival/departure tariffs, hotels, connections, meals, and so forth. This data was organized by calling-city. If a booking was requested, the agent checked the Availability Status Boards and when feasible, booked the passenger. The agent then filled out a standard T-124 booking card and placed the card in the appropriate path on a conveyor belt for transmittal to the Records subgroup. See Figures 9-2 and 9-3 for a diagram of Vancouver Reservations Control.

The Availability Status Boards were continually updated via messages coming in from the Payload Control Area by teletype. The information thus transmitted was copied manually, in chalk, on to the Boards.

The T-124 cards generated by the Sales subsection were intercepted on the conveyor belt by the teletype group in the Records area. Each card caused a teletype message to be sent to Payload Control or to other reservation centers. The Payload Control messages concerned flight status, aircraft configuration changes, schedule changes, and routing changes.

After processing by the teletype section, the T-124 cards were allowed to pass via conveyor to the appropriate records desk. There were eight separate desks: B. C. District, Trans-Continental, International, California, Special Accounts, Group Tours, Pre-Paid Ticket Advice, and Manifests. At each of these desks the T-124 cards were filed under the appropriate flight. The T-124 cards were destroyed after thirty days for domestic flights and after sixty days for International flights.

Payload Control

The basic reservation-oriented input to the Payload Control Section consisted of teletype messages from the several national and international reservations centers. The largest volume came over the local line from the Reservations office in Vancouver. Teletype messages for Payload Control were desk-routed via a conveyor belt operation similar to that in Vancouver Reservations Control.

The Payload Control agent desks were divided into three areas: California and International, B. C. District and Trans-continental, New bookings, cancellations, new requirements, itinerary changes, and so forth, arrived by conveyor belt at the appropriate desk. Status Charts, known as T-4 charts, were kept at these desks. One chart or group of charts existed for each flight, on a per-day basis. Occasionally, several flights were grouped in one chart. These charts contained a cross-reference list of passengers by class booked on each leg of the

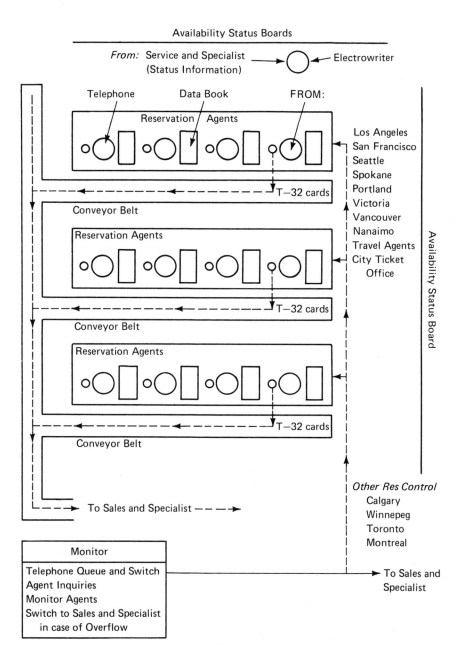

Figure 9-2. Vancouver Reservations Section

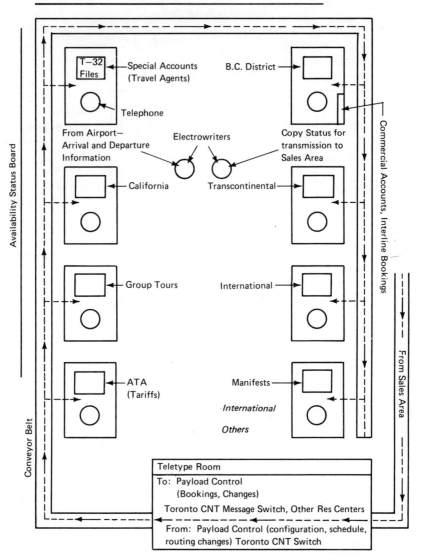

Figure 9-3. Vancouver Reservations Office—Records Area

flight. Special meals, stretcher cases, cargo expectancies, exceptional situations, or other data, were also included on the T-4 charts. The agent's main duties consisted of keeping these charts up-to-date and becoming aware of possible availability status changes. The T-4 files at the agent positions averaged about three months in length. These charts were kept for one year after the flight.

The major supervising functions were performed by a group of controllers. These people determined when a change in availability status had occurred and communicated this information to the reservation centers. The controllers decided when to waitlist and when to impose availability restrictions. In addition, the controller could make preliminary decisions to undersell a flight in hope of long-haul passage or to hold for late (and usually more reliable) bookings. As a further responsibility, the controllers had to be aware of special conventions, cargo requirements and past flight histories. They also obtained and prepared information for Marketing Research. (See Figure 9-4 for a diagram of the Payload Control Section.)

Administrative responsibility for day-to-day reservations control was held by two directors of customer service (Figure 9-5), one responsible for North America and the other for International. Customer Service Development was the responsibility of a third director, Bill Murphy.

Shared Computer Systems

One alternative to a manual system was to share a computer system with another company. CPA had received several such proposals of which two (those by Air Canada and Continental Airlines) received serious consideration.

The Air Canada Reservation System utilized a custom built Univac system. This system was unique to Air Canada and hence any changes and improvements could not be acquired from other carriers but had to be developed at full cost by Air Canada. The systems, as proposed by Air Canada, would function as one airline with Air Canada and CPA information intermixed in the computer but inaccessible to each others' agents. If Air Canada changed any of their systems, then CPA would be directly affected, as a result of the information intermixing. A number of Canada's five regional airlines had joined the Air Canada reservation system, and the others were considering this in 1973.

The Continental Airlines System utilized the IBM PARS programming package. This system would treat each customer as a separate airline within the computer (that is, a multi-host system). Unlike the Air Canada system where any changes or improvements had to be developed internally, the IBM system base allowed such changes to be purchased from any of the other airlines utilizing IBM equipment.

Several CPA managers had expressed their concerns regarding shared computer systems. Three factors were seen to be of major importance: flexibility, program availability and security. In direct comment on the Air Canada proposal, Mr. Ellwood, Director of Computer Services, stated that "they are one of six airlines with the Univac reservations system, all of which are different, so that improvements have to be made individually. The other twenty or so reservations systems are IBM, PARS, or IPARS, which are virtually the

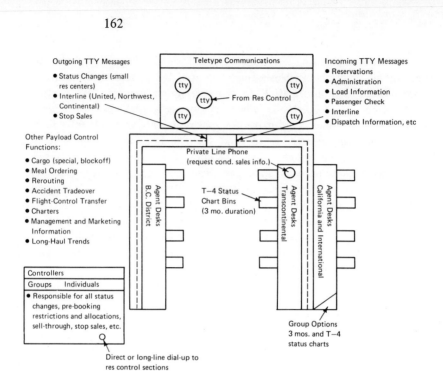

Figure 9-4. Payload Control Section

same. This means that improvements could be purchased from other carriers at a fraction of cost."

Another CPA executive, Mr. Bill Murphy, Director of Customer Services Development stated that with a shared computer system there was no real education of employees and when a stand-alone system became a necessity in the future, then CPA employees would still need more education in the operations of a computer reservations system.

Both Air Canada and Continental Airlines indicated to CPA that they would require a five-year contract to allow equipment planning. Some of the CPA computer services personnel believed that such a long term commitment could result in CPA losing substantial cost reductions due to computer technology changes.

One of the potential advantages (or perhaps, disadvantages) of joining the Air Canada System would be the possibility that reservations personnel for one airline could be aware of the bookings status of other airlines and make reservations on their behalf. At some time in the future, it might be possible to place remote terminals in the offices of travel agents who could thus enquire directly as to the reservations status of any Canadian flight.

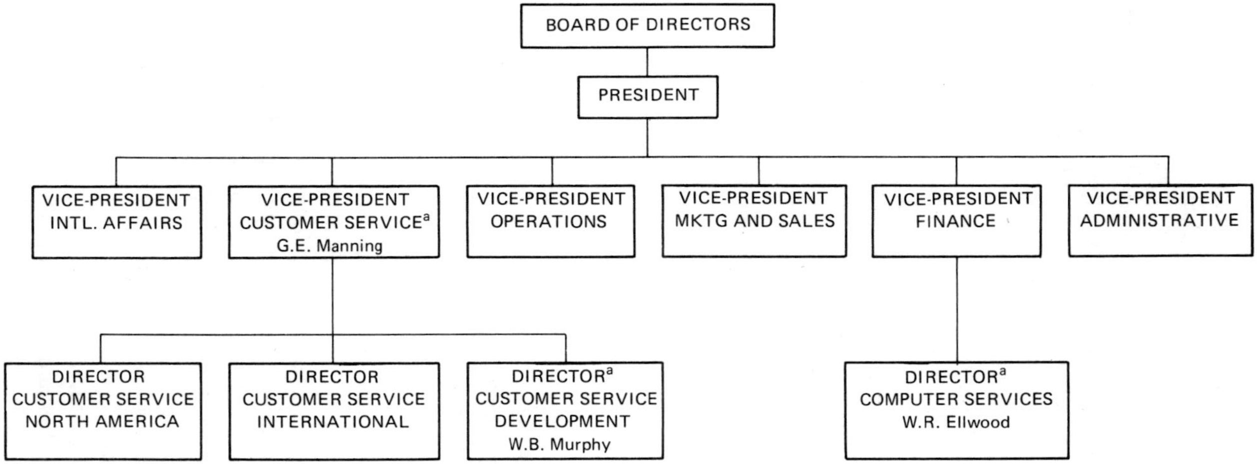

[a]MEMBER OF THE RESERVATIONS PLANNING COMMITTEE

Figure 9-5. Partial Organization Chart

IBM Stand-Alone System

A proposal had been made in 1967 by IBM for a stand-alone reservations system which would utilize the IPARS programming package. (The development of this proposal had been performed in consultation with CPA's Reservations Planning Committee, composed of Gerry Manning (Vice-President of Customer Service), Bill Murphy and W. R. Ellwood (Director of Computer Services).) The International Programmed Airlines Reservation System, or IPARS, was developed by IBM to meet the unique requirements of the international airline. IPARS was a functional extention of the PARS system.

The philosophy of IPARS was based on the centralized control of all reservations information which, together with a communications facility, provided speedy retrieval and updating of stored information. The stored reservations data included the names of all passengers holding reservations, flight schedules and inventory information, and a list of cities serviced by these flights. Medium and low-speed communications facilities provided the access to this information.

The facilities provided by IPARS to assist the sales agents in the performance of their tasks included:

1. Agent Schedule and Availability Information
2. Passenger Name Record Information
3. Inventory Control
4. Agent Communication
5. Teletype Message Processing
6. Departure Control Information
7. Message Switching Capability
8. Management Reservations Information

The schedule and availability information pertaining to the flights maintained by the IPARS System could be accessed directly by the sales agent. Schedule information was requested by specifying the departure date, board point, off-point, and the requested type of display. Up to ten flights could be displayed to the agent regardless of the availability or type of flight. Availability information was displayed by specifying the departure date, board point, off-point and code requesting the display. In response, the system would attempt to display four host airline flights for which one or more seats were available. For flights not under the direct control of IPARS, availability status messages would be received or generated by IPARS.

A passenger-name record would be maintained by the IPARS System for each passenger or group of passengers who have a reservation processed by the System. This record could contain names, telephone numbers, host airline data, general remarks, or other data, and would generally be created when the reservation was originally made. This information could be assessed or modified by any agent and would remain active in the System until the complete itinerary had been flown.

IPARS could provide CPA with the ability to rigidly control space sold on its flights. Since it was extremely important that Central Reservations Control be advised of fluctuations in bookings, upper and lower notification levels could be specified for each segment, which when reached, would automatically initiate messages to Central Reservations Control.

As a result of these messages, IPARS would provide the facility to exercise three types of actions. The first, limiting sales control, would restrict the request for availability on the specified flight, segment or class. The second, planned authorization control, would permit the adjustment of the availability space above or below initial authorization levels. The third, posting level control, would advise those agents without agent sets when bookings rise above the posting level or fall below twice the posting level.

IPARS would have the ability to communicate via medium and low-speed communications lines. The medium speed facility would permit an interactive conversation between the Reservations System and the agent via a Video Display Terminal. For those locations where the medium speed lines were not economically justified, IPARS would support the normal teletype terminal. As a result, the same basic reservations functions would be available to each of CPA's locations throughout the world.

The IPARS System would provide departure-related information for catering, the check-in agent, and the departure agent. This would be achieved by passing control of reservations to the check-in location. The departure control agents would be able to request up-to-date beverage and meal counts that could be directed to the catering personnel.

The departure control agents would also be able to request check-in and departure information relating to:

1. General flight information
2. Number of passengers boarded by class
3. Number of down line reservations
4. Passenger boardings
5. Passengers with in and out-board connections
6. Unticketed passengers
7. Passengers cleared but not confirmed from the wait list.

Following flight departure, the agent would be able to adjust the actual passengers boarded, thus ensuring the accuracy of sales at down-line locations.

An extension to the IPARS Reservation Function would support message switching. The Message Switching System would edit for correctness all low-speed traffic, rejecting any invalid messages. Messages that were related to reservations would be passed on for reservations processing. The Message Switching System would automatically log all messages, thus ensuring the recovery of messages that could be lost due to communications or systems failures.

Management information related to reservations and message switching functions could be extracted from the tape files that were created daily by the IPARS System. This data could be used to produce various reports regarding booking patterns, load factors, or message analysis.

Consultant's Review

In 1970 the Reservations Planning Committee of CPA requested that a well-known national consultant do an economic analysis of the various reservation options available to the company. The objective of the report was to determine when CPA could economically justify the installation of a computer-based reservations system.

This report determined that:

1. Using CPA's current passenger forecast, the total costs of an IBM IPARS System as a representative computer reservation service, and CPA's current manual system, CPA could not justify a stand-alone computer reservation system on the basis of strictly economic factors until well after 1976.

2. Based on the boarding forecasts for 1974, the total initial investment for a computer reservation system would be $8.2 million. This figure includes equipment purchases, initial programming and testing, and reservation system conversion costs.

3. The yearly operating costs for a computer system in 1974 would be $735,000. These costs include the total computer operating costs (not including payload control) of $343,000 and the field costs (including communication and agent set maintenance costs) of $392,000. They do not include any annualization of the initial investment. The costs for operating Central Reservation Control would be $525,000. These payload costs would replace the manual system costs of $820,000.

4. Twenty-five percent of the field office clerical costs were used to carry out functions that would be changed with electronics. Therefore, no more than 25 percent of the present field reservation system costs can be affected by an electronic reservation system. There will be some reduction of costs in payload; in 1974, this would amount to a net savings of $295,000. Thus, in 1974, the net savings when using an electronic reservations system could not exceed $1.3 million. These net savings account for computer operating costs but do not reflect annualization of the large initial investment. This is an upper limit of the net savings attributable to electronics.

5. If CPA were to go on a shared computer reservation system rather than a

"go it alone" system, they could expect to save part of the central computer, programming, testing, and operating costs. The consultant amortized the initial investment costs over a six-year period (with a 15 percent discount rate) and included these costs with the operating costs to achieve an annual expense. Based on our split between field and central costs, and on our analysis, CPA, using a shared system, might save 25 percent of the annualized central costs and, therefore, approximately 15 percent of the total annualized field of central computer system costs. The split between field and central costs may be reassigned, but the total costs for a "go it alone" system remain the same. Costs for a shared arrangement should be compared with the split that we have applied. In our split we have allocated a central cost per boarding of 88 cents out of a total cost per boarding of $1.45. Our estimate of replacing the 88 cents with a cost of 67 cents takes into account our split of the total costs and our estimates of the rational behavior of the supplier of such a system.

The report separated the costs of an electronic system into three main categories:

1. Equipment Costs, including field agent sets and central hardware,
2. Non-recurring Costs, including set-up and conversion costs,
3. Continuing Costs, including the costs necessary to operate a system.

Table 9-4 shows the added costs of an electronic system, the direct offsetting savings in central reservation control, and the level of savings required in field equipment costs if the net system cost was to remain constant. The consultant stated that "since we have assumed that no more than 25 percent of the manual system costs for field office record keeping can be affected by

Table 9-4
Added Costs of Electronic System

Year	Boardings[b] (000s)	Gross Cost/ Board for Electronics[c]	Central Savings per Board[d]	Field Savings/ Board Needed for Breakeven[e]	Needed Savings As % of Manual Costs[f]
1972	1,541	$1.62	$0.14	$1.48	40%
1974	1,887	1.45	0.16	1.29	35%
1976[a]	2,311	1.31	0.17	1.14	31%

[a]Based on consultant's extrapolation of IBM cost figures.

[b]North American only. Based on CP Air forecast.

[c]Based on IBM proposal, all costs annualized.

[d]Reduction in central reservation control costs expected from electronics.

[e]Column 3 less column 4.

[f]Based on a constant manual cost/board of $3.70.

electronics, we believe that an electronic system could not be justified as long as this balance exceeded that percentage. On this basis a computer system solely dedicated to reservations could not be justified until well after 1976."

Table 9-5 compares the manual system costs with the go-it-alone and shared system electronic costs, and Table 9-6 gives the cost breakdown for an electronic system.

Management Views

The consultant's report had determined the economics of the reservations alternatives available to CPA. On the basis of this report the top management committee of CPA (composed of the President and Vice-Presidents), which had to approve major capital expenditures, decided that the manual system was satisfactory at least until 1976. As a result, the customer service managers were told to "make do" with the manual system. However, some of these managers expressed concern about the strict economic orientation of the Report. Bill Murphy stated that "more than just the economic crossroads must be considered—other factors are involved." "A reservations system," as Bill Murphy said, "must not just service—the name of the game is the initial customer contact. The reservations system must be able to establish quick contact with the potential customer and also provide quick service. Our manual system was designed to answer 90 percent of all calls within 20 seconds. At projected peak volumes we felt that the manual system would not be able to cope with the volume of calls." By October 1973 the volume of traffic had risen to such a level that Mr. Murphy and Mr. Manning believed that there was a need to bring the computerized reservations system on-line before 1976. At peak volumes, as few as 40 percent of calls received were being handled within 20 seconds, and Mr. Murphy estimated that between 5 and 15 percent of callers were hanging up before being connected. Together with Mr. Manning, he wondered how he could

Table 9-5
Alternate Systems Cost Comparison

	Manual	Go It Alone Electronic	Shared
Reservation Agents	$2.78	$2.78	$2.78
Payload	0.43	0.27	0.27
Field Office Record Keeping	0.92	0 to 0.92	0 to 0.92
Field Equipment and Operation	–	0.57	0.57
Central Equipment and Operation	0.00	0.88	0.67 to 0.88
Total	4.13	4.50 to 5.42	4.29 to 5.42

Table 9-6
Cost Breakdown for Electronic System

	Cost $	Annualized (6-year, 15% discount) $
Non-recurring Costs		
Central (Go It Alone)		
Equipment Delivery	10,000	
Facilities and Conversion	190,000	
Programming and Testing	1,000,000	
Total	1,200,000	292,000
Central (Any Electronic)		
File Conversion	105,000	
Programming and Testing	235,000	
Total	340,000	82,734
Field (Any Electronic)		
Training	178,000	
Manuals	21,000	
Total	199,000	48,424
Equipment Costs		
Central (Go It Alone)		
Hardware-Central	3,612,065	
Power Supply	250,000	
Total	3,862,065	939,770
Field (Any Electronic)		
Agent Sets	2,539,702	
Cable and Connectors	75,000	
Total	2,614,702	636,245
Continuing		
Central (Go It Alone)		
Operations	120,000	
Space and Facilities	90,000	
Programming and System Support	75,000	
Hardware Maintenance	58,560	
Total	343,560	343,560
Central (Any Electronic)		
Payload Agents	525,000	525,000
Field (Any Electronic)		
Communications	300,000	
Hardware Maintenance	92,601	
Total	392,601	392,601
Total Annualized		3,260,334

make a convincing case to top management for early implementation of the computer reservations system.

Note

1. Although different in detail, the basic structure of airline regulation in Canada is similar to that in the United States. A regulating agency (since 1967 the Air Transport Committee of the Canadian Transport Commission) has authority over entry, rates, mergers, interline agreements and other matters. The Canadian airline industry's structure is similar to that of the United States— divided officially into transcontinental carriers, regional airlines (of which there are five, each serving reasonably distinct areas) and local service carriers.

10 Federal Express Corporation (2)

Introduction

After the completion of the long-term financing (see Chapter 7), Federal Express Corporation (FEC) turned its attention to implementing control procedures to ensure the smooth operation of its small-package jet delivery service. In February 1974, FEC also began to develop plans for future growth and activities.

The last two weeks in December 1973 and the first two weeks in January 1974 were disastrous for FEC. A severe ice storm hit Memphis and other areas in the system and substantial delays in service occurred. However, business began to pick up again as operations were restored to their former efficiency (Table 10-1). By late February, twenty-three aircraft were in use by the company in its mail and package activities, and a total of forty-two cities were being served.

Financing

FEC successfully raised $50 million to support its small-package jet service. When the deal was finally closed in New York, there were over fifty people in the room. Legal fees for all participants were estimated at $1 million, and the paperwork involved was such that Federal Express's own jet delivery service was needed to deliver all documents to all parties on time.

Major investors included the Prudential Insurance Company ($5 million), General Dynamics ($4 million), New Court Private Equity Fund, Inc. ($1.6 million), Allstate Insurance Company ($2 million), and many others. Total placement was $24.5 million in equity, $2.5 million in subordinated loans, and $25 million in senior debt at 2.5 to 3 percent over prime, placed with Chase ($15 million) and the First National Bank of Chicago ($10 million). Fred Smith and his family ended up with about 14 percent of the equity and invested a total of $9 million in debt and equity. General Dynamics owned 22 to 23 percent.

The success of the financing was a unique achievement. It constituted the largest single start-up investment in the history of venture capital in the United States, both in terms of dollar amount and number of participants. The fact that the president of the company was only twenty-nine also made the venture unique for a start-up of this size. Many factors contributed to the success, but all participants stressed the drive and forcefulness of Fred Smith in selling the FEC

171

Table 10-1
Package Volume by Week (Total System)

Week Ending	Priority One	Economy Air	Courier-pak	Hazardous Materials	Total
11/23/73	9,000	2,100	600	95	11,795
11/30/73	10,100	2,900	700	200	13,900
12/7/73	13,050	3,800	750	250	17,850
12/14/73	14,900	5,100	810	310	21,120
12/22/73	13,800	5,300	890	220	20,210
12/29/73	11,400	4,800	695	180	17,075
1/5/74	10,100	5,000	590	185	15,875
1/12/74	10,500	6,000	630	250	17,380
1/19/74	12,200	7,000	845	305	20,350
1/26/74	13,000	7,000	930	270	21,200
2/2/74	13,600	7,500	1,005	350	22,455
2/9/74					27,750
2/16/74					30,550

concept. The extensive analysis performed by the GD research team gave New Court strong evidence with which to persuade investors that FEC was both a viable concept and one that could not be implemented in stages, but had to start large.

Many other factors marked Federal as a unique organization. Not only was it integrated in that it performed a full door-to-door service, but it performed the conversion of its aircraft according to its own design, trained its own pilots, ran its own payroll, and so on. Of particular note was the spirit of the company throughout the extensive period of bankruptcy (June to November). Executives put their checks into the drawer rather than cash them, and in one instance a driver-courier "hocked" his watch so that he could purchase gasoline in order to complete his rounds.

Control Systems

Commencing in January, the company instituted a new control procedure based on the MIS (Management Information System) sheet. Selected data from this sheet are shown in Table 10-2. Total costs of operation were allocated among the mail, charter, and package services, so the cost figures shown in Table 10-2 represent those for the package service only. Revenue per package, which was $11.94 in the week of December 8, fell to $10.55 in the week of February 2 (revenue per pound was 78 cents). In the same week, the aircraft averaged 8.7 block hours per day, and the crews averaged 2.9 block hours per day.

Management committee meetings were held every Wednesday and Friday to review operations. Other management reports included the Daily Service Report for the Memphis hub and weekly summary reports for each city. Incentive schemes based on these reports had been established as described below in the section on labor relations.

Marketing

FEC had engaged in an extensive advertising program in the distribution and transportation journals even before the package operation began. This tactic was viewed primarily as a means to make the company's name and image known, and the program was cut back in the early months of 1974. As of February 1974, one FEC executive noted, "ten percent of our sales are original selling, and the remainder is diversion from other modes of transportation. We can do a better job on the original selling, and that percentage ought to rise." FEC planned to launch a promotional campaign, primarily by direct mail, aimed at the consignees of the packages. Screened prospects would be sent, along with other promotional materials, a complimentary shipping label that they could pass on to a supplier. The supplier could then send a package to the consignee free of charge. In this way, FEC would obtain two qualified sales leads, the shipper and the consignee.

Labor Relations

No employee at FEC belonged to a union. Attempts had been made to unionize FEC, beginning with maintenance workers, but it had never come to a vote. Fred Smith believed that unionization would be disastrous for FEC in its early stages, because it needed to remain flexible as systems and procedures were developed. The pilots, mostly exservicemen and all trained on Fanjet Falcons by FEC, planned to form a "Federal Express Pilots Association," an organization the company did not oppose.

Because of the "community spirit" generated during the period of bankruptcy, labor relations were excellent at FEC. Carroll Fitzgerald, manager of the hub facility, commenting on the low claims rate experienced by the company said, "Although we do have someone constantly watching the hub floor, we do not need tight security procedures. I am convinced that if any of our workers saw another attempting to pilfer a package, that man would, at the very least, be ostracized. These guys are all pulling for Federal."

However, Fred Smith was not relying on goodwill alone to foster good worker-management relations. The company provided extensive medical and dental coverage for each worker, up to $250,000 for the employee's whole family. Smith believed that wage scales were above average, with good reason:

Table 10-2
MIS: Summary Report

	Week Ending				
	1/12	*1/19*	*1/26*	*2/02*	*2/09*
Revenue					
Packages (000)	20.7	23.5	24.1	25.8	27.7
1. Training	0	0	0	17	42
2. Mail	54	67	67	62	62
3. Charter	0	2	7[c]	0	6
4. Corporate maintenance	0	(1)	6	17	17
5. Package	224	243	263	278	292
6. Other	0	0	0	0	0
7. Total revenue	278	311	343	374	419
8. Package goal	394	472	576	566[d]	337
9. Total goal		631	631	631	899
10. Revenue per package	10.81	10.81	10.81	10.55	
Cost per package[a]					
Goal					
11. Total	21.81	19.78	19.13	18.31	17.79
12. Training	.36	.36	.31	.39	.36
13. Flight operations	10.51	8.96	8.41	8.02	7.72
14. Maintenance	3.23	2.23	2.78	2.98	3.67
15. Sales and customer service	6.03	5.82	5.43	4.76	4.08
16. Hub	.20	.36	.31	.35	.28
17. All other	1.43[b]	2.05	1.89	1.81	1.68
Miscellaneous					
18. Total people	804	804	823	823	881
19. Service level	84.1%	84.4%	93.0%	93.0%	89.6%
20. Average load factor	44%	44%	43%	44%	51%
Packages					
1. % of goal	61.9	52.8	46.0	97.0[e]	82.2
2. Number of cities above goal	2	–	–	16	11
3. Number of cities below goal	37	40	39	23	29
Service					
4. Service failures–field	1757	1446	1159	1217	1390
5. hub	21	24	20	25	20
6. other	1627	1920	514	494	1239
7. Customer tracers	351	353	357	358	417
8. Claims issued (loss/damage)	4/1	0/2	6/3	1/6	4/3

Table 10-2 (cont.)

	Week Ending				
	1/12	*1/19*	*1/26*	*2/02*	*2/09*
People					
9. Field operating	285	291	301	303	344
10. Field sales	34	34	34	34	34
11. Other	40	38	38	36	38
12. Total	359	363	373	373	416
Sales					
13. Calls per close	9.3	10.5	14	13	9
14. Average calls per salesman wk.	20.0	25.6	25.5	25.5	24.5
15. Total closes	73	83	62	67	59
16. Average closes per salesman wk.	2.2	2.4	1.8	2.0	1.7
Performance					
17. Packages per courier day	44.9	42.2	29.8	51.5	51.0
18. Stops per courier day	17.0	18.6	18.4	21.2	20.1
19. Packages per pick up stop	3.6	3.4	3.8	3.3	3.4
20 Packages per delivery stop	2.1	1.6	2.1	1.9	2.0
21. Miles per courier day	106	106	112	123	113

[a]These figures represent only those portions of total costs that are allocated to the package service.

[b]Does not reflect adjustment in "all other."

[c]Includes prior weeks activity.

[d]Adjustment made to package goal.

[e]Reflects adjusted goals.

"We are not aiming for cheap labor. That implies a high turnover, and we can't afford to retrain people. So we pay well."

The main instrument used for labor relations at FEC was the incentive scheme for station personnel and salesmen implemented in January 1974. The scheme for station personnel, which included everyone from the city manager to the clerks and couriers, was based on the average cost per package at the city terminal. For each dollar reduction in cost per package, fifty cents per package handled went into a bonus pool for distribution to the employees. The basis of the calculation was the previous month's performance by that city; thus there was no intercity competition. Penalties were assessed against the bonus for avoidable delays (service failures) at $10 per package, and if a city manager attempted to "hide" a service failure (not report it) and it was discovered by Federal Express's "roving audit group," then a $100 per package penalty was assessed. The first month's incentive scheme results are shown in Table 10-3.

The salesmen's incentive scheme was based on the volume of *new* business

Table 10-3
Incentive Scheme Results, January 1974

City	Incentive Payout[a]	Cost/Pkg.	Employees
Albuquerque, N.M.	135.23	2.35	4
Atlanta, Ga.	220.30	1.51	9
Baltimore, Md.	1931.95	1.99	13
Bedford, Mass.	(3128.31)	1.73	13
Buffalo, N.Y.	(184.76)	2.86	5
Chicago (O'Hare)	(2089.42)	1.96	18
Cincinnati, Ohio	435.11	1.74	N/A
Cleveland, Ohio	597.74	2.15	8
Columbus, Ohio	298.28	1.76	N/A
Dallas, Texas	337.83	.96	11
Dayton, Ohio	312.08	2.39	7
Denver, Colo.	392.40	1.62	7
Des Moines, Iowa	(386.90)	2.57	3
Greensboro, N.C.	21.89	2.59	5
Hartford, Conn.	795.29	1.70	N/A
Indianapolis, Ind.	1490.85	1.62	6
Jacksonville, Fla.	(220.83)	2.43	3
Kansas City, Mo.	(278.85)	1.41	9
Little Rock, Ark.	143.78	.69	5
Los Angeles, Calif.	(4494.25)	1.59	14
Louisville, Ky.	420.06	1.16	N/A
Memphis, Tenn.	300.50	1.31	7
Miami, Fla.	604.04	1.29	9
Milwaukee, Wis.	(155.15)	1.67	7
Minneapolis, Minn.	1504.18	1.86	9
Moline, Ill.	(266.77)	3.42	4
Nashville, Tenn.	1102.64	1.34	4
Newark, N.J.	(201.25)	1.74	10
New Orleans, La.	224.67	1.70	N/A
LaGuardia, N.Y.	1144.25	1.08	N/A
Oakland, Calif.	(646.44)	1.78	10
Oklahoma City, Okla.	281.55	1.42	5
Philadelphia, Pa.	(781.13)	1.47	13
Pittsburgh, Pa.	376.37	2.32	7
Rochester, N.Y.	291.21	1.30	7
St. Louis, Mo.	(486.38)	1.88	9
Wichita, Kans.	59.38	1.83	5

Note: N/A = not available.

[a]( ) = penalties greater than bonus.

generated. Each salesman had a target of 360 packages of new business per month, and for the first 60 packages above the target the salesman received $24 as a bonus. The next 60 packages earned him a bonus of $30; the next 60, $36; and so forth. A salesman commented that the target was set very high and, therefore, the incentive scheme was not entirely satisfactory because it was not achievable. In the week of 9 February, 270 leads were called upon, 219 were "qualified," and 66 were closed.

However, FEC recognized that the nature of these schemes was temporary because they represented the needs of a young and growing company. Smith planned to replace them when the time was appropriate. Management was also preparing incentive schemes for flight and maintenance personnel.

Major Projects

As of February 1974, Federal Express had three major projects under consideration, "STAR," "MLG," and "CPS." These are reviewed on the following pages. Also of concern was the timing of the implementation of the "Rapistan" automated sorting facility that had been proposed at the company's beginning but had not yet been put into operation (see Chapter 7).

STAR System

"Developing systems in a new business is at best difficult, but at Federal Express initial system development was tougher than usual. Because of a large initial investment in aircraft, the company has had to grow extremely fast. This meant that basic system ideas should be designed to grow with the company. However, since the concept had not been tried before, thorough definition of requirements was impossible. The system, as defined here, had to: provide information for invoicing management, aircraft scheduling and package tracing from shipper to receiver. The company, therefore, chose to begin with a relatively simple manual system with full knowledge that the system would have to be restructured during the high growth period."

These words began a communication to Federal Express's investor group introducing the STAR (Systemwide Tracking and Recording) system. The system was designed with three objectives: (1) to provide positive control of freight—that is, Federal Express should know where a package was in the system at any given time; (2) to minimize billing and handling costs; and (3) to provide an accurate and timely data base.

In the period of September to November 1973, a project team led by Mike Basch, senior vice president of corporate development, structured a rough outline of the proposed system. There were to be five major functions in the system, as described below.

Function 1: Recording

Each of FEC's subscribers would be provided with an "Addressograph" data recorder. This machine, similar to those used in gas stations to process credit card purchases, allowed the customer to prepare the special FEC airbill with the aid of preprinted "consignee address cards." The airbill contained four parts, one of which was used as a label for the package. A machine readable bar code was preprinted on the package copy. Because each customer would have his own Addressograph with his account number on it, as well as the preprinted consignee address cards, he would be saved the effort of writing such information on the airbill.

Field tests on customer acceptance of the Addressograph proved very favorable. Some problems were anticipated with the fact that the system required one bill per package, but Federal Express believed that the benefits to the customer of the STAR system were such that it would not create an insuperable difficulty.

Function 2: Data Gathering

This function would be performed when the package arrived at FEC's city station. Each package would be scanned by a machine capable of reading the bar code on the airbill copy attached to the package. The information would then be communicated to the central computer in Memphis. The computer would summarize all the individual inputs from a station to calculate the lift demand into and out of each city. In this way, early warning of a large demand to or from any city would be available to the schedulers, who could route or reroute aircraft to assure service reliability at the least cost. Given the small size of FEC's fleet and the fact that all aircraft flew into Memphis, the scheduling could be done in sufficient time to be communicated, via the computer, to each of the stations and aircraft.

Function 3: Sorting

This function would be performed when the packages arrived in Memphis. As they were unloaded, they would be placed on a conveyor system which would take them to a "package inductor." Here they would be scanned again, to record the fact that they had arrived in Memphis. The scanning would also, via the computer, assign each package automatically to the "divert chute" on the conveyor appropriate to the destination zip code. In this way, sorting would be performed automatically using a tilt-tray sorter.

Function 4: Tracking

This function could be performed at any time. Every time a package was scanned, the computer would store the information and upon request give its "disposition." Scanning would take place first when the package was received at the city station, next when it was received in Memphis, and also when it arrived at the destination city. A fourth entry would take place when the package was delivered. When the courier obtained a signature as proof of delivery, he would remove the label from the package, and upon his return to the city station the bar code would be scanned to record the fact of delivery. This way FEC believed it could offer a tracing service as efficient as that of any other transportation company, and more efficient than most. It would also create a data base useful in evaluating various phases of its operations.

Function 5: Billing

This function would also be performed at Memphis. Airbills would be sent from the cities to Memphis. They would then be scanned and matched by the computer to confirm that the shipment had been delivered. They would also be microfilmed for permanent storage, so that the system would not accumulate paper. Each week the computer would print out air invoice for each customer that had used FEC, and this would be mailed, together with the air bill, for payment. The automation of the billing system would allow for efficient and effective billing.

The project team was convinced of the benefits of the proposed system, including ease of air bill preparation by the customer, automatic sorting, quick operational response to surges in demand, automatic billing, and efficient tracing. They recommended that implementation of the system begin when FEC began to handle 12,000 packages per day (twice their February 1974 volume) and/or when it had 1500 regular shippers. They also recommended five implementation stages: (I) installation of data recorders with a manual billing system; (II) data collection at the cities including communications and computer summarizing capability (tracking to be provided at origin and destination cities only); (III) automated billing system; (IV) automated sorting and hub tracking; (V) complete system, including flight planning, scheduling, calculation of weight and balance loading of aircraft, and so on.

Apart from the benefits outlined above, the project team estimated that operating cost savings would result in the areas of sales and customer service (in the form of freeing man-hours given over to the existing tracing service), flight operations, data processing, and elsewhere. It was projected that the "mis-sort" rate would fall from its current level of 1.4 percent of packages, to a level of 1.0 percent with the introduction of the sorter and to a level of 0.5 percent with the introduction of the scanner. Costs and benefits of the STAR system are presented in Table 10-4.

MLG Program

One of Federal Express's most revolutionary plans was to use "Mobile Loading Gates" (MLG). These forty-foot trailers would be loaded with containers at FEC

Table 10-4
STAR Costs and Savings[a]

| | Stage (× $1000) | | | | | |
	I	II	III	IV	V	Total
Savings per month @ 25,000 pkgs./day						
Sales and customer service	24.0	27.4	6.4	12.8	7.5	78.1
Flight operations		6.0			155[b]	161.0
Finance	8.7	2.6	1.0			12.3
Data processing "cost"	(2.0)		7.9			5.9
All other		44.7				44.7
Total	30.7	80.7	15.3	12.8	162.5	302.0
Hardware net cost/month	11.4	40.5	10.9		4.0	66.8
Net savings	19.3	40.2	4.4	12.8	158.5	235.2
Savings @ 12,000 packages (stages I and II only)	9.3	19.3				
Hardware commitment	379	825	462	62	668[b]	2396
One-time cost	68	94	8	5	46	221
Total commitment	447	919	470	67	714	2617

[a]Base day assumptions: 25,000 pkgs./day; 80 cities; 5000 regular accounts; 360 couriers.
[b]Most of the costs and savings in stage V are not STAR system dependent.

terminals and located at converted service stations in the city centers. The loaded trailer could be driven onto the ramp at the airport and backed up directly to the aircraft. Containers from the aircraft could be unloaded and the outbound containers loaded without touching the ground. The trailer could then be driven back to the city terminal, where its containers would be offloaded directly, if necessary, into the courier vans.

The handling efficiencies of the system were not its only significant benefits. The trailers, apart from carrying containers, could also carry fuel for the aircraft, and refueling could take place simultaneously with the unloading/loading operation. The trailer would also have the capability of deicing the aircraft should it be necessary. The implication of this plan was that FEC would not need to maintain any investment on the airport because all terminal facilities would be provided at the city-center location, and all fuel stored there (hence the objective of using service stations as the site of the terminals). Agreements with local fixed-base operators would provide for maintenance facilities. Apart from the ability to use less expensive off-airport terminal facilities, the largest advantage to Federal Express would be the ability to buy fuel in bulk and thus achieve significant savings in fuel costs as well as maintain its own inventories efficiently.

Central to the MLG concept was the use of a lightweight container that would float 1/8" above the floors of the aircraft and the trailer. The air pressure would come from yet another installation on the trailer. The use of the air-float system, which had been in use in industry for many years, would simplify handling and obviate the necessity for a roller bed in the aircraft and thereby increase its payload. Bids had been submitted for the design of the container, and Federal Express had settled upon an aluminum design that the manufacturer promised to make adaptable at no cost to the roller-bed system should the air-float concept be abandoned. It was projected that in the full 82-city system, 800 containers would be needed, at a cost of $687 each. The cheapest of the roller-bed-type containers investigated by FEC cost approximately the same amount.

The MLG itself would represent an investment of $30,000 per trailer (to be depreciated over seven years), and one trailer would be needed for each city. Handling devices at the Memphis hub, in the form of a chute to off-load containers onto dollies for transport into the sort facility, would cost $9000 each; thirty would be required. Conversion of the service-station tanks to hold jet fuel instead of gasoline would run to $3000 at each of eighty-two cities.

Savings from this system were expected to be substantial. Sixty-five percent of Federal Express's fuel was purchased at locations other than Memphis, and a conservative estimate of the savings from centralized purchasing was five cents per gallon, plus a saving of three cents a gallon that was currently being paid to fixed-base operations to perform the fueling for Federal. The Fanjet Falcon consumed 365 gallons per hour, and in the 82-city system it was projected that there would be 410 flight hours per day.

Savings estimated at $24,690 per month would result from speedier loading, as would faster aircraft turnaround. At the hub, it was estimated that for each of the 97 operations per day, turnaround could be reduced from 33.3 minutes to 15.8 minutes. At $77.60 per hour, the estimate of the value of time due to depreciation, increased utilization, and so on, every minute was valuable. Savings in turnaround at other cities were expected to be 7.5 minutes for each of 174 operations.

The implementation of the MLG program would not be an easy task. In some airports trailers were prohibited from driving onto the ramp, and FEC expected a hard fight to obtain permission at those airports. However, experiments had begun in training trailer operators to maneuver their trailer up to the aircraft. The difficulty of this task had been demonstrated in practice sessions, so FEC expected to invest a substantial amount in training. Total contingency expenses, including training, licensing, maintenance, and so on, were expected to run $42,000 per month.

Critical Parts Supply Inc.

CPS (Critical Parts Supply Inc.) was formed as a wholly owned subsidiary of Federal Express to provide a total distribution service for companies with inventories of "critical parts," that is, supplies needed to keep a machine in operation or to repair equipment in the event of a breakdown. Aimed primarily at electronics-based companies, the mode of operation can best be explained by the plan proposed for one prospective customer.

CPS would store the customer's inventory of spare parts at a public distribution center in Memphis, Tennessee. When any of the customer's service-men needed a part, they would contact CPS, which would ship the part to the serviceman, anywhere in the United States. The customer had the choice of four levels of service: "urgent," meaning the part would be on the next flight out of Memphis, on whichever airline happened to be flying that flight; "priority," meaning that the part would be delivered by the next morning on FEC's Priority One Service; "nonpriority," meaning that the part would be received by the second business day via FEC's Economy Air service; or "ground," meaning that the part would be shipped via United Parcel Service.

In this particular customer's case, the part that was being replaced was returned to the customer's headquarters for repair, so CPS would ship the replacement in a reusable container. The serviceman could then return the used part in the same container to CPS. After a week CPS would consolidate the used parts and ship them to the customer's headquarters for repair, after which they would be returned to CPS inventory.

To promote this service, CPS prepared a computer program that could be used by a portable time-sharing terminal. Upon request, the program would point out the cost and time of arrival of a package of any weight sent, by any of the four levels of service offered, to any destination in the United States.

It was projected that revenues would begin eleven weeks after the launching of the project, and that breakeven would be reached in the twenty-fourth week when weekly revenues reached $22,600. Of this amount, $12,600 would cover CPS expenses (of which only $1300 were fixed) and the remainder would be paid to FEC for transportation. Total loss until breakeven was projected at $62,500.

Long-term Future

Commenting on the long-term future of his company, Smith said "I see no limit to our expansion. This company is going to keep on growing. Eventually of course we will have to move to a larger aircraft. This will mean that we shall have to be certified by the CAB, but we will be ready for that in three to four years."

Charles Branden, head of technical services, had this comment about potential aircraft:

The Falcon 20 is not entirely economical for the short routes, and on the longer "hops" we have trouble because the Falcon 20 cannot make it from the West

Coast to Memphis without an intermediate fuel stop. We see ourselves with three aircraft when we are fully matured. Dassault is developing a larger version of the Falcon which, while it does not increase the range, will provide economies over the shorter routes. For the long routes, we might possibly go to a DC-9. We would like this to be "re-engined" so that we would have only one type of engine to perform maintenance for. I see us going to a three-aircraft-type fleet in about two to three years.

Smith also mentioned, only half-humorously, another of his long-term plans: "You know, the Concorde would make the perfect package aircraft. I've run the numbers, and I can see us operating a similar service to Europe, using the Concorde."

Appendix A
Glossary of Airline Industry Terminology

Accessorial Service   Services performed in addition to the usual transportation services.

Administrative Law Judge   A person appointed by the CAB to preside over a route application, rate investigation, or any other CAB proceeding.

Air Bill   Nonnegotiable shipping document containing shipping instructions, description of commodity, and applicable transportation charges.

Air Cargo   A comprehensive term referring to the total of air freight, express freight, parcels services, and air mail.

Air Express   The priority movement of goods by air. Until 1975, a joint service offered by the airlines and REA Air Express.

Air Freight   The movement of goods by air. Excludes air mail, small-parcels services, or various forms of priority (express) movement of goods by air.

Air Line Pilots Association (ALPA)   The union for pilots of most trunk airlines.

Air Taxi   Nonscheduled carrier using small aircraft for very short-haul travel on a charter basis. Not regulated by the CAB.

Air Transport Association of America   An industry association of scheduled carriers.

Air Waybill   Description of goods sent with an air-cargo shipment.

Air-freight Forwarder   A company that accepts small shipments for consolidation and movement by air. Licensed but not regulated by the CAB.

All Cargo   Correctly used, refers to an *airline* that carries only cargo, not passengers. Sometimes used to refer to aircraft that carry only cargo although the correct term is "freighter aircraft."

Available Seat-Miles (ASM)   A measure of the capacity provided by an aircraft or an airline. Calculated by multiplying the number of seats in an aircraft by the number of miles flown.

Available Ton-miles (ATM)   A measure of the capacity provided by an aircraft or an airline. Calculated by multiplying the payload (in tons) of the aircraft by the number of miles flown.

Belly   The lower cargo hold of an aircraft. Cargo carried here is called "belly cargo."

Big Four   A term used to refer to United, Eastern, Trans World and American Airlines.

Bill of Lading   A contract for transportation between the shipper and carrier.

Blanket Order   An order by the CAB that applies to all air carriers.

Block Hours   The time of a flight including taxiing time at airports. Measured from when the blocks are removed to when they are replaced at the next station.

Board   See CAB.

Breakeven Load Factor   The percentage of available seats filled at which all operating costs are covered.

Cabin Attendant   A term used to refer to an air hostess, stewardess, steward, or purser.

Capacity Agreement   An agreement between airlines to reduce capacity, e.g., frequency of operations or type of aircraft, on a given route or set of routes. Must be approved by the CAB.

Capacity Competition   A method of competing whereby carriers add capacity (numbers and types of aircraft) in order to increase market share.

Cargo   See Air Cargo.

Carload (CL)   A quantity of freight eligible for a (reduced) carload rate. Usually refers to a shipment in excess of 10,000 pounds. See Less than Carload (LCL).

Cartage   Surface hauling of air freight by a motor vehicle.

Certificate of Air-worthiness   A certificate that must be issued by the FAA before a new aircraft is allowed to be flown.

Certificate of Public Convenience and Necessity   Operating authority from the CAB to serve a route. Issued on a city-pair rather than on a complete route basis.

Certificated Carrier   Carrier holding a certificate of public convenience and necessity from the CAB.

City-Pair   A route or market between two cities.

Civil Aeronautics Board (CAB)   An agency of the federal government formed in 1938. It is responsible for the economic regulation (and promotion) of the air-transport industry.

Coach   A class of airline fare or service, lower than first class. Also called "economy."

COD   Collection delivery (cash, certified check, or money order).

Combination Carrier   An air carrier that transports both passengers and cargo.

Commodity Rate   A rate published for a specific geographical movement of a specific commodity.

Common Carrier   A carrier that offers service to the general public, rather than to specified customers.

Commuter Air Carrier   A carrier operating small aircraft on an irregular basis to serve small communities.

Connecting Carrier   The carrier to which a passenger and baggage or cargo are transferred to complete a trip.

Consignee   The party to whom a shipment is to be delivered.

Consolidator   A freight forwarder.

Container   An enclosed box in which shipments may be placed prior to loading onto a transport vehicle in order to facilitate handling as a single unit.

Contract Carrier   A carrier that offers service only to specified customers on a contract basis.

Cube   The available space in an aircraft.

Cube Out   An aircraft whose available *space* is filled is said to have "cubed out." See Weight Out.

CWT   Hundred-weight, or one hundred pounds.

DAFRI   The Domestic Air Freight Rate Investigation conducted by the CAB (since 1970).

Dimensional Weight   The weight per cubic foot of a shipment.

Direct Air Carrier   An airline.

Direct Flight   A flight that provides same-plane service between two points with intermediate stops. Not to be confused with nonstop flight.

Direct Operating Cost (DOC)   The costs of operating an aircraft, including flying costs, depreciation, maintenance, and maintenance burden.

Distribution Service   Service under which a carrier accepts a single shipment from a single shipper and separates it into a number of pieces at destination for delivery to more than one consignee.

DOT   United States Department of Transportation.

DPFI   The Domestic Passenger Fare Investigation conducted by the CAB (1970-1974).

Economy   See Coach.

Enplanements   The number of passengers boarded.

Enroute   On the way.

Express   See Air Express.

Federal Aviation Administration (FAA)   A federal government agency, part of the Department of Transportation, formed in 1958 to be responsible for the safety regulation of aircraft and airlines operations.

First Class   A class of fare service in which services (meals, seating space, liquor, etc.) are greater than in coach or economy class.

Freight   See Air Freight.

Freighter   An aircraft used to carry only cargo.

General Aviation   Includes flying operations performed by companies and individuals on their own behalf (private aviation), flying schools and flying clubs.

General Commodity Rate   A freight rate applicable to all commodities.

Grandfather Clause   A clause of the Civil Aeronautics Act whereby carriers operating given routes prior to the introduction of economic regulation automatically qualified for operating authorities on those routes.

Indirect Carrier   An air-freight forwarder.

Interline Traffic   A transfer of passengers from one airline to another as part of a single journey.

Intraline Transfer   A transfer of passengers between two flights (on separate aircraft) as part of a single journey.

Intrastate Carrier   A carrier operating solely within the boundaries of a single state.

Irregular Carrier   A nonscheduled carrier.

Leg   When an aircraft flies from A to C with an intermediate stop at B, the trips from A to B and from B to C are called "legs" or "stages" of the total routing.

Less than Carload (LCL)   A small shipment (usually less than 10,000 lbs.) carried by a railroad at a less than carload rate (usually higher on a per-pound basis than a carload (CL) shipment).

Less than Truckload (LTL)   A small shipment (usually less than 10,000 lbs.) carried by a motor carrier at a less than truckload rate (usually higher on a per-pound basis).

Load Factor   The percentage of available seats filled, or the percentage of available tons filled, with passengers or cargo. For passenger flights this figure is usually the ratio of RPM to ASM.

Local Service Carrier   A class of airline defined by the CAB. Normally smaller than a trunk airline and normally operates over a smaller geographical area.

Mutual Aid Agreement   An agreement between the airlines (approved by the CAB) whereby any carrier forced to cease operations due to union action is partially compensated by other carriers.

National Mediation Board (NMB)   A quasi-governmental agency that mediates labor disputes.

Nonscheduled Carrier (Nonsked)   A carrier that operates on a charter basis, that is, on irregular routes and irregular schedules.

Official Airline Guide (OAG)   A book published every three months showing all airline schedules by city.

Off-line Passenger   An off-line passenger is one who travels between A and B, but whose origin or destination (or both) is not A or B.

On-time Performance   The percentage of flights that arrive within 15 minutes of schedule.

Operating Ratio   Operating expenses (excluding interest charges) divided by operating revenues.

Overbooking   The practice of accepting a number of reservations in excess of the number of available seats to compensate for passengers with reservations who do not show up ("no-shows").

Passenger-mile   A measure of services performed. One passenger carried one mile.

Pitch   The distance between seats in a passenger aircraft seating configuration.

Revenue Passenger Emplanements   The total number of revenue passengers boarding aircraft in scheduled service, including origination, stopover, and on-line connecting passengers.

Revenue Passenger-miles (RPM)   A measure of services performed by a transportation company. One passenger moved one mile equals one revenue passenger-mile.

Revenue Ton-miles (RTM)   A measure of services performed by a transportation company. One ton moved one mile.

Route Authority   See Certificate of Public Convenience and Necessity.

Route Swap   An agreement between two or more airlines (which must be approved by the CAB) to exchange route authorities.

S-curve   A theory that the carrier in any market with the largest proportion of capacity will obtain a larger than proportional share of the traffic.

Segment   See Leg.

Service Competition   The process of competing by changing the type and level of services offered but keeping rate levels constant.

Specific Commodity Rate   A freight rate applicable to a specific commodity (or set of commodities) between specific geographical areas.

Stage   See Leg.

Subsidy Ineligible   A local service carrier route that is not eligible for subsidy from the CAB.

Supplemental Carrier   A nonscheduled airline.

Tariff   The published fare, charges, and/or related conditions of carriage of a carrier.

Truckload (TL)   A quantity of freight (usually over 10,000 pounds) eligible for a truckload rate (which is usually less on a per-pound basis than a less than truckload rate).

Trunk(-line)   A large air carrier operating over a wide geographical area.

Weight-Out   When an aircraft's load is such that maximum weight limits have been reached (and there is still space available), it is said to have "weighted out."

Wide-body   A generation of aircraft with wide bodies, including B-747, DC-10, and L-1011.

Yield   Refers to revenue received, as in "yield per passenger-mile."

Appendix B
Further Reading

Two books of general interest to students of airline management are *The Commercial Airline Industry*, by N. K. Teneja (Lexington, Mass.: Lexington Books, D. C. Heath and Company, 1976), and *The International Airline Industry*, by Mahlon R. Straszheim (Washington, D.C.: The Brookings Institution, 1969).

One of the best-known books on airline regulation in America is *Air Transport and Its Regulators*, by Richard E. Caves (Cambridge, Mass.: Harvard University Press, 1962). A more recent book dealing with the competition in the lightly regulated California intrastate market is *Airline Regulation in America: Effects and Imperfections*, by William A. Jordan (Baltimore, Md.: The Johns Hopkins Press, 1970).

The Fight for Competitive Advantage, by William E. Fruhan (Boston: Harvard University Business School, Division of Research, 1972) is a very useful study of the competitive behavior of the United States domestic trunk-line air carriers. *The Future of the U.S. Domestic Air Freight Industry: A Study of Management Strategies*, by Lewis M. Schneider (Boston: Harvard University Business School, Division of Research, 1973) will be of interest to readers with a concern for the development of air-freight services in the United States.

Aviation Week and *Air Transport World* are useful trade magazines that report the activities of the airline industry. The Air Transport Association of America annually publishes *Air Transport Facts and Figures*, which is a very useful compilation of airline operating statistics, as is *World Air Transport Statistics*, published by the International Air Transport Association.

About the Authors

D. Daryl Wyckoff is an associate professor at the Harvard University Graduate School of Business Administration, George F. Baker Foundation. He received the B.S. in aeronautical engineering from MIT, the M.B.A. from The University of Southern California, and the D.B.A. from Harvard University. As a doctoral student at Harvard he was a William Barclay Harding Fellow in aviation studies. In the past he has served as the vice president of the logistics systems group of a California-based aerospace conglomerate. He is a consultant in management, transportation, and logistics to companies, governments, and industrial organizations in the United States, United Kingdom, and several countries in the Middle East. He has specialized in intermodal and intramodal competition and capacity strategies.

Dr. Wyckoff is the author of *Organizational Formality and Performance in the Motor Carrier Industry* (Lexington Books, 1974) and *Railroad Management* (Lexington Books, 1976). He is the coauthor of *Operations Management: Text and Cases* (Richard D. Irwin, 1975) and the coauthor with David H. Maister of *The Owner-Operator: Independent Trucker* (Lexington Books, 1975) and *the Motor-Carrier Industry* (Lexington Books, 1977). His articles have appeared in *Traffic World, Modern Railroads, Handling and Shipping,* and *Transportation and Distribution Management.*

David H. Maister is an assistant professor in the Faculty of Commerce and Business Administration, University of British Columbia, Canada. He received the B.Soc.Sci. (in statistics and economics) from the University of Birmingham, England, the M.Sc. (in operations research) from the London School of Economics, and the D.B.A. (in transportation and logistics) from the Harvard Business School.

Dr. Maister is the coauthor with D. Daryl Wyckoff of *Owner-Operator: Independent Trucker* (Lexington Books, 1975) and *The Motor-Carrier Industry* (Lexington Books, 1977). His articles on transportation and logistics have appeared in the *International Journal of Physical Distribution* and the *Logistics and Transportation Review.* He is currently engaged in research concerning the Canadian trucking industry.